The Biology of Emotions

The Biology of Emotions

JEAN-DIDIER VINCENT

Translated by John Hughes

Basil Blackwell

Translation copyright © John Hughes 1990
Originally published in French as *La biologie des passions*,
copyright © Jean-Didier Vincent 1986

This translation first published 1990

Basil Blackwell Ltd
108 Cowley Road, Oxford, OX4 1JF, UK

Basil Blackwell, Inc.
3 Cambridge Center
Cambridge, Massachusetts 02142, USA

British Library Cataloguing in Publication Data

A CIP catalogue record for this book is available from the
British Library.

Library of Congress Cataloging in Publication Data

Vincent, Jean Didier.
[Biologie des passions. English]
The biology of emotions/Jean-Didier Vincent;
translated by John Hughes.
p.   cm.
Translation of: Biologie des passions.
Includes bibliographical references.
ISBN 0-631-16073-6
1. Emotions—Physiological aspects. I. Title.
QP401.V5613   1990   89-18610
152.4–dc20   CIP

Typeset in Sabon 10 on 11½ point
by Hope Services (Abingdon) Ltd.
Printed in Great Britain by
T. J. Press Ltd., Padstow, Cornwall

Contents

Preface

Why do mood, pain or being in love have such an influence, not only on the way we act, but also on the way we think? What are the common biological parameters of the sexual drive and the desire for power? These and other questions arising from introspection or naive observation are avoided by scientists who consider them as lacking in respectability. Jean-Didier Vincent's interpretation rejects this arrogant attitude. It simplifies without denying the complexities of the field being discussed. It uses the anecdote to go beyond the anecdotal. Without making spectacular concessions to the layman, it charms him by a certain use of paradox, and just when the paradox is in danger of being merely provoking, we find ourselves in the realm of epistemology or mythology, or viewing the confrontation of immaterial thought and the brain-machine being played out on the stage of a shadow theatre. We are faced with a brilliant dialectic which casts new light on the classic duality of the world and our representation of reality, of the internal milieu and consciousness. The text, however, is by no means a kind of conjuring trick: the great debates concerning modern neurobiology remain perfectly clear. When the brain was still unexplored territory, it was first described by pioneers from the fields of anatomy and physiology: they spoke mainly in terms of cables and electric potential. For them, mental pathology could be explained only by the existence of lesions. The second generation of explorers, from the fields of biochemistry, molecular biology and communication theory, see the nervous system mainly as an exchange of coded chemical signals. It sees psychiatric disorder as being caused by a lack or surfeit of mediators. The author of this book is a descendant of the first wave of pioneers but feels closer in heart and mind to the second generation. He sees in hormones a means of relating unreconciled conceptions. These signals which flow freely throughout the organism introduce a degree of uncertainty into the extremely strict concept of neuronal wirings. Many biologists sought for this uncertainty in the all too tightly organized neuronal network. Thirty years ago, Alfred Fessard already thought that, because of 'leaking currents', the action potential escaped from the straitjacket determinism of cerebral architecture. A space for liberty has slipped in between the two dominant overlords of knowledge: the emotional and the cognitive.

The fact of considering our noble mind as being immersed in a veritable witches' brew of humours allows us to go beyond the mechanistic conceptions of the nervous system, whether it be the telephone switchboard of the neuroanatomists or the locks and keys of the molecular pharmacologists. A few other accounts are settled: the illusory hierarchy of different brains — reptilian structures governing animal drives, cognitive structures appearing for the first time in primates, the question of the seat of the soul and the anthropomorphic fear we have of bringing our noble mind down to the level of one biological interaction amongst others.

Jean-Didier Vincent's book is a palace of the mind rather than a museum of knowledge, and its vision partakes simultaneously of the tradition of humanism and the age of the computer. His science takes natural root in our common culture. His sense of humour and tongue-in-cheek moralizing keep him well away from reductionism. This is a delicious book, which offers us a special bonus: the fleeting impression of being able to take in at a glance the many facets of the mind, the strangest of our attributes.

Claude Kordon

The whole man must
move together

Introduction

> There are times when one must drink a bit too much, have a good
> time, enjoy oneself . . . in short, sin a little, in hatred and scorn of
> the Devil . . .. Therefore, I shall drink because you forbid it, and
> furthermore, I shall drink a good deal! One must always do what
> Satan forbids! Ah! If only I could imagine some enormous sin to
> disappoint the Devil and make him understand that I admit the
> existence of no sin, and that my conscience accuses me of none.
>
> Martin Luther, *Correspondence*

'As far as I can remember, I have always been obsessed with you know
what.' Such was the deathbed confession of a contemporary philosopher
who was well known for the strictness of his morals.[1] His words were a
timely reminder that despite the successive linguistic veils that have been
drawn over this aspect of human nature since the darkest ages, man has in
fact never ceased to be a slave to his passions.

A great deal of a man's time is spent in being hungry, thirsty or
transported with desire, in repressing or satisfying a need for power or
affection, not to mention defecation. Add all this up and there is not much
time left for the exclusive exercise of the noble functions of the species,
namely language and thought. Sharing with our philosopher an education
based on the constant presence of sin, we discovered early that man could
suffer, as Thomas Aquinas tells us, from the contrast between the
intellectual appetite, dominated by the will, and the sensory appetite,
dominated by the passions.[2] But were these passions evil, as a violent moral
tradition inherited from the Stoics claimed? Were they a sickness of the soul
which had to be eradicated at all costs?[3] Was it not in the name of this
morality that doctors relegated the passions to the seediest parts of the brain
and the swamps of the humours, leaving to the exercise of reason the noble
stretches of the cortex, ever greater as evolution brought the beast nearer to

the angel? Asked to declare our allegiance either to the 'thought secretary' or the 'passions secretary' in a hypothetical ministry of life, we decided to take refuge in biological data and speak of passions only in relation to laboratory experiments.

Indeed, in the rest of this book, we shall deal exclusively with experiments and observations, mainly concerning animals. We shall counter the deep-rooted idea that blind instinct is exclusive to animals, in opposition to conscious human intelligence based on thought and language, an opinion reinforced by the Cartesian thesis of the beast–machine. Rather than launching out into an interminable discussion of the relative interest of animal models in understanding human phenomena, we prefer to subscribe to the opinion of Cureau de la Chambre, a contemporary of Descartes: he thought that instinct, far from being incompatible with reason, implied it. Instinct, he said, is 'the usual refuge of those who do not wish to admit that animals think; it is like a magic formula which can be used to put a stop to all arguments which are opposed to theirs.' All movements of the appetite are preceded by two propositions, one which tells us that something is good, and another which tells us that we can do it: the operation itself brings the two propositions to a conclusion.[4] There is no better definition of what we nowadays call the cognitive functions, which are recognized as playing a primordial role in animal and human behaviour, alongside the purely mechanical associations between stimulus and response.

But what do we mean by passions? When we consider man as master of his behaviour, we too easily forget the hunger and thirst that are caused by his basic bodily needs, the suffering caused by pain and the pleasure or frustration caused by his love-life. We shall call passions everything that a man or animal is subject to. The etymology of the term underlines the passive aspect we wish to emphasize, opposed to movement and the exercise of the will. It is perhaps significant that the word passions, used by classical philosophers and physiologists, has disappeared from the vocabulary of contemporary psychologists and biologists, only to be replaced by the word emotions, which, in contrast, implies the notion of movement. Descartes himself, who sees in movement the foremost criterion of passion, is responsible for this.[5] Both the movements of the sense organs and the nerve movements of the 'animal spirits' end up in the coronarion gland in the brain. The movements of this gland make the soul feel passion. We find this argument in the work of T. Ribot, who holds Anglo-Saxon authors responsible for it.[6] For Ribot, however, passions are only emotions, i.e. eruptive time-bound intellectualized emotive states. It is this use of the word passion which we still find today referring to the violent feelings that we may have for another person (love passion) or anything which obsesses our mind (a passion for gambling, for example).

The mechanistic materialism which inspires neuronal physiology is not interested in the passions. Neuronal ideology cannot do without movement. The neuronal self devises movement pictures, and action is witness to the brain's self-organizing capacity. Emotions are action induced and so are quite the opposite of passions. The passionate self is passive, humoral, influenced by its environment.

Nevertheless it would be a mistake to consider the passions as the purely passive result of the presence of the being in the world. In contrast, it seems to us that the passions are an integral part of the being and are the basis of its 'existential reality'. This is an idea developed by the German physiologist Johannes Müller (1826) who was himself indebted to Spinoza's theory of the passions.[7] 'All passions can be explained with reference to pleasure, sorrow, and desire. In all passions you find the idea of the self, the idea of exterior things which limit or heighten our existence, the tendency towards self-preservation and the power to further or counter this tendency.' He goes on to say that 'there is but one appetite, but one original tendency to maintain and extend the power of our own existence'.[8] Desire 'causes movements of the appetite by which the soul tries to approach good and escape evil'. Desire is perhaps not very far from what others call love. Bossuet, who lists eleven passions, adds that 'we can even say, if we consult our inner selves, that love alone is responsible for all our passions: it contains and excites them all . . . take but love away, and there is no more passion; put love back and all the passions reappear.'[9] Father Sénault writes: 'All the movements which trouble our soul are only love in disguise: our fears and desires, hope and despair, pleasure and pain, are merely masks that love adopts in success and failure.'[10] In our chapter on sex, you will find a text by Freud which says exactly the same thing. Biology, with Bowlby's notion of love attachment, shows the primordial role of love considered as an exclusive attribute of desire.[11]

This brief introduction is certainly not the place to explain Spinoza's theory of the passions. Unlike psychiatrists, biologists do not care much for Spinoza. They are wrong. His is a cosmological system, not a theory of experience. It is more convenient than others for people who want to hold an electrode in one hand and a rosary or ideological bible in the other. Claude Bernard, reputedly the most dualistic of scientists, makes much of concomitance, which derives from Spinoza's idea of psychophysical parallelism. He writes 'We will never reduce the movements of our soul to the mere properties of the nervous system, any more than we will understand beautiful music in terms of the mere properties of the wood or strings of the violin which produces it.'[12]

In contrast, scientists love Descartes, even if they have read only chosen extracts. It is true that thanks to him the immortal soul was irredeemably separated from the body, leaving plenty of room for the mechanistic scientists to explore the brain. However, because of this too violent expulsion from the body, did the soul become too noisy? Henceforth, the soul would never be so present as in the words of those who wished to denounce it. This perversion of Cartesian thought is particularly striking in the doctrine of cerebral localization. As Riese says, 'Attributing mental functions to different parts of the brain is totally incompatible with the Cartesian conception of thought as non-spatial.'[13] Some scientists may seem to be using a cheap conjuring trick when they give exclusively mechanistic explanations of thought processes: the greater the illusion we are to swallow, the louder are the conjurer's protests. Therefore, faced with over-loud claims of scientific rigour, we have no option but to follow Spinoza, who affirms the independence of the mental and the physical. 'The elimination of laws concerning the consciousness, analysis, interpretation and localization of cerebral activity is the touchstone of Jacksonian neurology',[14] in which we find a hierarchy of structures which cannot be conceived separately and which leads to the principle of the parallelism of the psychic and the physical as a manifestation of the basic unity of being. Hence our definition of a fluctuating central state which will serve as a basis for our description of the chemistry of the passions.

It must be recognized, however, that while we announce that being is not just the sum total of the parts of the machine, this very machine shows itself to be more and more complex as it gradually yields up the secrets of its inner workings. It is indeed astonishing that we can analyse networks of billions of interconnected elements of an extraordinary complexity and at the same time develop a single molecule capable of causing or correcting the most inextricable disorders of the mind. On the one hand the brain appears as a kind of celestial computer, and on the other as a gland with an abnormal secretion which we have only to correct for everything to function normally. Take a typical schizophrenic patient. He walks about like a robot, his eyes gazing blankly from an expressionless face. A few grams of a neuroleptic drug are enough to transform a fury with a tortured mind into that zombie wandering in the gardens of the asylum. Mere medicine absorbed by the diffuse humours of the body is enough to reduce the marvellous machine which creates and perceives to an aimless automaton. The scientist is not the only one accused of reductionism: nature itself gives an example of radical simplification.

Even a unicellular being has a certain degree of freedom between the information receptors on the cell surface and the effectors on the inside.[15] The evolution of a species consists in a gradual increase in the number of intermediaries between information from the outside world and effectors responsible for actions. An animal's freedom grows in proportion to the number of these intermediaries. Yet it is only because the liquid element and the substances it transports bring a solution of continuity to cell organization that this freedom is possible. Our treatment of the passions will therefore be preceded by a study of the humours, i.e. the liquid environment of the organism and the substances which allow communication therein.

We shall therefore deal with what is called the constancy of the internal milieu. The internal milieu is supposed to reconstitute around the cells the characteristics of the original marine environment. In homeostasis, any departure from the norm draws mechanisms into play which tend to bring the trouble spot back to its initial state. Passions could thus be interpreted as a kind of neurosis of the normal, itself a fictitious immobile system of reference. In fact, behind the impassivity of the internal milieu a confused mesh of false constants is hidden, all of which are more or less dependent and variable from one species to the next, from one individual to the next and, within each individual, from one situation to the next. We can see the kind of safeguard that the constant agitation of the humours of the internal milieu offers the nervous system and its operational flexibility: perhaps the brain runs the risk of falling victim (losing its soul?) to such a commotion. For its own protection, it can organize its own disorder: the brain-gland reveals itself as grand master of the humours by its multiple secretions of neurohormones. Like the brain-machine, the humoral brain simultaneously undergoes and acts the passionate victim and the orchestrator of its own passion.

Another protection for the brain is the existence of a barrier of blood and meninges which isolates the cerebral milieu from the rest of the internal milieu: it is a barrier with doors through which selective information passes. But in its retreat behind these walls the brain took with it the elements of the peripheral disorder. Alongside the rigorous organization of neurones in intricate networks of synapses, we can suppose the existence inside the brain of a double set of hormone secretions modulating the functioning of the main neuronal groups at the whim of diffuse humours.

Far from enslaving man, we can see that the passions help to free him from the limits of his environment. Following the tradition of seventeenth-century philosophy, we shall finally study the good use of the passions which brings out their adjustment value. Descartes proclaims in article 211 of *The Passions of the Soul*: 'they are all good by nature and all we have to avoid is their abuse or excess'.[16] Far from being an affliction, as long as they remain in the happy mean, far from the extremes that Aristotle abhorred, the passions are the essence of virtue. Furthermore, not only do they form the basis of a being's experience, but they are also the source of communication between beings.

At this point, we feel we should not try to hoodwink the reader by giving the violent and poetic name of passions to what is only a collection of biological discussions. But perhaps this is just a metaphorical pretext for describing the concepts of a new biological discipline: neuroendocrinology. The sciences of life have always used metaphorical language, which can hardly avoid being reductionistic. The humours, for example, are used to describe our happy or sad behaviour as well as the bodily fluids which are held responsible for it. We speak about psychic functions slowing up just as we speak of slow encephalogram rhythms. We could give a host of examples of physiological terminology hesitating between a literal and a figurative meaning. At the risk of disappointing the reader, we shall limit ourselves to the glands and humours of the brain. But once we start playing with metaphors it is sometimes difficult not to succumb to the delights of metaphysiology: we shall see what we shall see . . .

Notes

1   We do not wish to show any lack of respect, and so the philosopher will remain anonymous.
2   Thomas Aquinas defines passions as acts of the sensory appetite in so far as they are linked to bodily changes: 'Actus appetitus sensitivi, in quantum habent transmutationem corporalem annexam' (Thomas Aquinas, *Summa Theologica*, I 20, 1–10).
3   Chrysippus, quoted by J. Hengelbrock, 'Affect', in J. Ritter (ed.), *Historisches Wörterbuch der Philosophie*, Wissenschaftliche Buchgesellschaft, Darmstadt, 1971.
4   In this paragraph, we quote W. Riese, *La Théorie des passions à la lumière de la pensée médicale du XVII° siècle*, Basle, 1965.
5   Descartes, *Les Passions de l'âme*, Paris, 1649.
6   T. Ribot, *Essai sur les passions*, Paris, 1907. 'The term "passions" is not used in contemporary psychology. I have carefully researched this point. I have read a score of books in different languages. They are all popular works with the public, but only two or three of them contain anything on the passions. Many authors never use the word "passions" (Bain, W. James, etc.). Others use it in passing, but interchangeably with "emotions" or "sentiments", and they affirm that emotions and passions are the same thing. Others rightly remark that it is a vague and elastic term, without supposing that an accurate meaning may be given. Exceptions to this universal laxity are few and far between.'
7   J. Müller, *Handbuch der Physiologie des Menschen für Vorlesungen*, J. Holscher, Koblenz, 1840.
8   This text gives a first approximation of the libido in the language of scientific biology. It is worth recalling that Müller was the teacher of Ernst Brücke, who greatly influenced Freud.
9   J.B. Bossuet, 'De la connaissance de Dieu et de soi-même', *Sermons* I, VI, 1722.
10 J.F. Sénault, *De l'usage des passions*, Paris, 1641.
11 J. Bowlby, *Attachment and Loss*, London, 1970.
12 C. Bernard, *Lettres beaujolaises*, Villefranche, 1950.
13 Riese, *Théorie des passions*.
14 Ibid.
15 R.B. Livingston, 'Sensory processing, perception and behavior', in R.G. Grenell and S. Gabay (eds), *Biological Foundations of Psychiatry*, New York, 1976.
16 Descartes, *Les Passions de l'âme*.

PART I
Fluids

1

Humour, Humours

But say it is my humour.

Shakespeare, *The Merchant of Venice*

The humours, substances secreted by the cells and fluids which transport them, make of our body a veritable witches' brew, and our sweet or ill humour varies with its composition. The fact that the same words are used to refer to our bodily fluids and our feelings underlines the causal links which unite them. The primacy of the liquid element in the organization of life was the basis of Hippocratic humorism, which would later clash with mechanistic theory.

The morning light filtering through the curtains tells me that it will be a grey day. Is it the coming rain or the substances my sleepy brain has carted about during the night that has put me out of humour? Our path lies between this humour and the humours that permeate our body.

According to J. Delay, humour is 'that basic instinctive and emotional disposition which gives each of our moods its pleasant or unpleasant character, oscillating between the extremes of pleasure and pain. Humour is to the thymic or emotional sphere what consciousness is to the noetic or intellectual sphere: that is to say its most basic and general manifestation.'[1] This definition introduces the affective and intellectual contestants for the endless battle between the emotional and the cognitive: the mashy pulp in one corner versus the dry rigour in the other. A little semantic musing on the word 'humour' leads us inevitably to the liquid element – a good example of 'substantial imagination' where the symbol includes both cause and effect.[2] Humour and passion are both singular and plural: the vast fleet of the passions drifts at the mercy of currents and winds upon the sea of humour. This sea, alternately calm or violent, has its own humours which becalm the ship or hurl it to the darkest depths. Confronted with humour and its humours, reason invokes the rigour of its nerve mechanisms. This dualism has been present throughout the history of physiology.

The wet brain

The birth of neurophysiology dates back to the end of the eighteenth century, and from the outset it sought to study functions and relations such as movements and perceptions which were best suited to mechanistic explanations. The main thing was to be able to dismantle the living being and the nervous system, to reduce them to a heap of spare parts. 'It is neither the growth of the vegetable nor the visceral and viscous palpation of the mollusc which gave rise to mechanistic explanations, but the distinct successiveness of movement in the vertebrate whose central nervous system controls and coordinates segmentary reactions: those very reactions which lend themselves . . . to mechanistic simulation. As von Uexkull says, an amoeba is less mechanical than a horse.'[3]

Faced with this dry mechanism, the wet was long neglected. The field Bichat calls 'vegetative life' as opposed to 'animal life' is less amenable to mechanistic explanation. Vegetative functions are emotional by nature. Langley's description of a so-called 'autonomous' vegetative nervous system, responsible for these functions, does not allow the mechanisms to be materialized.[4] With the idea of the internal milieu and the discovery of hormones, back comes the wet to its rightful place. Neuroendocrinology and neuropharmacology have allowed humour-transported gland secretions to invade the brain and explain changes of humour. The brain itself has acquired the status of a gland. From Hippocrates to Guillemin the paradigms have been dancing in circles.[5]

In the beginning was the water

The *Kosmos* stands with its feet in water; such is the principle of nature according to Thales of Miletus (about 630 BC). The three elements of earth, air and fire spring from this primeval element, water. This cosmogony, based on the observation of the Nile floods, may be naive, but it signed the scientific mind's birth certificate. Water is the origin and the substance of the universe: *natura naturans*, creator and creature. *Physis* is incorruptible matter, the principle of unity which engenders things and makes them evolve. This is the first time that we find the objective conception of a physical world issuing from itself, with no outside intervention.

A question of principle

Empedocles (485–435 BC) states more clearly the doctrine of the four eternal incorruptible elements – water, earth, air and fire – which constitute everything. This fourfold division corresponds to the Pythagorean *tetractys*, the first four cardinal numbers 1, 2, 3, 4 (the sum of which is 10), symbolizing the four cardinal points from which the four winds blow, as well as the four seasons and the four ages of life (figure 1). This structure divides itself up into a system of binary coordinates which groups the qualities in two opposite pairs: hot/cold and dry/wet.[6] The universe exists in two forms: a stable form which corresponds to the chaos in which elements are united in an immobile, eternal and incorruptible manner, and an unstable form which corresponds to the *Kosmos*, the result of the splitting up of the universe into a multitude of minute particles known as germs. These in turn aggregate to form the perceptible world. Two forces are constantly at work: repulsion (*nerkos*) or discord (*eris*) which separates opposites, and attraction (*philotis*) which unites kindred elements. 'Not only does the creation of the world's organic and inorganic beings go on incessantly but their destruction also, according to mutual domination. Creation and destruction take place successively.'[7] Bodies and organs are made up of a mixture of the elements and their qualities derive from the different proportions of this mixture. Generation results from the attraction by love of male and female seeds. The senses also follow the law of attraction. The organ which perceives and the object perceived are similar in nature.[8] Particles detach themselves from the object and enter the pores of the sense organ. Therefore 'we see the earth with earth, the water with water, the air with air and the fire with fire.'

The soul is also material, linked to the blood, and moves just like the minute particles through the pores. Thinking and feeling are one and the same thing. Joy and pleasure, according to Empedocles, come from the uniting of kindred elements, whereas sadness is the result of the repulsion of opposites. Desire, which aspires to the possession of what is similar, is the consequence of the mixture being incomplete. 'Appetite comes from a lack of food; desire for what is lacking in the mixture can only be satisfied by what is similar.' As for suffering, 'it is caused by opposites, because of the distance separating the various components of the mixture due to their difference'.[9]

These statements are forerunners of Hippocratic humorism and modern physiology. The quest for precursors often leads to exaggerations, and it is hard to find a modern scientific theory without an ancient Greek in its family tree. However, without enthroning Empedocles, as some people do, as the founding father of modern chemistry and physics, let us give Meton's son credit for having erected love and hate as the powerhouse of the world while at the same time giving us an example of purely materialistic thought in a doctrine centred on the passions.

A few Greeks

According to Anaxagoras (500–428 BC), the universe is made up of infinitely small identical particles, *homeomeres*, ruled by an organizing spirit, *nous*. *Nous* does not mix with anything, but instigates everything. It knows the qualities of the *homeomeres* which are beyond human

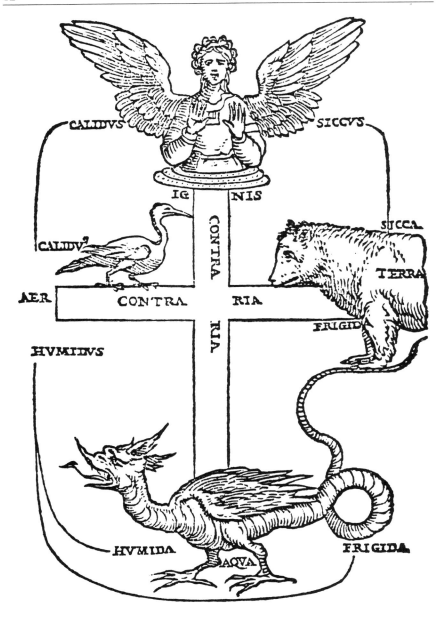

FIGURE 1   The four elements.

understanding and organizes things. This spiritualist mistakes *nous*, the creative spirit (*deus ex machina*), for the material spirit contained in things. Anaxagoras belongs to those coming armies solely preoccupied with the things of the spirit rather than the spirit of things, who will dither between spiritualism and mechanistic materialism, leaving the passions to fight it out alone in the messy swamp of the humours.

The doctrines of Alcmeon and Philolaos, nearer humorism but still marred by animistic Pythagoreanism, are amongst the immediate forerunners of the Hippocratic tradition. Alcmeon (about 500 BC) is rightly considered as 'the real father of experimental medicine'.[10] He was a famous vivisectionist and dissector, and his experiments show the encephalon to be at the 'heart' of mental activities and sensations. Nerves link the brain to the different sense organs. The study of their anatomical structure and qualities reveals their functions. We hear with the ear because it is hollow and dry; we see with the eye because it is mobile and its black back reflects a diaphanous humour; we taste with the tongue because it is soft, warm and wet; we smell with the nostrils which conduct air to the encephalon when we breathe in. Alcmeon, who showed the brain and not the heart to be the seat of the passions, is dear to neurobiologists. The immortal soul of the Pythagoreans is now a tenant of the upper floors. Alcmeon shows above all an extraordinary substantial realism: qualities come to life, confront each other, swell up or wither away inside the human body (*soma*), which is the privileged stage for the play of nature. The passions express themselves in the flesh and the mind moves amidst the passions. Alcmeon believes in justice which is responsible for the normal state of the world. Good health comes from isonomy, which is the balance of forces and the perfect proportion of qualities grouped in opposing pairs: wet/dry, cold/hot, sweet/sour etc. This balance is dynamic and needs regulating: an excess of cold is counterbalanced by exposure to heat. 'A force dominated by one quality alone (monarchy) leads to illness, because of its isolated power to corrupt. Illness is caused by an excess of heat or cold.'[11] This is the theoretical basis of humorism taken up in the writings of Hippocrates or, nearer to us, the basis of homeostasis, the internal stability of an organism.

A similar doctrine can be found in the writings of Philolaos (550 BC), a disciple of Pythagoras, who based his conception of the world on the symbolism of numbers and the perfect analogy between man and the universe. Just as the earth has its central fire, the human body has its heat principle in the genitals, which are the source of life. Desire is an attribute of the body, which tries to temper its inner heat by inhaling cold air. The humours, whose role is recognized more and more clearly, spread and change in volume according to the alternate and reciprocal influence of heat and cold. They cause illness.

Another figure from our gallery of Greeks is Diogenes (469–410 BC). The spirit (or soul) comes from the incorruptible divine air and returns there. It lodges in the encephalon which represents the unity of consciousness and serves as a mediator with the organism. Amidst this metaphysical hotchpotch, the somatic origin of pleasure and sadness is nevertheless stated. Pleasure is felt 'when a large quantity of air mixes with the blood which spreads throughout the body according to the laws of nature. When the air is thick, unnatural, and of poor quality, it does not mix and brings about a feeling of sadness.'[12]

The theory of the humours

Hippocrates is not the father of the theory of the humours. However, we find in his writings the first coherent statement of the doctrine which would serve as the basis for physiology and medicine for many centuries. A good example here is 'melancholy', an illness with a history which is intimately linked with that of our conception of the humours. From the seventeenth and eighteenth centuries onwards the nervous system would replace the humours in the explanation of natural illness.

Hippocrates and humorism

Hippocrates (460–377 BC), in his treatise on ancient medicine, refutes the opinion of those predecessors who attribute the world to one element – air, earth, fire or water – as 'that would mean there is only one illness and consequently only one cure'. On the contrary, the organism is a balanced mixture of several substances which permit the coexistence of opposite qualities: hot/cold, sweet/sour and acid/tasteless. All qualities are tempered by their opposites. 'As long as these forces are evenly mixed, hot and cold in balanced coexistence, there is no effect, for there forms a kind of corrective symmetry of cold compensated by heat and vice versa; and being separate, they can come together without help or preparation.'[13] There is no better description of the principle of homeostasis. The rules of hygiene and therapeutics follow. Diet should not stray from a balanced mixture of qualities (*dietetics*). If nature maintains a balance, any untimely intervention which may hinder the action of its forces should be avoided. Illness is a break in equilibrium. There may be a constitutional predisposition to this imbalance (*diathesis*). Diet, which is the link between the organism and its environment, should aim at restoring this synergy. Treatment consists of drugs and operations which strengthen or lessen the qualities which are wanting or overabundant. More than by its formal description of the system of the four humours, it is by the living dialectic of its dynamic balance that Hippocratic humorism announces modern physiology.

The body is an aggregate of fluids, the humours, and the solids which contain them. Vital phenomena are born from the action of these fluids. The cardinal humours are blood, phlegm, yellow bile and black bile. The balance of the humours constitutes *crasis*; its breakdown constitutes *dyscrasia*. This balance has a natural tendency to restore itself. By analogy with food, which we have seen to be the substantial link between man and nature, a humour with an excess of qualities causing trouble should be cooked for it to cease being harmful. This process allows the sinful humour to be transformed, favouring expulsion during an attack or fit. As these events follow each other in time, the illness can be followed and a prognosis established. In explaining the illness, symbolic unity is always respected and the quality of the humours corresponds to the quality of the symptoms.

The old picture of bleeders in pointed hats should not obscure the fact that the Hippocratic tradition is responsible for a rigorous thought system which would later give birth to the physiology of thermotaxis. Whereas the Cnidians developed an exclusively functional organ pathology, the followers of Hippocrates, while profiting from the anatomical knowledge of the former, consider the organism as a whole. This whole is made up of interdependent parts, linked by the humours considered as systems of communication and action, the very roles which will later be attributed to hormones. The doctrine of the temperaments extends this notion of interdependence to the whole universe. Temperament is the individual's attitude to the world and governs his capacity for reaction. It is a dynamic and diachronic constitution in opposition to the static structural constitution extolled by the Cnidians.[14] The isonomy of the humours and the harmony of qualities establish a relationship with the world. The proportion of humours varies according to the temperament and influences the nature of the relationship. Each individual reacts according to his temperament to the action of the environment: climate, place, produce of the earth etc. Temperament is not stable and, like nature, changes with the seasons and the ages of man.

Black humour

Amongst the humours, a special place must be set aside for black bile or melancholy, an excess of which is responsible for the ailment of the same name. The name given to the substance has such metaphorical power that it also serves for the illness it causes. Black bile is a concentrated humour which through evaporation has accumulated the piercing, corrosive and aggressive properties of yellow bile (choler). Like the melancholic patient, it is self-consuming. Its blackness conjures up the patient's depression, the dark night that surrounds him and the death he desires. It is the most capricious of the humours, passing in a trice from freezing to boiling point. Metaphorical richness should not make us forget the substantial reality of the humour. It offers a natural and coherent explanation for the disturbances of the mind: excess or alteration, accumulation, cooling down or heating up – such are the common misadventures of black bile. If black bile affects the body, we observe epilepsy, and if it affects the brain we observe melancholy. Since all the causes are physical, the treatment will be of the same order and aim at restoring the right proportion, correct temperature, easy drainage and balanced distribution of the humour.

The role of black bile in the birth of a mental disorder provides the first example of physicians recognizing a causal relationship between psychic trouble and a biochemical anomaly. The second half of the twentieth century is strewn with attempts to explain mental illness by means of a chemical substance. The corresponding treatment still follows Hippocratic logic by trying to restore the disturbed metabolism of the substance or by neutralizing its harmful effects. We can only regret that words like dopamine and serotonin do not have the metaphorical power of melancholy or black bile.

The words black bile or melancholy are so evocative that they were easier for the Hippocratic psychotherapist to use than the esoteric names of today's medicines are for the modern doctor. Even if thick black bile has lost its substantial reality, it has kept its allegorical power. A lack of materiality has never deprived a word of its operational or explicatory potential. If this were the case, what would become of the repressions, displacements, condensations and other manoeuvres of the unconscious still spoken of by disciples of Freud?

Galen and medical tradition

Whether it be Freud or Galen, western medicine has always held masters aloft to strengthen its power to persuade. Galen (130–201 AD) innovated little, but dissected, classified and wrote a great deal. For centuries he remained the authority who inspired physiology and medicine. The humorism which was never clearly stated in the writings of Hippocrates acquires in Galen a doctrinal rigidity which leaves little room for variations. Linked with the humours are the places where they exercise their influence. The hypochondrium, where we find the stomach and the spleen, is a place where black bile accumulates through congestion. Laughter helps to evacuate this bile by dilating the spleen. The accumulation of black bile in the stomach causes hypochondria: nausea, flatulence and slow digestion. In the stomach, the black bile gives off vapours which rise to the encephalon causing fear, sadness, dark thoughts – a gloomy reflection of the humour responsible for them – and the death wish. There are mental disorders in which black bile strictly situated in the encephalon causes hallucinations, and others in which it spreads throughout the body including the brain. The organ here recovers its rights over the system. The humour, however, remains the driving force behind the disorder, which varies according to where the bile flows.

The end of the humours

The humours thus reigned for centuries, providing an irreplaceable metaphor for the circulation of the passions. They dried up when the imagination rose to those lofty peaks where the soul could bask calmly in the sunlight of the mind. The fear of sin, even when washed away by the baptismal waters, kept the soul away from those wet regions where uncontrollable desires proliferated. Cartesian dualism only confirmed the divorce. Between the immaterial soul and the brain-machine, the passions were now cut off from the humours. Whether he be dualistic or vitalistic, materialistic or spiritualistic, the classical scientist needs rods and springs to animate the living being. Systematic medicine, with Hoffman (1660–1742), rejects humorism and speaks of striction and spasms. Melancholy is due to a *status strictus* of the brain's covering.[15] For Lorry (1726–83), the cause of disorders is attributable to the degree of fusion of the fibres which constitute the organism. Good health depends on the tone of the different organs and the harmonious tension of the fibres. There would be nothing new in this rehashing of the ideas of *laxus* and *strictus* if progress in anatomy and physiology did not provide organic support in the form of nerve fibres. Henceforth the brain and its nerves have an undisputed primacy, and melancholy can become a nervous breakdown.

Whether we shake the world or only perceive it, it is now the brain which is in question. 'Every man in his humour' has been superseded by neuronal man.

Notes

1   J. Delay, *Les Dérèglements de l'humeur*, Paris, 1961.
2   G. Bachelard, *La Formation de l'esprit scientifique*, Paris, 1980.
3   G. Canguilhem, 'La constitution de la physiologie comme une science', in C. Kayser (ed.), *Physiologie*, Paris, 1970.
4   J.N. Langley, 'On nerve-endings and on special excitable substances in cells', *Proc. R. Soc. London, Ser. B*, 78, 170–94, 1906.
5   R. Guillemin, 'Biochemical and physiological correlates of hypothalamic peptides. The new endocrinology of the neuron', in S. Reichlin, R.J. Baldessarini and J.B. Martin (eds), *The Hypothalamus*, New York, 1978.
6   The school of Pythagoras defined ten principles for categorizing everything. They are binary oppositions: finite/infinite, even/odd, unity/plurality, right/left, male/female, fixed/mobile, straight/curved, light/dark, good/bad and regular/irregular. Empedocles reduced the oppositions to two: hot/cold and dry/wet.
7   A.A. Phylactos, *Les Doctrines des philosophes physiologues présocratiques grecs mises par Hippocrate avec profit au service de la médecine*, Athens, 1979.
8   This proposition can be compared with our concept of the fluctuating central state, which includes the extracorporal and corporal dimensions of the individual.
9   This is the reduction drive theory which links motivation to the satisfaction of a need (see chapter 8).
10 G. Baissette, 'La médecine grecque jusqu'à la mort d'Hippocrate', in M. Laignel-Lavastine (ed.), *Histoire générale de la médecine*, Paris, 1936.
11 Phylactos, *Doctrines des philosophes physiologues*.
12 Ibid.
13 Ibid.
14 The Cnidian school was a neighbour and a rival to Hippocrates' school. It specialized in the study of organs and their diseases, linking the disorder to the

lesion, whereas Hippocratic medicine considers the organism as inseparable from environment and time, lending importance to evolution and prognosis.

15 The methodist school was important in Rome in the first centuries of the empire. One brilliant representative of this school had a simple 'method', which consisted in linking the affection to one of two morbid states: tension (*status strictus*) or relaxation (*status laxus*).

2

The Internal Milieu

The fixity of the internal milieu is the *sine qua non* of free, independent life.

Claude Bernard, 1878

The external milieu was a Greek invention, but the internal milieu[1] was invented by Claude Bernard (1813–78). For Greek doctors and their disciples, man lived in harmony with nature. Temperament fixed the conditions of this harmony. However, the living being had no real identity or biological unity: the humours were nothing but a kind of reproduction, inside the animal, of the surrounding natural elements; there was no substantial difference between nutrients and living matter. The internal milieu ensures the biological unity of the animal and confers a certain autonomy relative to the external milieu.

The living body

The existence of a fluid milieu linking the different cells of an organism is vital to the functioning of the whole. The cells draw the materials necessary for life from this milieu and discharge their secretions into it.

The great unifier

Cell theory is inseparable from the concept of the internal milieu. The organism is composed of a host of cells which are scattered or grouped together in tissues. Each cell, individualized by its plasmatic membrane, plays out its fate under the genetic control of the nucleus. The cells are surrounded by water, more water and, beyond the membrane which encloses the cell, yet more water. Claude Bernard, comparing the weight of a mummy with that of a living human being of the same size, estimated the water content of the latter to be 90 per cent. To be more precise, let us say two-thirds water for one-third dry matter. The mixture in a crucible would be as consistent as thick soup. Today chemical tracers provide us with accurate means of measuring the fluid compartments of an organism. A compartment corresponds to the volume of diffusion of a specific substance.[2] Some molecules, like the radioactive sodium isotope, remain exclusively outside the cell and diffuse throughout the extracellular space; others are limited to blood plasma. There are three compartments, as follows: the water contained in the cells (the intracellular compartment), the water around the cells (the interstitial compartment) and the water which circulates in the form of blood plasma and lymph (circulating compartment). The very idea of a tracer, which is injected into the organism at a specific point and which spreads uniformly throughout a compartment, corresponds perfectly to one of the functions of the internal milieu, namely to provide a medium for diffusion and homogenization around the cells. The internal milieu defined by Claude Bernard – the blood and the fluids in which the cells are bathed – is thus the unifier of the organism. The cell draws from the extracellular fluid the nutrients it needs, the fuel and oxygen which provide its energy and the chemical factors which keep it in working order. It discharges into this milieu its waste and the produce of its activity. Here we have Claude Bernard's second idea, internal secretion, which is inseparable from the concept of the internal milieu.

Internal secretions

Claude Bernard discovered internal secretion while describing the glycogenic function of the liver. The hepatic cell draws from its reserves of glycogen the sugar that the organism calls for and reintroduces it into the bloodstream. Internal secretion, which differs from excretion, demands a fluid medium which can receive the cell's outpourings. The term endocrinology, introduced by Nicolas Pende (1909) to refer to the study of internal secretions, was finally used only for the secretions of the so-called vascular glands, later to be called the endocrine glands. The function of these glands, which have no excretory canal, cannot be deduced from their appearance or anatomical location. We now know that they provide the internal milieu with substances called hormones. The hormone concept, which is much narrower than that of internal secretion, refers to a cellular secretion with no strictly metabolic function, but which has a communicative role. We shall deal with the various hormones in detail later.

Homeostasis

The concept of homeostasis explains the stability of the internal milieu and serves as a theoretical basis for the physiology of regulation.

A conservative milieu

The internal milieu was discovered only a century ago, but its existence goes back to the birth of life. Life, the last word in negative entropy, appears in a rudimentary form in the primeval ocean – a vast salty medium becoming even saltier by licking the earth's feet. Let us consider this brine for a moment. It furnishes the physical and chemical conditions necessary for life to be born. It is life's medium and its prison. Any change means that the living being is done for. In order to survive, it organizes and marks out its own milieu so as to ensure a certain stability. This internal milieu reproduces for the cells the physicochemical conditions of the mother ocean which allowed life to appear. The autonomy acquired by the organism relative to the external milieu gives it independence and freedom to evolve. Indeed, unlike the external milieu which is inert and subject to uncontrollable changes, the internal milieu is elastic. 'There is an elasticity which, within limits, allows life to resist the causes of disorders that are to be found in the immediate environment.'[3] This elasticity is due to forces which are brought into play each time that a characteristic of the internal milieu tends to move away from its normal value under the influence of variations in the external milieu. A rise in the surrounding temperature sets off cooling mechanisms, whereas the presence of cold temperatures stimulates an increased generation of heat. We could give many other examples of what W. Cannon named 'homeostasis'.

The internal milieu takes the form of a certain number of volumes called regulated variables. Without regulation, the changes in the external milieu and the functioning of the cells would make these volumes vary, when the very survival of the organism depends on their stability. Stability is obtained as the result of a regulating system comprising several subsystems, each of which is subject to control mechanisms and responsible for controlled variables. A regulated variable thus remains fixed within strict limits because of the intervention of controlled variables which have a much wider scope for variation.

The regulated volumes define the constancy of the internal milieu. The most important are the gas content of the blood, acidity or pH, temperature, sugar content, blood pressure and osmotic pressure. The latter offers an example we shall often return to. The more salty a solution, the higher its osmotic pressure. If for any reason an animal loses water, the salt concentration in the internal milieu (in other words the osmotic pressure) rises. As it is a regulated variable, osmotic pressure will be kept constant by regulating mechanisms: diminishing the outflow of water and/or increasing the intake. The outflow is reduced by slowing down the elimination process through the kidneys. Vasopressin, an antidiuretic hormone secreted by the brain, takes on this job. The amount of this antidiuretic hormone circulating in the blood is a controlled variable which increases in response to any rise in osmotic pressure. This is an example of hormonal regulation. The best way of increasing intake is to drink. Beyond a certain level, the rise in osmotic pressure causes thirst and an urgent need to drink. This is an example of behavioural regulation. Therefore the regulating mechanisms can be of two kinds: hormonal or behavioural. A camel, despite the dry heat of the desert, does not suffer from a much higher osmotic pressure than a barman; it merely possesses more powerful regulating mechanisms which are adapted to the external milieu and which give the controlled variables, diuresis and water intake, a wider scope for action.

Nevertheless there is a hierarchy to be respected. The most important constants must be maintained at all costs, even if this means sacrificing one of the lower orders. In case of need, a regulated variable can become a controlled variable. For example, blood pressure is constant, but if the oxygen content of the blood is endangered, as it is a hierarchical superior, blood pressure will rise in order to provide a higher flow of gas and will thus temporarily become a controlled variable instead of remaining a regulated variable.

The homeostatic order

The healthy reader will have understood that all is for the best in the best of all possible organisms. Stability and adaptability are the life and soul of the homeostatic order; with the internal milieu guaranteeing biological freedom and progress! Cannon entitled one of his books *The Wisdom of the Body*, a title which is not without dualistic and moralistic overtones. The wisdom of the body, as exemplary as solid middle-class industrial management, is implicitly contrasted with the folly of the mind, the root of all evil. After all, in the context of mental homeostasis, the unconscious is perhaps nothing more than a (badly) regulated variable . . .

The real lesson to be learnt from the internal milieu is not so much the idea of the perfection of the functions, as the fact that living beings are less and less passively subjected to their immediate environment. The constancy of the internal milieu does not mean fixity but on the contrary the possibility to evolve while resisting the limits imposed by changes in the external milieu. Freedom does not mean indeterminacy but a causal link between the regulating mechanisms and the disturbances which bring them into play.

The internal milieu is a medium for communication

The internal milieu serves as a medium for the diffusion and circulation of various chemical messengers. A traditional distinction is drawn between messengers from the nervous system and those from the endocrine system.

A cultivated milieu

What is the difference between the internal milieu and lentil soup? The former is a cultivated milieu in which information circulates; the latter is

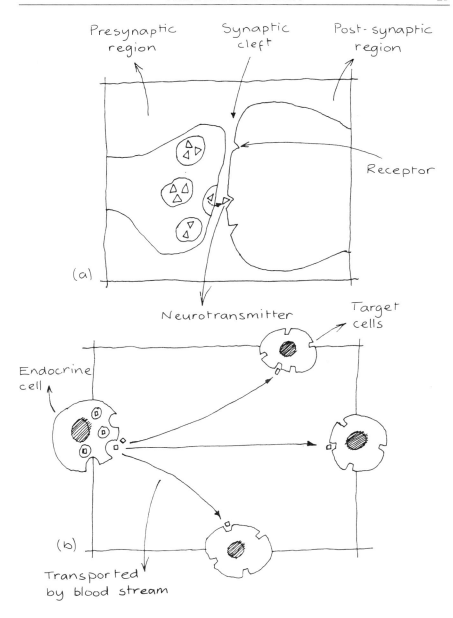

FIGURE 2 (a) Simplified sketch of synaptic communication; (b) hormonal communication. The main difference lies in the distance covered by the messenger (hormone or neurotransmitter) between its emission and reception sites: a few thousandths of a millimetre for the synapse, and varying distances in the bloodstream for the hormone.

nothing more than inert soup heading for faecal chaos. For there to be life, there must be organization, and for there to be organization, there must be communication, i.e. an exchange of information between cells and, within the same cell, between the elements from which it is made. In organized beings there are two modes of communication, through nerves and hormones, which we shall first try to distinguish and then relate by minimizing the differences.

The sprinter and the long-distance runner

From a traditional point of view, the nervous system is a mesh of knotted cables functioning as a network through which a brief electric signal (lasting a few thousandths of a second) can pass: this is the nerve impulse. During the first half of the twentieth century, the physiologists studying the nervous system were more or less electricians. The endocrine system uses chemical messengers, hormones, which can act at a distance from their seat of origin (after circulating in the fluids of the organism) on a more or less scattered group of target cells over a prolonged period of time ranging from a few minutes to several hours. The first physiologists studying the hormone systems were more or less chemists. More recently, chemistry became interested in the nervous system as soon as it became clear that communication between the nerve cells also took place through chemical messengers, namely the neuromediators which are released under the action of the nerve impulse and which are capable of modifying the electrical properties of adjacent cells. Therefore from electricity we move to chemistry before moving back to electricity again. Nevertheless, the distinction between hormones and neuromediators is quite clear cut. In traditional parlance, the transmission of information via the nervous system is a dialogue between contiguous excitable elements, whereas hormonal information is diffused to the target cells scattered at a distance from the source cell (figure 2). The action of the neuromediator is local, immediate and discrete, whereas the hormone acts at a distance, by diffusion and over a certain time span.

Notes

1 *Translator's note*: 'Milieu interne' is usually either translated as 'internal environment' or left in French. I wished to make the term a little more transparent for the English-speaking reader and at the same time respect the French origin, hence 'internal milieu'.
2 A compartment is the volume of distribution of a substance in a given part of the organism. The liquid compartments are the volumes of distribution of water in the body. The water contained in the cells forms the intracellular compartment and represents about 40 per cent of the total mass of the organism. The water outside the cells, or extracellular compartment, accounts for 20 per cent of the total mass.
3 C. Bernard, *Pensées, Notes détachées*, Paris, 1937.

3

Hormones

These chemical messengers, or hormones (from the Greek *hormaô* ≡ I excite), as we could call them, must be transported by the bloodstream from the organ that produces them to the organ they affect.

Hardy

All's well that endocrines well

A bearded woman dances with a hermaphrodite, a dwarf teases a fat man, mental defectives file by and nymphs shake it up to the sound of a band of goitrous musicians, while a placid giant beats time with his hand (figure 3). Here was a common view of people suffering from endocrine disorders before the role played by hormones through insufficient or excessive internal secretion was discovered. As a result of experiments on animals and advances in chemistry, rapid progress was made. In less than a century the causes of the main endocrine disorders were identified, along with the glands and their respective secretions. In under a century the hormones were isolated and analysed and the mechanisms governing their activity understood – how the chemical messenger recognizes its target cell thanks to the receptors on the membrane or in the cell, and how this recognition leads to a concrete effect thanks to a second messenger acting inside the cell. Within a century most endocrine disorders could be cured by medicine, and hormones could be extracted from glands or synthesized from basic elements. The Breughel-like vision can be replaced by a group portrait including some forty Nobel prize-winners and a few hundred researchers of different nationalities.

FIGURE 3   The endocrine ball (François Durkheim).

The birth of endocrinology

The example of the thyroid shows how the methods of endocrinology have developed, and certain events in the history of science serve to illustrate the beginnings of hormonal therapeutics. Hormones are secreted by about ten glands scattered about the body and by the brain itself.

The methods of endocrinology

The methods of endocrinology are exemplary, and their simplicity is perfectly compatible with a great practical and conceptual efficiency. The first step consists in removing the gland from an animal and observing the effects which are more or less exactly the same as the disorders caused by deficiency in the patient. The second step seeks to correct those effects by means of a gland graft. In a later step the active principle which can compensate the effects of the extraction is obtained from the gland. Later still, a pure product, the hormone, can be obtained. It is then possible to ascertain its chemical formula and perhaps produce it artificially.

The case of the thyroid is a good illustration of the advantages and drawbacks of this type of procedure. In 1859, Morritz Schiff, then teaching in Berne, extracted the thyroid from a dog and observed the animal's death. He falsely concluded that 'thyroidectomy' led to death, not realizing that the parathyroids he had taken out at the same time were the culprits, and not the thyroid itself.

The surgeons Koch and Reverdin advanced further. They observed the appearance of a myxoedema after successful removal of the thyroid in goitrous patients, i.e. the same symptoms as those noticed in the Bicêtre idiots whose congenital lack of the thyroid was described by Bourneville. After thinking the problem over for twenty-five years and after carrying out the first successful thyroid transplant, Schiff, now teaching in Geneva, concluded that the gland functioned by secreting into the bloodstream as a result of the vascularization of the graft.

At the end of the nineteenth century, the method of removal and graft had been applied more or less successfully to the other glands, leading people to accept the idea that the vascular glands function by secreting into the bloodstream. If this is so, we should be able to reproduce the physiological functions of the gland and compensate any sign of insufficiency observed in the patient by injecting an extract. Charles Brown-Séquard, Claude Bernard's successor at the Collège de France, drew some over-hasty conclusions from this hypothesis. In the space of two weeks at the end of May 1889, the intrepid old man injected himself with a watery extract obtained from dog and guinea-pig testicles. On 1 June he reported the results of his experiment to his colleagues at the Society of Biology.[1] After the injections, Brown-Séquard noticed an increased vigour. With exquisite suggestiveness, he noted that 'other forces, which were not lost but considerably diminished, improved spectacularly'. We must admit that Brown-Séquard's new-found virility gave birth to modern hormone therapy and led to thousands of patients being cured. Nevertheless, his interpretation was erroneous. The substance used by Brown-Séquard contained no male hormones. Testicles produce but do not stock hormones, and the quantity of active substances which can be extracted from them is infinitesimal compared with the daily secretion of a gland. The effects observed by Brown-Séquard were the result of auto-suggestion, what we would call today a placebo effect. This is neither the first nor the last example of a correct hypothesis being confirmed by false results.

In 1881, Murray successfully treated a patient suffering from myxoedema by repeated injections of thyroid extract. Unlike the testicles, this gland contains a considerable stock of hormones. Thousands of patients suffering from thyroid insufficiency were going to be cured. In late 1914 Kendall finished preparing purified thyroid hormone or thyroxine, of which he obtained 33 grams from 3 tons of cattle glands: this was the beginning of the long contribution of slaughterhouses to endocrinology. Sheep and rabbits as well as cattle would henceforth contribute their glands to the good cause. Each discovery of a new hormone is a story full of strange twists, red herrings, partial successes, disappointed hopes and forgotten heroes. For each gland, the story ends with pure products being obtained for analysis and successful synthesis. Once a hormone has been isolated and its biological effects catalogued, it becomes possible to measure it in the blood and to discover the amounts in circulation during different physiological and pathological circumstances. The hormone can be marked with a radioactive tracer in order to follow its destiny: how it spreads to different parts of the body, how proteins carry it to target cells, how it recognizes its receptor and fixes itself there, and how it is inactivated, degraded and finally eliminated. Each hormone could be the subject of a treatise, but such is not our purpose.

We now open the door on boring generalities reminiscent of the introductory display in a museum. Biologists will be on familiar ground; they can stroll quickly through to the inner halls. The neophyte must patiently gather a few rudiments in order to understand what lies further on.

The endocrine glands

Scattered about the body, specialized cells secrete hormones into the bloodstream. They are called endocrine to distinguish them from the exocrine glands which secrete liquids into the digestive tube or out of the body (saliva, sweat etc.). Today, the endocrine glands are a familiar part of the anatomical landscape: the thyroid and parathyroids, the adrenal glands which cap the kidneys, the gonads in the womb or between the legs according to sex, the pituitary gland attached to the brain like a basket to its balloon, and lastly the pancreas coiled up in the intestines (appendix 1).

A gland generally contains several cell types. The anterior pituitary has at least five kinds of cells, each secreting one or more hormones. The endocrine pancreas, which coexists in the same organ with an exocrine gland possessing a digestive function, secretes three hormones: insulin which lowers the sugar content of the blood, glucagon which increases it and somatostatin which inhibits the first two. A hormone can also come from two different sources: glucagon is secreted by the pancreas and by the intestinal wall. Many hormones produced by the digestive tube are also produced by the brain. The intestinal wall constitutes a great gland with a wide range of endocrine secretions: the gastro-intestinal hormones (gut hormones). Other indirectly endocrine organs and tissues can also secrete hormones: the liver, the kidney, some blood cells etc. The nervous system also behaves like a multiple gland secreting neurohormones and neurotransmitters with hormonal functions. We shall study the brain-gland in detail later, as it is a happy hunting ground for the humours.

Different classes of hormone

Hormones can be classed in three groups according to their structure: steroids derived from cholesterol, peptide hormones made up of a chain of amino acids and a more disparate group made up of molecules obtained by transformation of an amino acid.

Steroids

Steroids all have the same form, that of the cholesterol molecule they derive from. Look at its formula (figure 4), it is well worth it. On paper, it resembles a kind of kite, the angles of which are carbon atoms with various ornaments and appendices attached. Minimal variations in this structure or the addition of a lateral chain determine the variations in affinity of the receptors and the biological properties of the molecule. Of course, this picture on paper is only a formal representation remote from reality. As it stands, the formula is recognized by chemists: a symbol of the three-dimensional sign which the hormone molecule, recognized only by its own receptor, really is.

Steroids are characterized by their solubility in fat and their versatility. The former property allows them to pass without difficulty through fatty biological membranes and penetrate the brain. Their versatility comes from a structure which facilitates the passage from one steroid to another as long as the right enzyme is present in the gland: female hormones are the daughters of male hormones and, conversely, the main male sex hormone testosterone can be transformed into the female hormone oestradiol. And it is not a lesser paradox that in order to work on the brain, testosterone must be transformed into oestradiol in order to acquire its male functions.

Different kinds of steroids can be present in the same gland. On top of cortisol and aldosterone, the corticosteroids, the adrenal cortex secretes

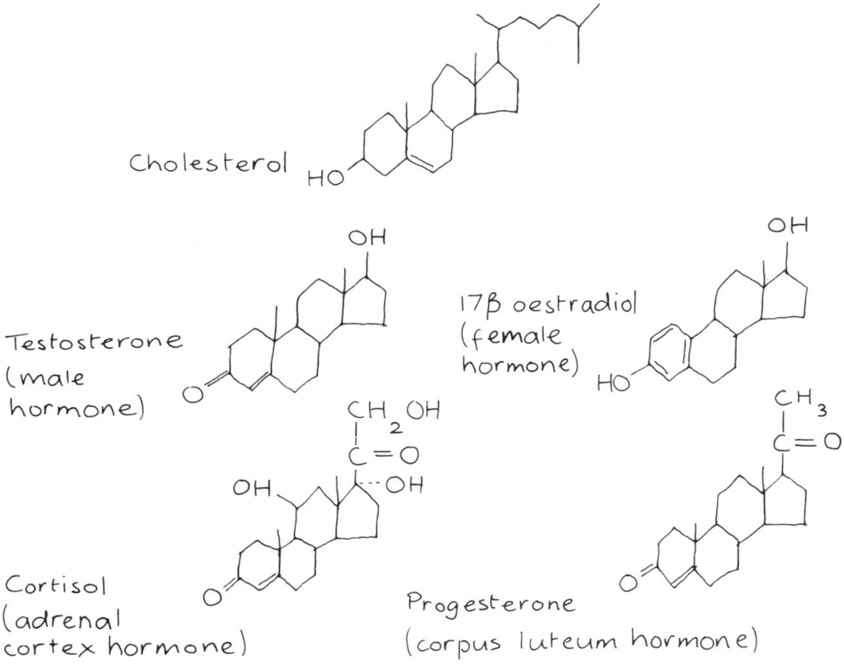

FIGURE 4   Formulae of the main steroid hormones. The intermediate stages, their
numerous derivatives and the pathways between different forms are not shown.

androgens or male hormones. Thus the organism makes female with male,
masculine with feminine. What a confusion of sexes there would be if these
series of transformations were not perfectly controlled! One chromosomal
anomaly, one missing enzyme, one extra hormone, and the little boy
becomes a little girl, the bearded woman weds the fertile eunuch . . . strange
things which modern endocrinology is able to explain.

Peptide hormones

Peptide hormones make up the second group of hormonal signs. They can
be compared to words or sentences according to their size. The letters which
compose them are amino acids. There are about a score of these, some of
which are manufactured inside the organism while other indispensable ones
are supplied by our food. The words are of varying length, from the simple
peptide compound of two to ten amino acids, to the protein made up of
hundreds of amino acids. Sometimes we are dealing with a sentence made
up of several words or subunits. But the comparison has gone far enough.
We must not imagine a linear structure but a veritable three-dimensional
sculpture with curves and bends due to the reciprocal attraction of different

parts and the odd foreign element which attaches itself to a point in the chain. These peptides are insoluble in fat and so do not pass through the cell membrane. In order to act, they must fix themselves on the membrane and either pass the baton on to an intermediary facing inwards or locally modify the properties of the membrane. The list of these hormones is long, but it is just as well to know the names of the characters in order to follow events in the rest of the novel. Some are extremely well known, like insulin; others have strange names due either to chance, like 'substance P', or to the Hellenistic leanings of their discoverer, like cholecystokinin, bradykinin, endomorphine etc. In future, the masses will have to get to know this hidden language of our inner life. People will soon say 'my cholecystokinin is rising' instead of 'I'm full up', or 'my hypothalamus is bathed in luliberin' instead of a banal 'I love you'. I am, of course, only joking. A better knowledge of the names of peptide hormones may help us to recognize their origins and understand their meanings, but will never be able to replace the mysterious power of the words that make up human language.

Hormones derived from an amino acid

Hormones derived from an amino acid can be compared to interjections of one or two letters since they are the result of a transformation from one amino acid (appendix 2): serotonin comes from tryptophan, histamine from histidine, and the catecholamines (dopamine, noradrenaline and adrenaline) from the same amino acid, tyrosine. The latter, decked out with iodine, gives us the thyroid hormone, the isolation of which marks the beginning of the endocrinological era and the end of our stroll through the hormonal garden.

Manufacture and action of hormones

Hormones have a double role. On the one hand, by handling intercellular communication, they integrate the chemical and physiological functions in order to maintain certain constants and adapt the response of the organism to environmental changes. On the other hand, they are essential for the complete and harmonious development of infants and for the growth of the individual or one of his organs until adulthood. The manufacture of a hormone molecule by the endocrine cell and the action of this molecule on a target cell can today be described in their main outlines.

The messenger hormone

It is not just a coincidence that Hermes, the founder of alchemy, should also be the messenger of the gods. Hermetic science is nothing more than a coded discourse, a catalogue of signs and symbols which carry messages and call for action. In the world of alchemy, life is just a struggle to escape from the chaos to which entropy destines everything that exists. With each higher degree of organization which is reached, a little more information circulates, more messages are sent out and received. To the question 'What is man?', Peirce replies: 'He's a symbol'.[2] That is to say, a system of signs working to establish an organization and keep it throughout all the vicissitudes of being. The ultimate incarnation of communication is the snake eating its own tail (*serpens qui caudam devoravit*), enclosing in its impenetrable circle the infallible hermetic axiom which proclaims the unity of matter: *en to pan* (all one).[3] It is fascinating to note that the fundamental principle of hormone regulation is based on the feedback that takes place as far as secretion is concerned, so that a rise in the presence of hormones in the bloodstream slows down their secretion and vice versa (principle of Moore and Price) (figure 5).

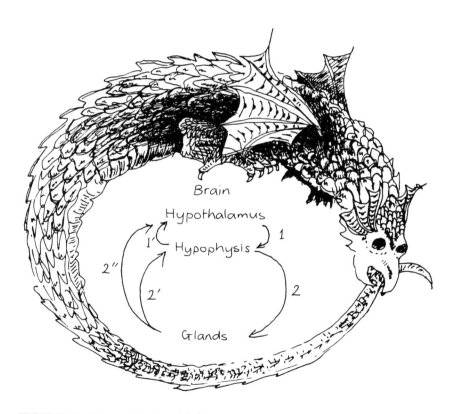

FIGURE 5 Extremely simplified sketch of neuroendocrine feedback: 1, the hypothalamus orders the secretion of adenohypophyseal hormones; 2, the adeno-hypophysis orders the secretion of hormones by the peripheral glands; 2', feedback from these hormones working on the adenohypophysis or (2″) on the hypothalamus; 1', short feedback from the hypophyseal hormones working on the hypothalamus.

Another principle of alchemy is the bringing together of opposites which leads to mutual recognition and union: male and female, the empty and the full, the greater and the lesser. We may smile at this seemingly unscientific language, but is Engels, that esteemed philosopher, less ridiculous when he applies dialectics to biology, expalining that the barley seed negates itself when it grows into a stalk and produces the flower, which negates itself in its turn by producing the seed?[4] The bringing together of opposites allows us to understand how a hormonal messenger of a given chemical nature recognizes a receptor of an opposite yet complementary nature, how their union gives birth to information which is converted into action, which in its turn produces a new messenger and so on. Life is just an uninterrupted circulation of information, as we said before. Similarly the forming of a messenger ribonucleic acid (mRNA) in the nucleus comprises the successive assembly of bases which are complementary to those of the deoxyribonucleic acid (DNA) of the gene. Everything a cell can do or has others do comes from the nucleus in the form of coded messages from the genomic library which are then translated into proteins in the ribosomes (figure 6). Some of these proteins will become hormones after several snippings and reshufflings and will be secreted from the cell. Others will be enzymes, i.e. crucibles where chemical reactions which are impossible at body temperature will be able to take place.

The vasopressin molecule provides a good example of these successive transformations. The entire history of its birth has been reconstructed *in vitro*, artificially, outside the organism. Like all peptide hormones, vasopressin issues from a precursor, a protein larger than itself. The mRNA, a long filament carrying the coded message from the gene of this protein, leaves the nucleus of the cell and is read and translated in the ribosomes into acceptable amino acids which, in the prescribed order, form the protein. This precursor is then wrapped up in the membrane of a granule which protects it from the aggression of the cellular environment. The granule then travels to a terminal where its contents are released (exocytosis) (figure 7). But the story is not over. The hormone is only a fragment of the long chain of amino acids in the precursor. This chain begins with a sequence of twenty-three amino acids (signal peptide), followed by the nine amino acids which make up the vasopressin. Next comes a short sequence of three amino acids preceding the long string of ninety-three amino acids of neurophysin, a protein associated with vasopressin which it apparently protects from damage during transport. Lastly, we find a series of thirty-five amino acids associated with sugar, forming a glycoprotein of unknown function. When the granule matures, enzymes called peptidases snip parts off the precursor, individualizing the different fragments: vasopressin, neurophysin and glycoprotein. These peptidases have no special characteristic a priori. They are to be found everywhere. They are workers who know how to separate two amino acids of a given type in whatever protein chain they may occur. Peptidases which are specific to a given hormone may exist; Snyder has apparently found one which participates in the manufacture of

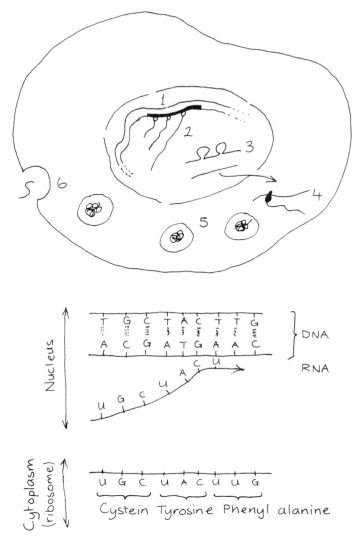

FIGURE 6 Protein synthesis. The gene (1), a segment of the chromosomal DNA, is translated into mRNA whose chain of nucleotides becomes progressively longer (2). Some fragments of the mRNA are excised (3). The mRNA enters the cytoplasm and is translated into a polypeptide chain (protein) by means of the ribosomes (4). The newly synthesized proteins can be packaged into granules (5), mature and be secreted by exocytosis (6). The DNA is formed of two strands of nucleotides with complementary bases linked two by two (adenine–thymine (A–T), and guanine cytosine (G–C)) by hydrogen bonds. The nucleotide sequence of the mRNA is complementary to that of the bit of DNA from which it derives. In this case the complementary base for A is uracil (U). The combination of three consecutive bases corresponds to a particular amino acid. The various possible combinations constitute the genetic code. The mRNA is decoded in the ribosomes which translate it into a chain of amino acids.

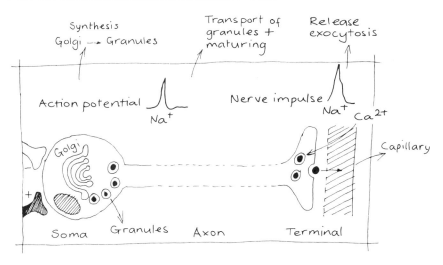

FIGURE 7   Destiny of a hormone in the neurosecretory cell. The precursor is packaged into granules by means of the Golgi apparatus. These granules are transported to the nerve terminals by the axonal flux. During the axonal transport, the precursor matures and the hormone appears in its final form. The release of the hormone takes place when the granule attaches itself to the cellular membrane and ruptures outside it (exocytosis). Axonal transport is not the same thing as nerve impulse. The latter, arriving at the terminal in the form of action potential, causes calcium to enter the cell. This calcium is the main agent in exocytosis.

encephalin. This is an important discovery, as it opens up the possibility of preventing the forming of a hormone by blocking the action of the enzyme. If we can act on the synthesis of certain hormones from the brain we may finally be able to influence the origins of certain kinds of behaviour . . .[5] However, for the moment, peptidases specific to the manufacture of vasopressin have not been found. As we have just seen, the story of the hormone is complicated. It is wonderful that the relay can be run without the baton being dropped. Sometimes it is dropped. The Brattleboro rat does not secrete vasopressin.[6] This miserable animal suffers from hereditary diabetes insipidus: it urinates excessively and compensates for this by drinking an extraordinary amount of water. A simple base error in the gene which codes for the precursor and the message transcribed on the RNA is wrong, making the ribosomal reading impossible or aberrant; this leads to an abnormal precursor which is incapable of furnishing the right hormone.

The cell receives two information flows: one from inside the nucleus, giving birth to the hormones, and the other from outside, transported by the hormones.

Secreted into the internal milieu, the hormone goes off in search of its target. The amount of hormone which arrives in the vicinity of its destination depends not only on the amount secreted but also on losses along the way. The target or receptor is a large molecule situated on the membrane of peptide hormones and inside the cell in the case of steroids. As opposites attract, the hormone recognizes its receptor and attaches itself to it. It is a reversible relationship based on a dynamic balance between the partners. The affinity that a hormone feels for its receptor measures the force which brings them together and unites them. Therefore the number of hormone–receptor unions depends on the number of partners present and their affinity. The intrinsic activity of the hormone is expressed by the force of the effect of the union. The affinity between receptor and hormone is indeed very selective, but may not be exclusive. Other substances called analogues are recognized by the hormone receptor. They attach themselves to it with an affinity which is sometimes greater than that of the hormone whose place they have taken. If the union results in an effect comparable with that of the hormone, the analogue is an agonist; if there is no effect, it is an antagonist. These facts are important, as they allow the experimenter or doctor to intervene in the hormone–receptor dialogue by introducing a foreign substance which can inhibit or reproduce the action of the hormone. For a hormone to act, it must find its receptor. The apparently charming young lady we meet in the street or see on a music-hall stage may have perfectly formed testicles. The absence of male hormone receptors means that the hormone has no effect and leads to a secondary feminization.

The binding of a hormone and its receptor brings about a change in the latter or in its immediate environment. The receptor is said to be activated. This is the first stage in a cascade of events which lead to the hormone producing its effect (figure 8). When the receptor is situated on the membrane, a second messenger is needed. The best-known example concerns the action of adrenaline on the hepatic cell in which the second messenger is the famous cyclic adenosine $3',5'$-monophosphate (cAMP) which, from one enzyme activation to another, finally transforms stored sugar into usable sugar. cAMP is not the universal intracellular mediator. The hormone–receptor binding can, depending on the hormone concerned, solicit other factors, modify the structure of the neighbouring membrane, open or close canals . . .

As for steroids, the receptor is inside the cell. The complex formed by the hormone–receptor union migrates in the nucleus and attaches itself to the chromosomes, where it induces the synthesis of proteins, i.e. enzymes ready for action (figure 9).

The final result of the hormonal message is to ensure a certain cellular function in a particular type of cell, the one which possesses the corresponding hormone receptor. A hormone can even carry several messages destined for different receptors. Vasopressin or antidiuretic hormone (ADH), two different names for two different effects of the same substance, acts on the kidney through the action of receptors quite distinct from those through which it brings about the contraction of the blood vessels. Each receptor recognizes a different part of the hormone molecule and there exist different analogues for these different receptors.

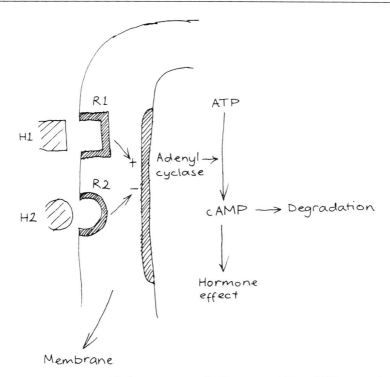

FIGURE 8   How peptide hormones work. Hormones H1 and H2 recognize their respective specific receptors R1 and R2 situated on the cell membrane. The interaction of the hormone and its receptor brings about activation (in the case of H1–R1) or inhibition (in the case of H2–R2) of an enzyme which is also situated in the membrane: adenyl cyclase. The latter transforms adenosine triphosphate (ATP) into cyclic adenosine 3',5'-monophosphate (cAMP), which is considered to be the real second messenger, responsible for the effect the hormone has on the cell.

The fairy hormone

A caterpillar changes into a butterfly, a tadpole into a frog, a little boy into a girl; we could give other examples, but in any case, a hormone did it. Here the hormone is no longer a messenger with one clearly defined function; it works on the whole organism, bringing about a transformation in the individual. The most striking example is furnished by ecdysone. When injected into the body of a grub, this steroid hormone penetrates cell nuclei and brings out puffs on the chromosomes which are perfectly visible under a microscope. This great upheaval results in the synthesis of mRNAs and the formation of new enzymes which change the grub into a fly.

In man, several hormones, in addition to their messenger role, have a trophic function which contributes to the complete harmonious development

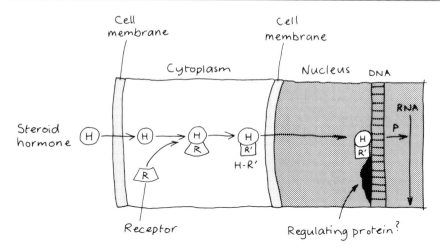

FIGURE 9   How steroid hormones work. Hormone H passes freely through the membrane and attaches itself inside the cell to a cytolytic receptor R, thereby composing an active complex H–R′. This complex reaches the DNA in the cell nucleus and leads to its translation into RNA. A regulating protein can either prevent the complex from reaching the translation promoter P or help the link.

of the infant, the growth of the individual or one of his organs as we said before. The hormone acts and transforms the cell by inducing the synthesis of new enzymes. A tadpole injected with thyroid hormone changes into a small frog as a result of the appearance of different enzymes which work on building up the lungs and liver and resorbing the tail. In man, testosterone is responsible not only for the sexually secondary characteristics of the voice, but also, and above all, for the differentiation of the sexual organs. Testosterone does everything if it gets going in time. If not, only the embryonic female sexual organs, which originally coexist with the male organs, develop. The manufacture of a total adult is, then, the result of cooperation in the work of several hormones: glucocorticoids, sex hormones, growth hormones, thyroid hormone. As we read in the song of Solomon: 'We have a little sister, and she hath no breasts.' In order to make a female breast, the coordinated action of gonadotrophins, growth hormone, oestrogens, progesterone and prolactin is necessary. Therefore those blessed with the best breasts should thank their lucky hormones.

Notes

1   C. Brown-Séquard, 'Des effets produits chez l'homme par des injections sous-cutanées d'un liquide retiré des testicules frais de cobaye et de chien', *C.R. Soc. Biol.*, 1 June 1889, 15 June 1889.

2   C.S. Peirce, *Collected Papers of Charles Saunders Peirce*, Cambridge, MA, 1931.
3   E. Canseliet, *Alchimie*, Paris, 1964.
4   F. Engels, *Dialectique de la nature*, Paris, 1952.
5   G. Kolata, 'Unique enzyme target neuropeptide', *Science*, 224, 14–17, 1984.
6   H. Valtin and H.A. Schroeder, 'Familial hypothalamic diabetes insipidus in rats (Brattleboro Strain)', *Am. J. Physiol.*, 206, 425–530, 1964.

4

The Cerebral Environment

Immense the stretching of the waters, greater still the empire
Of secret chambers of our desire.

Saint-John Perse, *Amers*, IX, 1

The barrier

There is a barrier around the brain which allows it to evolve independently, free of the limitations of the internal milieu. This barrier can only be passed at specific entry and exit points which exist so that the brain can receive the latest news from the internal milieu and take the necessary action.

The haemato-encephalic barrier: myth or reality

Vital colouring injected into an animal's bloodstream uniformly stains every organ except the brain which keeps its original hue. Ehrlich concluded from this single experiment, which is a forerunner of modern tracer techniques, that the brain is protected from the invasion of foreign substances transported in the bloodstream by the haemato-encephalic barrier.[1] There is no need to strangle one's neighbour in order to grasp the importance of the blood flow to the brain. No organ is more completely vascularized, and the circulation of the blood is so rich and complex that a partial or total stoppage, whether diffuse or not, causes irreparable damage in only a few minutes; no nerve cell is further than 0.005 mm from a capillary. These capillaries, however, are very different from those which irrigate the rest of the body. The walls of the latter are made up of a layer of separate endothelial cells with spaces between them for the flow of liquids and substances in solution. Blood plasma, except for the presence of large protein molecules, is like extracellular fluid: they mutually reflect each other's variations in composition. The endothelial cells of the cerebral capillaries, however, are tightly bound together, leaving no room for the passage of liquids and the substances dissolved in them. In order to pass through the wall, the cells themselves, in other words two plasmic membranes, have to be passed through (figure 10). The barrier is certainly there, but it is a semi-permeable barrier like the plasmic membranes themselves, allowing water and solutions to come and go according to precise physical rules, with regular gradients and various modes of transport according to the solution involved. If we were to push the comparison further, the brain could be likened to a vast cell protected by a double membrane with the cerebral environment of the nerve cells inside, and the internal milieu of the rest of the body outside.

Passing through this barrier requires systems of transport which vary according to the substances involved. Electrolytes, for example, which give neurons their electrical properties, follow strict rules. The slightest change in their concentration in the cerebral environment would modify the excitability of nerve cells quite dangerously. A simple experiment can demonstrate the independence of the electrolyte concentration in the cerebral environment compared with that of the internal milieu. When small mud-dwelling amphibians called necturus are raised in a potassium-enriched environment, the concentration of this ion in the blood can rise by as much as 50 per cent, whereas the variation in the brain is negligible. Therefore electrolytic upheavals of the plasma have only an attenuated effect on the nerve cell. The haemato-encephalic barrier ensures a veritable homeostasis of the ion content of the brain. There are also transporters for sugars: glucose is the only neuron energy source and is important for the precursors of nucleic acids, for choline, the precursor of acetycholine, and for certain amino acids which are precursors of neurotransmitters and neurohormones. If there is no transporter, there is no message. This is the case for dopamine, and so all attempts to make up for its shortage in the brain in the treatment of Parkinson's disease have failed. However, its precursor L-dopa passes through the barrier and is therapeutically useful. Here we should mention the general problem posed by the existence of this barrier for the use of medicine destined for the brain. Certain substances which are effective when administered directly to the brain are often seen to lose their efficiency when injected into the bloodstream. Research is directed towards finding an active product with a chemical make-up allowing it to pass through the barrier: such a product is called a mime, a molecule which is different but which has the same affinities and effects as the molecule it imitates.

Like any embarrassing reality, the haemato-encephalic barrier raises doubts and flirts with myth. The possibility of transport inside vesicles formed from membranes has been evoked. Black radish peroxydase, an enzyme with a trajectory which can be followed under the microscope, has been used as a marker to confirm the existence of the barrier: the enzyme cannot pass through in either direction. Neither can peptides and proteins. Hormones cannot get into or out of the brain, except for steroids, which are

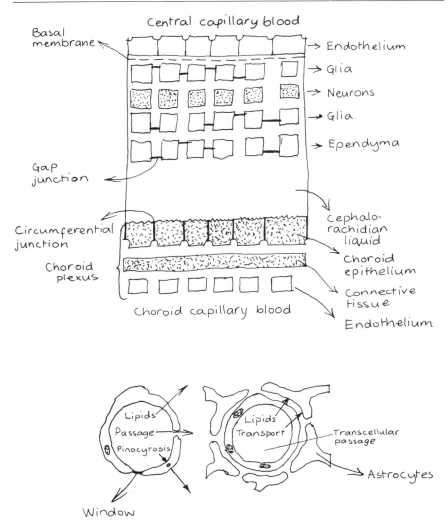

FIGURE 10   The haemato-encephalic barrier. The choroid epithelium cells secrete the cephalo-rachidian liquid. They are sealed together by circumferential junctions which prevent any diffusion. The endothelium of the choroid capillaries is loose and allows the diffusion of substances between the cells. That of the cerebral capillaries, however, prevents the diffusion of blood molecules towards the brain. The difference between the cerebral and general capillaries can be seen at the bottom of the figure. There is no endothelial window or passage in the cerebral capillary; in contrast, there are tight junctions between the cells. The only passage is through the cell.

soluble in the membrane. The hormonal communication system in the cerebral environment is therefore not the same as in the internal milieu. However, some exits for hormones from the brain do exist: these exits are strictly limited to certain special areas where the barrier is not present.

Therefore a protective wall and specialized transport systems help to constitute the autonomous environment round the nerve cell. The most important thing is for this environment to remain stable and for it to be able to observe in an independent way whatever disturbs the internal milieu. In other words, the internal milieu plays the same role for the organism relative to outside influences as the cerebral environment plays for the brain relative to the internal milieu. We shall see that this homeostasis of the cerebral environment must be submitted to the same restrictions as that of internal milieu: it varies in space and time.

In, out

The brain is often said to be a representation of the world – *imago mundi* – and, reciprocally, a shaper of the world – *anima mundi* – according to innate or acquired knowledge. The stability of these images and programmes requires an isolation to which the haemato-encephalic barrier contributes.

There are only two possible paths into the brain, the nervous and the humoral. The latter, as we have seen, is perfectly controlled by the haemato-encephalic barrier. The former allows into the brain data collected and shaped by the sense organs and specialized receptors where the process of representation has already begun, whether concerning the outside world (exteroceptors), the position of the subject in the world (proprioceptors) or the internal milieu (interoceptors).

The two paths out are the nervous, responsible for effecting motor programmes, and the humoral, in the form of the releasing of hormones in a specialized region or hypothalamo-hypophyseal crossroads (figure 11). This hormonal and motor output can be a response to stimulations from the body and the outside world or may be centrally programmed. In the latter case, some of the output is regulated by clocks in the brain which resemble Salvador Dali's soft and strangely shaped watches: they lengthen and shorten at the drop of a humour or an outside stimulus.

The environment as metaphor

The cerebral environment is not only separated from the internal milieu, it is also a representation of it. The hormones which cannot pass the barrier are also secreted inside the brain for its own use: their cerebral play mimics their activity on the outside.

The isolation and autonomy of the brain constitutes a step forward in the evolution of intelligent beings. The higher we climb in the hierarchy of the species, the more hermetic and selective the barrier becomes and the more

External face

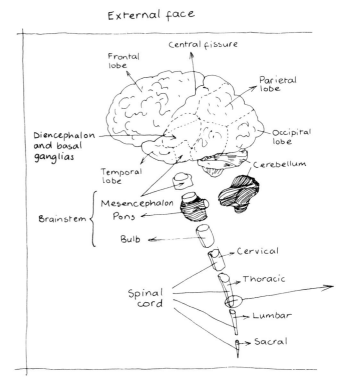

FIGURE 11 Simplified sketch of a human central nervous system. There are two openings: the hypothalamo-hypophyseal region which allows a humoral communication of the brain with the rest of the body, and the spinal cord and

independent the brain. We can take the reproductive function as an example. The ovulation cycle of the female rat lasts four days. This cycle depends on a cerebral clock which at fixed times every four days delivers a message to the ovary in the form of a massive release of hormones. The ovary in its turn influences the activity of the nerve centres through its steroid hormones. Besides undergoing the modulating effect of the ovarian hormones, the nerve centres are influenced by outside factors such as light, temperature and noise. The ovulation cycle is therefore both rigid and fragile, chained to the workings of the central clock and heavily dependent, like the clock itself, on outside factors.

Things are different in the primate – ape or human – where the ovulation cycle lasts twenty-eight days. As Knobil has shown,[2] the functioning of the ovary depends permanently on the rhythmic pulsatile discharge of a cerebral hormone, luliberin, which stimulates it through the hypophysis.

This process lasts throughout the cycle, which is consequently regulated outside the brain by the retroaction of the ovarian hormones on the

Internal face

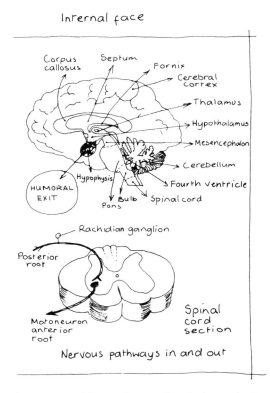

Corpus callosus
Septum
Fornix
Cerebral cortex
Thalamus
Hypothalamus
Mesencephalon
Cerebellum
Hypophysis
HUMORAL EXIT
Fourth ventricle
Bulb
Pons
Spinal cord

Rachidian ganglion
Posterior root
Motoneuron anterior root
Spinal cord section

Nervous pathways in and out

brainstem with, on the one hand, the paths in through the posterior roots of the spinal cord and sensory cranial nerves of the brainstem and, on the other hand, the paths out through the anterior roots of the spinal cord and the motor cranial nerves.

hypophysis. The interaction between ovary and hypophysis is consummated exclusively in the internal milieu. The ovulation cycle in the primate, by freeing itself from the cerebral clock, not only protects itself from outside factors, but also gives the brain a greater liberty of action by freeing it from its reproductive duties.

By escaping from certain biological limitations, man and his brain have become less time bound. Should we conclude that, just as the internal milieu allowed the animal to rise above the water, the cerebral environment will allow man to rise above the animal?

Cerebral hydraulics

Within the brain flow fluids long believed to be its most vital component. Cavities filled with cephalo-rachidian liquid drain intracerebral environment and provide a path for communication between the various cerebral structures.

A tap on the head for the water in your mind

The idea that living beings are mechanisms depends on the machines that man invents, and the explanation depends on what can be described. Whether it be a sand machine which measures time with gravity, a water machine which goes against the grain, a wind machine wielded by the strong arm of Louis (Armstrong), or a fire machine which makes the walls come tumbling down, man's machines respect the order of things and the four elements of nature. It was inevitable that the scientist, who places the brain at the centre of man, should place the functions of the mind in what can be described, namely the cavities, the only parts accessible to his observation and imagination. The four ventricles of the brain thus naturally become the seats of the workings of the mind, according to the Platonic sequence which leads from sensation to memory. The lateral ventricles, the seats of *sensu communae*, receive the results of sensorial analysis, evolve pictures and transmit them to the median ventricle, the seat of *ratio* (reason), *cognatio* (thought) and *aestimatio* (judgement); the pictures are then transferred and retained (memory) in the fourth and last ventricle.

The exact shape of the cavities has been known since Leonardo da Vinci used his skill as a sculptor to make a mould of the ventricles of an ox's brain, showing the structure of these spaces where a fluid secreted from the grey matter circulates. In order to evolve his concept of the brain-machine, Descartes took the church organ for a model. The ventricles push a fluid through pipes and vents which distribute the animal spirits amongst the muscles. The brain-machine hypothesis cannot of course be proved. The living machine is here clearly a metaphor, an 'unmarried machine' (see part II); conceived only for the use of the mind, it is a tool for the creative imagination. However, in a truly immaculate conception, the unmarried machine gives birth to scientific progress. When Kant reintroduces the idea that man is radically different from any machine because of his capacity for goal-oriented activity, the divorce seems complete and mechanistic materialism utterly defeated. Then, unexpectedly, the living being becomes the model for organized autoregulating machines, and these computers in their turn serve as models for the brain. The unmarried machine is back, but with a difference. The fluids once necessary have been forgotten. Computers do not need watering, and yet their metaphoric harvest is immense. What is to be done with all the water? The mills have stopped turning, the hour-glasses have served their time, Louis plays an electronic synthesizer and computers manage our affairs in war and peace. Only the cavities of the brain are still there!

The cavities

In a brain weighing 1400 grams, the cavities filled with liquid represent about 100 millilitres, or two wineglasses (figure 12). In each hemisphere, the lateral ventricles contain most of this cephalo-rachidian liquid. A narrow orifice leads from them to the third ventricle, a funnel-shaped container around which are found the nervous structures concerned with the passions: the limbic lobe and the hypothalamus. This space communicates rearwards, by the sylviduct, with the fourth ventricle, a lozenge-shaped basin whose floor covers the vital centres (respiratory, cardiac and vascular) and whose roof forms the base of the cerebellum. A narrow canal prolongs this last ventricle inside the spinal cord and, through small openings at its lower end, allows it to communicate with the spaces round the brain and the spinal marrow. These openings allow the liquid to flow over the convexity of the hemispheres and deep into the fissures as well as bathe the base of the brain and the entire spinal cord. The fountains which supply the liquid spaces are situated inside the lateral ventricles. These choroid plexuses are made up of capillary vessels covered with contiguous epithelial cells which draw from

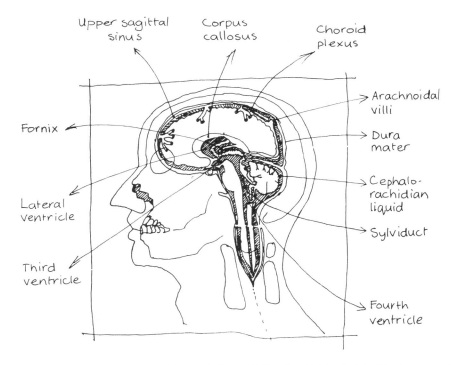

FIGURE 12   Distribution of the cephalo-rachidian liquid (shaded) inside the central nervous system.

the blood plasma and secrete into the cephalic cavities a liquid of the same composition as the cerebral extracellular environment. With a flow of 0.35 millilitres per minute, the choroid plexuses are responsible for the flow of about 0.5 litres of cephalo-rachidian liquid inside the lateral ventricles, whence it flows through the median ventricles towards the base and convexity of the brain.

The liquid from the cavities spreads throughout the liquid bathing the nerve cells. No barrier prevents the diffusion of the substances contained in the cephalo-rachidian liquid within the cerebral extracellular space. In their turn, the products secreted by the neurons can spread throughout the cerebral structures by means of the cephalo-rachidian liquid. This liquid can be considered as a veritable supply and drainage system for the brain. It is a medium for what Rémy Colin has called hydrocrinia,[3] the diffusion of hormones through a liquid medium inside the cerebral environment. The liquid secreted is taken up by the veins through granular formations which are a type of small valve allowing the cephalo-rachidian liquid and its solutions to be released into the blood. The water-tightness of the choroid plexuses and exit valves should be insisted upon. They do not interrupt the haemato-encephalic barrier, whereas the cephalo-rachidian liquid passes freely into the cerebral extracellular space.

Thus the cephalo-rachidian liquid is to the cerebral extracellular environment what the blood plasma is to the internal milieu. It brings an element of continuity and uniformization to neuronal discontinuity and heterogeneity.

Neurons and those other cells

There are two classes of cells in the nervous system: the nerve cells proper, or neurons, and the neuroglial cells. Neurons transport electric signals because of the properties of their membrane. They form cabled networks amongst themselves and communicate by means of synapses. The neuroglial cells, which are ten times more numerous, have various trophic functions.

Neurons

There are about 10^{12} neurons in the human brain, and about a thousand different types (figure 13). A nerve cell is divided into four regions: the soma, the dendrites, the axon and the axonal terminals. The nucleus and large-molecule construction unit are situated in the soma, the seat of enzyme and precursor synthesis. From the soma comes an axon which can reach 1 metre in length and which is sometimes coated with a fatty insulator, myelin. The axon divides itself up into terminal branches which make contact with other cells at the synapses. These are made up of the terminal part of a cell (presynaptic) and the receptor surface of another cell

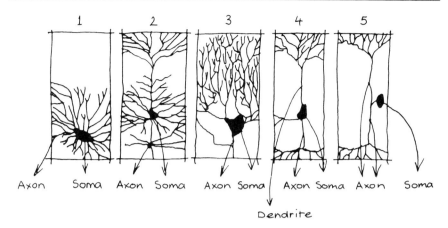

FIGURE 13   Different types of neurons: 1, multipolar cell, here a motoneuron; 2, pyramidal cell to be found in the cortex and the hippocampus; 3, Purkinje cell which is a neuron of the cerebellum; 4, bipolar cell, here a cell from the retina with a dendrite which transmits the information towards the cellular body or soma and an axon which transmits the information to the periphery; 5, T-shaped monopolar cell typical of a sensory neuron with a branch coming from the skin or muscle and another going towards the spinal cord. (After E.R. Kandel and J.H. Schwartz, *Principles of Neural Science*, North-Holland, Amsterdam, 1981.)

(postsynaptic). The receptor surfaces are often situated on extensions called dendrites.

Neurons are able to transmit signals of an electric nature. At rest, the neuron membrane, like that of any living cell, is polarized with a separation of the ionic charges between the inside and the outside, where the inside is negative (-60 millivolts). With the passing of charges through the membrane, the difference in potential can increase (hyperpolarization) or decrease (depolarization).

At the receptor sites (sensorial receptors or postsynaptic zones) the passing of charges can be locally modified by the opening or closing of ionic canals. The result is a local variation in the membrane potential (receptor or postsynaptic potential). These potentials spread over the membrane according to the laws which govern the conduction of electricity in a cable. The different potentials cumulate algebraically and affect the rest potential. When the latter reaches a threshold of approximately -40 millivolts, there occurs a sudden impulsive movement of charges called the action potential, which consists of an inverted, brief and reversible polarization of the membrane. This action potential or impulse, which is remarkably constant, spreads along the axon to the terminals at a varying speed of about 1 metre per second. It is a universal signal which does not differ from one neuron to another. For each neuron, the integration of the local potentials which tend to bring together (depolarizing, excitor potentials) or separate (hyperpolarizing, inhibitor potentials) establishes the membrane potential which corresponds to the trigger threshold of the impulse (figure 14).

Once it has arrived at the axonal terminals, the action potential induces a local potential, linked to the taking in of calcium, which causes a vesicle containing a package of neurotransmitter substance to open. This substance, once released, affects the postsynaptic membrane, creates in its turn a local potential and thus carries on the transmission of information from one cell to the next. Each cell can receive several hundred local potentials and establish contacts with several hundred other cells. Of course, this is only an extremely general and simplified description.

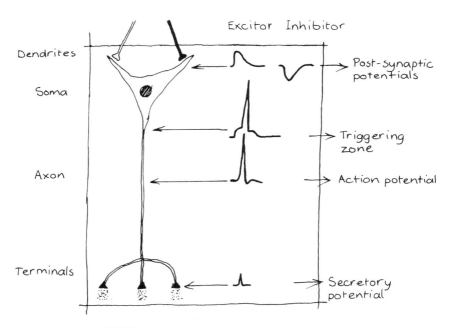

FIGURE 14   General sketch of neural function.

Glial cells

The other brain cells are the unfamiliar and often forgotten glial cells. Neurons and glial cells are like masters and servants. Because of their excitability, neurons can converse with one another, as we have seen. However unfamiliar they may be, there are ten times as many glial cells as neurons, but they are not excitable, have no synapses and were long thought to have only humble functions: maintenance, packaging, protection, nutrition etc. Books about the brain often ignore the glial cells. There is no place for the soft and sticky amidst the fine lacework of the neurons!

The glial cells and neurons are nevertheless inseparable. They have a common origin in the embryo, and are linked by their anatomical distribution. The glial cells occupy the space left free by the neurons between their cell bodies so that the remaining extracellular space does not exceed a few millionths of a millimetre. This very small space is nevertheless uninterrupted and so the free circulation of solutions is possible. Physiological properties also link the two kinds of cell, as glial cells fulfil their functions only in liaison with neighbouring neurons. Whereas the latter are individualized, and communicate with one another only through the synapses, the glial cells establish junctions or short-circuits between one another, and this confers on them a continuity and a kind of common identity. The glia make up non-discrete ensembles around discrete neuronal units.

The membrane sheath formed by the glial cells around the axons contains a fatty substance, myelin, which is responsible for the whitish colour of cerebral matter and nerves. Interrupted at regular intervals by nodes of Ranvier, this insulating sheath forces the impulse to jump from one node to the next, accelerating its progression. Therefore the glia condition the speed at which signals are transmitted. The absence of myelin for congenital reasons or because of illness seriously affects nerve functions, as can be observed in the Jimpy strain of mutant mice whose myelin does not develop normally.

The secretory role of the glia was plainly indicated by Nageotte, a French histologist of the early twentieth century: 'the neuroglia is an interstitial gland annexed to the nervous system'. Indeed, the glial cells secrete neurotransmitters despite the absence of synapses. Dennis and Miledi have shown that when a motor nerve is severed, the glial cells which come to take the place of the degenerate nerve fibres are able to release acetylcholine spontaneously or in response to an electric stimulation, exactly as the intact neurons would have done.[4] In the last few years, a lot has been said about the ability of glial cells to secrete γ-aminobutyric acid (GABA), a substance which, in the brain, is the main inhibitory neurotransmitter. This ability is coupled with that of being able to intercept the GABA present in the extracellular space. This can be checked by exposing a photographic emulsion to the radioactive GABA molecules intercepted by the cell, a technique called autoradiography. Here we discover a possible function of the glia: the stocking and release of neurotransmitters in certain conditions in parallel with the synaptic role played by these interneuronal liaison officers.

Without anyone really knowing what is involved, the nutritive function of the glia is often taken for granted. The glial cells may indeed intercept and bring neurotransmitter precursors to the neurons, constituting a kind of stock-cupboard. It is more important, however, to insist upon the ability of glial cells to divide, unlike neuronal cells. Rakic and Sidlan, in a series of studies of the development of the cerebral cortex and cerebellum in man and ape, have shown that the glial cells and their extensions form a kind of net on which the neurons migrate towards their final destination.[5] Their reproductive faculty allows the glial cells to play a role in the repair of nerve lesions by occupying the lost space and guiding and helping the growth of substitute nerve elements through the secretion of growth factors. A protein (nerve growth factor (NGF)) which encourages the growth of nerve cells can be extracted from glial tumours.

Given the absence of excitability and synapse in glial cells, it may seem paradoxical to study their electrical properties, but this is what we shall do now. As with neurons, their membrane is polarized, with the internal face being negative relative to the extracellular face, and this negative membrane potential, higher than that of the neighbouring neurons, could constitute a kind of well of negativity attracting the neighbouring positive charges. This potential mainly depends on the distribution of a positive ion, potassium, on each side of the membrane. When the potassium concentration rises on the outside, this positive ion tends to penetrate the cell and depolarize the negative internal face of the membrane. The slow variations in potential which can be recorded with an electrode inside the cell faithfully translate the movements of the potassium ion through the membrane, which are dependent on the extracellular concentration of the ion. This concentration depends on the electrical activity of the neighbouring neurons. A neuron which produces action potentials spits potassium. When the neuron beats repetitively, the potassium accumulates outside the cell. As neuronal excitability depends on the amount of extracellular potassium, the more the neuron discharges, the more excitable it becomes. By pumping the potassium which builds up outside the neuron, the glial cell absorbs the ion excess and prevents the situation from getting out of control.

As we have just seen, the glial cell intake of potassium causes slow variations in potentials which shadow the activity of neighbouring neurons. This glial participation in the electrical activity of the brain has been elegantly demonstrated in an experiment carried out by Kelly and Van Essen.[6] A glass electrode is placed inside a glial cell in the visual cortex of a cat. It is known that certain neurons in the visual cortex region are activated in a specific way when a luminous target is moved in a given direction. The glial cell shows slow variations in potential, the amplitude of which depends on the movements of the luminous target. These variations probably correspond to the activation of a column of neighbouring neurons. While these slow variations do not generate an impulse, they may possibly release substances which could affect the workings of the neighbouring synapses.

The glial response, which is non-specific in character, only indicates the amount of traffic in the neighbouring neurons. The effect is not limited to one synapse, and the electrical communication amongst the glial cells themselves increases this character of diffuseness.

Two examples can be taken to illustrate these possible roles of the glia. The first is taken from pathology. An abnormal functioning of the glia could contribute to the accumulation of potassium in the regions of the brain and thereby cause their electrical firing, leading to an epileptic fit. The second example is taken from physiology. Dennise Théodosis, in the Bordeaux neuroendocrinology laboratory, has observed a strange phenomenon in the rat during lactation (figure 15). Immediately after giving birth and later, throughout the period when the animal suckles its young, a total upheaval of the nervous architecture resulting in the disappearance of the glial cells, can be observed in a particular region of the hypothalamus, the magnocellular nuclei. The nerve cells are consequently in direct contact, as the glial insulation has vanished. These neurons secrete oxytocin, a hormone released into the bloodstream periodically and paroxystically in response to the sucking of the young, which causes the milk to be ejected. It

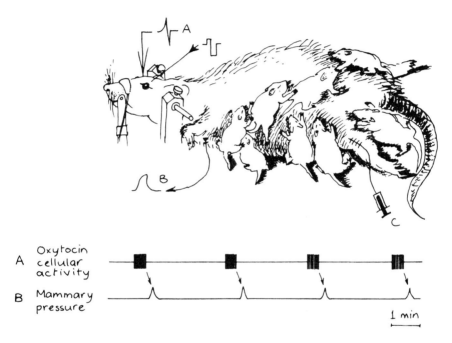

FIGURE 15   The electrical activity (A) of an oxytocin cell is recorded in the brain of an anaesthetized female rat while the young feed. The electrode is placed by stereotaxis in the magnocellular nuclei of the hypothalamus containing oxytocin cells. The oxytocin cell is identified using electrophysiological criteria. While the young feed, the variations in mammary pressure are recorded by a pressure captor (C). The sudden periodic rises in pressure are due to a pulsatile release of oxytocin into the blood by the neurosecretory cells. During the pulsatile discharges of oxytocin, it is observed that all the cells releasing the hormone have synchronous electrical activity. This simultaneous activity is linked to a deep structural reorganization which takes place during lactation in the hypothalamus of the female rat. (After D.A. Poulain and J.B. Wakerley, 'Electro-physiology of hypothalamic magnocellular neuron secreting oxytocin and vasopressin', *Neuroscience*, 7, 773–808, 1982.)

is thought that the relative disappearance of the glia helps the paroxystic activation of the nervous structures which manufacture oxytocin, a hormone which also has a role to play in generating and maintaining maternal behaviour. Here we can see how movements of the glia, in a certain region of the brain, can bring about a physiological upheaval in the animal, simultaneously setting up a certain type of behaviour and triggering hormonal secretion adapted to the new situation. At the end of the lactation period, the brain goes back to normal.[7] Thus the entire manner of being of an individual (maternal passion) and the survival of its young are here conditioned by the movements of a few thousand non-neuronal cells in an extremely limited region of the brain. It is quite possible to imagine that other behavioural changes may be very generally linked to modifications in the organization and functioning of glial cells.

Notes

1   P. Ehrlich, *Das Sauerstoff Bedürfnis des Organismus, Eine farbenanalytische Studie*, Berlin, 1985.
2   E. Knobil, 'Neuroendocrine control of the menstrual cycle', *Rec. Prog. Hormone Res.*, 36, 53–88, 1980; E. Knobil et al., 'Control of the rhesus monkey menstrual cycle: permissive role of hypothalamic gonadotropin-releasing hormone', *Science*, 207, 1371–3, 1980.
3   Rémy Colin can be considered as a pioneer in the neurosecretion field alongside its discoverers, Ernst and Berta Scharrer, although his contribution came after theirs. Colin suggested that there was endocrine secretion inside the brain by the neurons themselves. He went so far as to posit the existence of veritable neurosecretory synapses, an idea taken up by Barry and generally accepted today as a result of the discovery of neuropeptides. In addition to the transportation of the products of secretion by the neurons, a diffusion pathway using the cephalo-rachidian liquid would also seem to exist within the nervous system. Therefore hormones could spread throughout the organism using three means of transportation: the blood, the cephalo-rachidian liquid and the neurons. This is a very modernistic classification. (R. Colin and J. Barry, 'Histophysiologie de la neurosécrétion', *Ann. Endocrinol.* 153–92, 1957.
4   M.J. Dennis and R. Miledi, 'Electrically induced release of acetylcholine from denervated Schwann cells', *J. Physiol. London*, 237, 431–52, 1974.
5   P. Rakic, 'Neuron–glia relationship during granule cell migration in developing cerebellar cortex. A Golgi and electromicroscopic study in *Macacus rhesus*', *J. Comp. Neurol.*, 141, 283–312, 1971; R.L. Sidman and P. Rakic, 'Neuronal migration, with special reference to developing human brain: a review', *Brain Res.*, 62, 1–35, 1973.
6   J.P. Kelly and D.C. Van Essen, 'Cell structure and function in the visual cortex of the cat', *J. Physiol. London*, 238, 515–47, 1974; S.W. Kuffler and J.G. Nicholls, *From Neuron to Brain*, Sinauer, Sunderland, 1984.
7   D.T. Théodosis et al., 'Possible morphological bases for synchronization of neuronal firing in the rat supraoptic nucleus during lactation', *Neuroscience*, 6, 919–29, 1981.

5

The Humours of the Brain

What potions have I drunk of Siren tears
Distilled from limbecks foul as hell within,

Shakespeare, *Sonnet 119*

The chemistry of the passions

*Certain substances, most often of a peptide nature, when injected in very
small quantities into particular regions of the animal brain, bring about a
series of actions which are called behavioural: eating, drinking, mating etc.
A few examples follow.*

Tristram and the rat

Take a normally constituted individual and sprinkle a pinch of luliberin
over a small part of his hypothalamus. Your subject, if he has a consenting
partner within reach, will immediately engage in energetic and repeated
sexual intercourse. The story may seem a little worrying, until you realize
that the individual in question is only a laboratory rat. Isolde did not use
luliberin to make Tristram fall in love with her; King Mark's ship was not a
psychophysiological laboratory.

Nevertheless, the experimental fact remains. Just inject an infinitesimal
amount of a certain peptide into a given region of the encephalon, and you
bring about in the animal the complete sequence of mating behaviour, from
approach manoeuvres to consummation.

However, the chemical adventure does not stop there. Measurements
have shown that the final coital explosion is accompanied by a massive
release of endorphins. These peptides are apparently responsible for the
feeling of post-ejaculatory satisfaction, through their inhibitory action on
the nerve cells of the hypothalamus. In other words, after the peptide-

induced desire, we have the peptide-induced repose of the warrior. Let us push on a little further. The injection of endorphins into the hypothalamus causes a feeding reflex in the rat. Conclusion: the sexual act makes you hungry! Do desire, sexual activity and hunger result simply from the serial release of chemical substances inside the brain? We are not so naive as to succumb to the temptation of such romantic reductionism, even if certain mythological texts loudly proclaimed on psychoanalytical shores have no qualms about similar simplifications. After all, what do we know about the peptides secreted by the brain of the young Oedipus when he was deprived of his mother's breast? What interests us is to know that a single substance applied experimentally or released naturally in the brain is capable of initiating the complete uninterrupted sequence of infinitely complex and varied actions which make up a given behaviour pattern.

Chemistry and behaviour

Sexual activity is not the only example of behaviour brought about by the intracerebral injection of a peptide. Wounded and bleeding soldiers are unquenchably thirsty. We now know that this is due to the release of a peptide hormone called angiotensin, which is manufactured jointly by the liver and the kidney in the struggle against the sudden lowering in blood volume that can follow a haemorrhage, for example. The effect of the hormone is to contract the blood vessels (adapting the vascular container to the diminished blood content) and thereby avoid a dangerous fall in blood pressure. If a few billionths of a gram of angiotensin is injected into certain regions of the brain, the animal will immediately seek to quench its thirst. Even with an animal which has drunk to bursting point, water becomes its only desire. As with luliberin, the initiated behaviour pattern is enacted in full, from the frenzied search for water to compulsive and prolonged drinking.[1]

What more tender scene is there than a mother tending her young? The heart of the most hardened spectator softens at the sight and feels in communion with nature: beauty and the beast are reconciled!

The injection of oxytocin (a hypophyseal hormone which brings the milk springing from a mother's teats) into the cerebral ventricles of a virgin female rat induces perfect maternal behaviour within a few minutes: a nest is hastily flung together, young rats of no family relation planted in the cage are rounded up and protected, and any strays are licked and brought back to the fold.[2]

The golden hamster is a charming little hibernator who sometimes competes with the rat in the hearts of behaviourists. The hamster habitually stakes out its territory by rubbing its flanks, which are equipped with scent glands, on the walls of its cage. This is a highly significant behaviour pattern which bears witness simultaneously to the identity of the species and the individual. A micro-injection of vasopressin into a minute part of the hypothalamus quickly triggers a characteristic performance: the hamster carefully cleans its muzzle with its front feet, then it energetically licks and combs its flanks, arousing its scent glands before rubbing them compulsively along the sides of the cage. Thus a long series of stereotyped actions, characteristic of a well-brought-up hamster, is once again triggered by the appearance of a hormone in a given part of the brain.[3]

This type of behaviour induction is not exclusive to peptides or vertebrates. Kravitz and a team of Harvard researchers have shown that the injection of a lobster with serotonin (a classical neurotransmitter in vertebrates), not into the brain, since the lobster does not have one, but into its circulation, induces a posture characteristic of the love-struck male on the defensive: tail up, legs tense and pincers open. Another amine, octopamine, induces the opposite posture of submission in the female: tail down, legs relaxed and pincers closed.[4]

These behaviour patterns are stereotyped and identically repeated within each species. Man is a very different matter, of course. However, rather than being totally absent, the characteristic is masked, as the sequence of actions can be long-drawn-out, disordered and even delayed. It is not our purpose here to analyse the different phases of the behaviour of men and women in love, nor are we qualified to do this. However, it will be conceded that this behaviour has certain repetitive aspects, and that, once triggered, the action sequence is often irresistibly carried through to the end. The sad cohorts of premature ejaculators bear witness to this fact. Is it superfluous to suggest that the overpowering attraction which draws the lover into the arms of his mistress may sometimes (according to what people say) resemble the irrepressible urge of an animal in heat?

We could say the same about the various passion-dominated behaviour patterns that we shall study: hunger, thirst, anger or joy. They follow an invariable sequence, and they are explosive, overwhelming and hegemonic in character. The absence of these behaviour patterns is perhaps even more spectacular than their presence. Take the sad case of those young women suffering from mental anorexia. The illness is characterized by a state of non-hunger so absolute as to force the sufferers to refuse all food, condemning themselves to a mortal thinness. The intelligence remains intact, but the anorexic person is totally transformed by the absence of a vital behaviour pattern, the non-desire which is stronger than desire, the negation of a vital need, the refusal to admit her thinness, the obsessive fear of food. We have here a typical example of negative passion-dominated madness where the unaffected reasoning faculty is nevertheless incapable of surmounting the passion-induced obstacle. We do not intend to deny the importance of socio-affective factors and particularly the role of the family in the origin of such an illness, but we may imagine, in the absence of any definite proof, that some biochemical factor is at work in the brain of the anorexia sufferer. It may be the absence of an appetite-inducing substance or, conversely, the excess of a factor responsible for the feeling of satiety. We see here how all the social and cultural conditioning which surrounds and organizes the act of eating can be cancelled out by a behavioural shortcoming. In all the behaviour patterns that we have called passion dominated, a hard, invariable and stereotyped nucleus can be found that the exercise of thought, language and custom has masked, deformed, stretched and repositioned, but which constitutes the basic structure of behaviour.

Even in its negative version, the global character of passion-dominated behaviour (it can be triggered by the injection of a single chemical substance) should be underlined. The fact that behaviour appears as irreducible to the mere physical actions which it is composed of goes against the Platonic concept of the fragmentary nature of knowledge and reason which, according to Hobbes, is the result of discrete operations. We can also find here the roots of the traditional opposition between reason and passion.

The common humour

The chemical compounds which act in the brain to trigger a certain kind of behaviour are the same as those which maintain homeostasis in the internal milieu by inducing visceral reactions which contribute to regulation.

Regulating behaviour patterns

A characteristic trait of passion-dominated behaviour, as we have defined it, is the regulating role it plays in the survival of the individual or the species. The great systems of homeostasis all repose on two kinds of action: behavioural and metabolic. To fight against the cold and avoid a fall in body temperature, an animal not only seeks shelter and fluffs its feathers or makes its hair stand on end (behavioural means), but also increases the heat produced by its cells (metabolic means). To compensate a loss in water and maintain a constant degree of hydration, the individual drinks (behaviour) and reduces the elimination of water through the kidney (metabolism). To maintain a constant weight, he eats (behaviour) and uses his reserves (metabolism). In the preservation of the species, reproduction represents a harmonious combination of cellular phenomena (maturing of sex cells) and behaviour. In caring for the young, maternal behaviour is associated with the production of milk.

Any cut-and-dried separation which would put the brain (behaviour) on one side and the hormones and glands (metabolism) on the other is unacceptable. When you study the detail of the chemical processes, you discover that the substances which intervene in the behavioural response mechanisms are often the same as those in the metabolic response. The substance acts in the blood in the form of a hormone, and in the brain as a neurohumour. In reproduction, luliberin, which in the brain triggers sexual behaviour, is also the hypothalamic hormone which regulates the maturing of sex cells through the action of the pituitary gland. Luliberin is also to be found in the ovary, where it acts as a local hormone. Angiotensin, which induces the contraction of the blood vessels, is present in the brain, where it not only triggers drinking behaviour but also participates in the nervous regulation of blood pressure and orders the release of ADH. The substance is astonishingly omnipresent: it is a hormone in the blood, a neurotransmitter in the ganglia of the sympathetic nervous system and a neurotransmitter again or a neurohormone at different levels of the central nervous system. The digestive hormones insulin and gastrin also have a double destiny, as they are to be found in the brain participating in the mechanisms of feeding behaviour.

In the cerebral environment, what we see is the organization of functional ensembles which regulate the vital processes necessary for the survival of the individual and the species. The formation of an internal milieu in multicellular beings calls for the creation of organs specialized in given functions. Similarly, the appearance of a cerebral environment is accompanied by the formation in the brain of complex regulating units, and their overall task is carried out by the same chemical entities as those used in the peripheral organs. Just as the homeostatic functions of the internal milieu are not limited to one specialized organ, liver or kidney, the homeostatic units in the brain overflow from their narrow 'headquarters' (dealing with hunger, reproduction or breathing, for example) and spread to widely dispersed territories, sometimes covering the whole encephalon. On either side of the haemato-encephalic barrier therefore, the same liaison officers become double agents of regulation.

Yeast and snails and puppy-dogs' tails

In a jar of baker's yeast (*saccharomyces cerevisae*), millions of cells make love. Unicellular, neither animal nor vegetable, a yeast cell is the most primitive of eukaryotes. It can reproduce sexually, in so far as a new diploid cell is born from the fusion of two haploid cells. A factor has been isolated in yeast cell membranes: by recognizing a specific receptor, it triggers the reciprocal attraction of two partners. Furthermore, this peptide possesses an amino acid chain which is very close to that of luliberin, and it recognizes the luliberin receptor; it is also capable of stimulating the reproductive function in mammals. From the jar of yeast to Juliet's balcony the same peptide is at work.[5]

Take the verb 'love' on a blank page. In the beginning, there is a gene which codes for the manufacture of a molecule in charge of communicating for a given function (feeding, reproduction etc). The species become more complicated and various: from the ancestral gene there descend new genes which code for new molecules acting within an increasingly complex function. As they originate from the same shelf in the genomic library, all those molecules which take part in the function will have a family resemblance, a common root which makes them recognizable. Alongside 'love', there will be 'lover', 'lovely', 'loving', 'lovingly', 'unloving', 'loveless', a family of words united by a common root but bearers of a different message. A woman in love will not respond in the same way to her lover and to an unloving person. Similarly, the peptides coded by a family of genes will have different roles within the same function. All the adjustments that nature can make in a gene, substituting a nucleotide here, doubling it there, eliminating it somewhere else, are left to the imagination of the reader and the scientific examination of molecular biologists.

It is high time we used the sea-snail as an example. The sea-snail is an almost mythical beast for the neurobiologist, so great has been its contribution, along with its marine colleague the squid, to progress in this discipline. In its annual life cycle there comes a moment when this non-onanistic hermaphrodite lays eggs by the million on a suitable support. The eggs are expelled from the genital tube situated near the head by oscillating movements of the latter. They form irregular heaps rather like toothpaste on a toothbrush. This behaviour is associated with a pause in feeding and locomotion, and an acceleration of the respiratory pump. This is just one of a number of equally stereotyped behaviour patterns which make up the life story of a sea-snail. What makes the sea-snail so precious to us are its twenty thousand neurons, almost negligible by comparison with the millions in the human brain. They programme and direct the execution of different behaviour patterns and can all be observed, counted and coloured. Eight hundred nerve cells, the bag cells, orchestrate the egg-laying process. When the electrical activity of these neurons is recorded, their firing is observed half an hour before the laying begins. These rushes of action potentials cause the release of neurohormones which in their turn bring into play other neurons responsible for carrying out the programme. Also released into the circulation, the substances act directly on the sex glands. They are thus simultaneously hormones and neurotransmitters, a double role with which we are now familiar. It is surgically possible to remove the bag cells and extract from them a preparation which triggers the laying behaviour when injected into the circulation of an adult sea-snail. An active peptide, ELH, can be obtained from this extract. ELH is made up of a chain of thirty-six amino acids. Researchers from the University of Columbia have cloned the DNA which codes for ELH.[6] Using this probe, they have been able to identify nine genes which all seem to play a part in controlling the laying process. For three of them, the whole chain of nucleotides is now known. These genes are present in all the cells of the sea-snail, but express themselves individually only in certain areas of the organism. The gene coding for ELH is active only in the bag cells. It contains the instructions for the synthesis of a large protein, a precursor, which, when broken down later, produces other peptides besides ELH, all released simultaneously by the cell. Their action associates and cooperates with that of the ELH. The other two genes act on the atrial gland, appended to the genital organs. They code for two proteins, which when split up lead respectively to two peptides, A and B, which are able to activate the bag cells when injected into the animal. With eight hundred neurons and one gland we are already faced with all the complexity of the neuroendocrine organization of the higher animals. Here we have precursors giving birth to a host of peptides which are both hormones and neurotransmitters, a family of genes expressing themselves in different places where they code for various peptides but take part in the same function. For a single ELH, what an army of associated peptides! And yet we are only on the lower branches of the genealogical tree. In what nook or cranny of our body or brain does the ELH peptide hide out? Does the sea-snail drowsing in our past wake up when the crook and nanny mate? What function does the ELH take part in, if it still exists in our organism? Is its gene forgotten and now expressionless?

The substances responsible for communication are present in the living being even before the different organs are differentiated. Hormones and neurotransmitters appear before the endocrine and nervous systems. One could almost say that the mediators precede the appearance of life. Adenine derivatives and especially adenosine triphosphate (ATP) appear as the first neurotransmitter candidates. Adenine can be synthesized in the laboratory by simulating the conditions and composition of the primeval atmosphere (water, ammonia and methane) which reigned on earth before life appeared. The steroid hormones, oestrogens and cortisol, are manufactured by the yeast cells that the corresponding receptors possess. At this stage in evolution we can already observe that these hormones regulate the development of the cells, their reproduction and their relationship with their host. Hormones and neuromediators (at this stage, the distinction is pointless) are present in protozoa. Endorphins, insulin and somatostatin are to be found in tetrahymena. These substances secreted by the unicellular being can act at a distance on other individuals (pheromone-type action) or through the cell itself by linking with autoreceptors (autocrine-type action). All these actions will be found again in the higher animals and man. A nervous system and a digestive tube are two continuous links with the outside world and two places where substances in charge of communication are secreted. In the hydra, a small freshwater coelenterate, there exists an advanced sketch of a nervous system made up of cells sensitive to outside stimuli and capable of transporting information through a network of extensions as well as secreting neurohumours. Amongst the latter we can already list dopamine, acetylcholine, serotonin and all kinds of peptides that immunology is in the process of discovering. The nervous system is initially neuroendocrine in a general sense, with the secreted substances being able to act at short or long range. When a new substance intervenes in the evolutionary tree, it first appears in the nervous system. The ancestral gene expresses itself in the neurons before its descendants appear in the digestive cells. In the worm, the formation of the nerve centres (a grouping of neurons and synapses) precedes that of the endocrine glands (appendix 3). The existence of endocrine glands which are clearly independent of the nervous system is a relatively recent evolutionary development characteristic of vertebrates and higher invertebrates.[7] As we have already suggested, the autonomy of the hormone systems seems to be a basic evolutionary prerequisite for the later development of the nerve centres (see chapter 3).

Without becoming enmeshed in the quarrel between those who defend a polygenic theory (multiple origins) and those who defend the theory of a common root for all nerve cells, evolution allows us to understand the extraordinary diversity and omnipresence of neurohumours in the nervous, digestive and endocrine systems. This diversity can be found in a single cell during the development of an individual. Pancreatic cells, for example, are apparently dopaminergic during a transition period before secreting insulin. Several substances can also be present in the same cell. Researchers who identify nerve cells by using antibodies directed at one substance or another are intrigued and even worried by the presence in the same neuron of several neurotransmitters (coexistence): a peptide and an amine, two or more peptides, acetylcholine and serotonin, acetylcholine and one or more peptides etc.[8] Hard times for Dale's principle of one neurotransmitter per neuron! Instead, we have one neuron for ten neurohumours (neurotransmitters or neuromodulators). Babel in the brain! Amidst this confusion of tongues, who can still speak of coding of information? It should be noted that the presence of a reputed neuromediator in a cell does not necessarily mean that it fulfils a function of communication. For example, why is acetylcholine present in the cells of the cornea? Are all the peptides found in a cell functional?

Evolution gives rise to another consideration concerning the variability of functions according to the organs concerned and the differentiation of the species. Peptides are born when a precursor fragments. The breakdown of the large protein takes place differently in different places. The different types of possible communication in an organism with a single precursor can be illustrated by taking pro-opiomelanocortin (POMC), the precursor of the corticotropic hypophyseal hormone, as an example (figure 16). In the

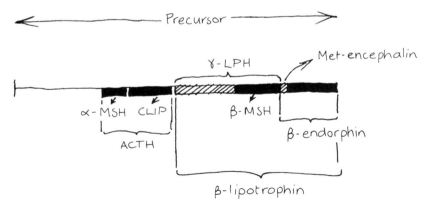

FIGURE 16   Sketch of the common precursor for adrenocorticotropic hormone (ACTH) and β-lipotrophin. Within these two compounds, there are amino acid sequences forming peptides which are already known, such as melanocyte-stimulating hormone (α-MSH), met-encephalin and β-endorphin. The derivatives which appear are consequently different according to the region of the precursor where the cuts take place.

brain, POMC is divided into neuropeptides which play the role of a neurotransmitter. In the hypothalamus cells, it gives birth to neurohormones released into the hypophyseal portal system. In the hypophysis, it is the starting point for the corticotropic hormone released into the general circulation system. Finally, in the digestive tube and reproductive organs, the substances derived from POMC and which are released on the spot have a paracrine function, i.e. the functions of a local hormone.

This variety of functions for the same substance can also be explained through the evolution of its receptors. The prolactin receptors found on the kidney explain that, in fish, this hormone takes part in the regulation of water. This function has disappeared in mammals, whose prolactin receptors are situated in the brain and the mammary gland.

With such confusion in the evolution process, it is not surprising to find confusion persisting in the individual and the traditional frontiers between hormones and neurotransmitters breaking down under examination.

The brain-gland

Glandulae vero non tam sanguini qua nervi famulantur.
Vesalius, *De humani corporis fabrica*, LVII (1543)

The brain is an endocrine gland which releases into the bloodstream a certain number of hormones and is subject to their feedback. Furthermore, without going outside itself, the brain uses typically neuronal modes of communication alongside information exchanges of a hormonal nature.

The brain is a gland

Up to now we have defined the brain as a closed citadel sheltering behind the haemato-encephalic barrier. Such isolation makes sense only in so far as it can be broken by paths of communication: inputs for nerve and hormone messages; outputs for the ordering of exterior actions. Alongside the nervous output concerning the motoneurons spread out all along the brainstem and spinal cord, there exists a hormonal output at the narrow funnel formed by the floor of the brain, the hypothalamus. Here the brain becomes a veritable endocrine gland which pours its secretions into the general bloodstream or into a local network which irrigates the hypophysis (figure 17). The hormones of the brain are no exceptions to the basic principles defining hormones: long-range action (Hardy) and autoregulation by feedback (Moore and Price).

Long-range action

We shall first consider the hypothalamic magnocellular system, which pours its oxytocin and vasopressin into the general bloodstream, and then the

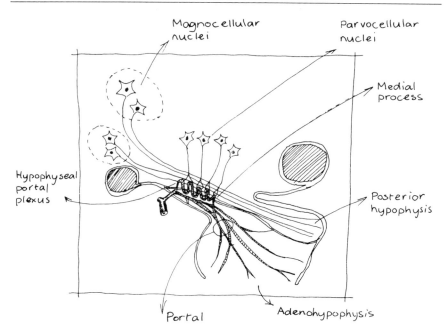

FIGURE 17 General organization of the hypothalamo-hypophyseal system. The posterior hypophysis is a nervous extension of the floor of the third ventricle. The axonal terminals of the magnocellular neurosecretory system (supra-optic and paraventricular nucleus) gather there in contact with capillaries from the general circulation system. The anterior hypophysis or adenohypophysis is a gland of ectodermal origin connected only secondarily to the nervous hypophysis. It is not connected to the brain by a nervous pathway, but only by a vascular pathway via a portal system. At the medial process, where the hypothalamic hormones manufactured by the parvocellular neurosecretory systems flow, a primary capillary network gives way to a second hypophyseal network where exchanges take place between hypothalamic factors transported to the hypophysis, and hypophyseal hormones poured into the general circulation system.

hypothalamic parvocellular system, which releases its hormones into the hypophyseal portal network where they exert their influence through the adenohypophysis.

The magnocellular neurosecretory cell, with its terminals gathered in the posterior hypophysis, is a typical example of a peptidergic cell. It has served as a model for the study of the synthesis, transport and release mechanisms of a neuropeptide (hormone or neurotransmitter). The peptide is first synthesized in the form of a large precursor. The precursor ripens during its transport towards the axonal terminal, while the electrical inhibitor and excitor factors, integrated by the neuronal membrane, are translated into action potentials which spread to the terminal. Here the action potential causes membrane doors to open and let calcium in. The calcium causes the granules to rupture outside the terminal (exocytosis) so that the peptides they contain are released. The release of these hormones (oxytocin and vasopressin) triggers true reflexes in which the stimuli induce a hormone release instead of the kind of motor response to be observed in sensorimotor reflexes. The study of these neurohormonal reflexes has clearly shown the complex organization of neurosecretory systems, and the special properties of the neurons which constitute them. Perhaps we should just point out that the vasopressor neuron seems to have an internal rhythmic activity and that oxytocin cells change their organization during lactation. In this latter case, a real upheaval of the architecture of the magnocellular nervous centres takes place, linked in a perfectly reversible way to the momentary physiological state of the animal. Another interesting property of these neurons is that they can be stimulated by the product of their own secretion (positive feedback or auto-amplification).

The parvocellular system releases a considerable number of hormones in a specialized region of the floor of the hypothalamus. There, the terminals of the neurosecretory cells are in contact with blood vessels which irrigate the anterior hypophysis (figure 18). The hormones released are either peptides,

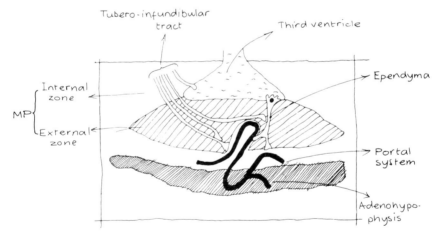

FIGURE 18   Structure of the medial process (MP). The sketch of this neurohaemal organ allows its role and function to be understood. The MP is the portion of the hypothalamus located in the floor of the third ventricle and separated from the adenohypophysis by the hypophyseal portal system. There is no haemato-meningeal barrier between the hypophyseal portal capillaries and the cells of the medial process. The internal zone is composed of ependymal cells, and the external palisade zone includes the nerve terminals and the portal capillaries. The tubero-infundibular tract is the main afferent system. It makes contact with the capillaries and forms axo-anoxic synapses, which are synaptoid contacts with the ependymal cells and terminals in the third ventricle. The ependymal cells also constitute a communication pathway between the ventricle and the portal capillaries.

which stimulate or inhibit the secretions of the anterior hypophysis, or traditional neurotransmitters (GABA, dopamine), which when released into the blood acquire a hormonal status. These hormones act on the different types of adenohypophyseal cells (appendix 4). The regulation is always multifactorial, as each hypophyseal hormone is dependent upon several agents, whether they be of cerebral origin or not, and one agent participating in the regulation of several hormones. This variety allows a wide spectrum of neuroendocrine responses which are part of the adaptive regulations. Take the adrenocorticotropic hormone (ACTH) and the milk-secretion hormone (prolactin) which are released in all sorts of circumstances where the body must respond to a new situation. These hormonal responses are modulated by the interaction of the multiple factors solicited by the change in environment.

Moreover it is quite remarkable that the adenohypophyseal cell combines the characteristics of a *stricto sensu* endocrine cell with those of a nerve cell. It is excitable, and the stimulus–secretion duo brings about ion movements which are comparable with those observed on a nerve terminal (figure 19).

Hormonal feedback

The steroid hormones cross the haemato-encephalic barrier and act directly on the functioning of the neurons (figure 20). An action generally exerts itself slowly through receptors situated inside the cell. These can modify the functioning of the genome and thereby influence the protein factory. This results in lasting changes in both behaviour and adaptive responses to stimuli, or again in feedback on hormonal secretions in the brain. There are as many examples as books and articles devoted to them. Inevitably, the complex action of the gonadic hormones (oestradiol, testosterone and progesterone) on sexual behaviour must be mentioned (see chapter 11).

The hormones secreted by the adrenal cortex (the cortisone family) are in the front line when it comes to defending the organism against aggressions or during the adaptive compromises to be studied in chapter 12. The release of these hormones depends upon ACTH, which is itself controlled by a hormone secreted by the hypothalamus (corticotrophin-releasing hormone (CRH)). Therefore the brain is central to the adrenal response and is consequently subject to the feedback of the adrenal hormones. If a subject is injected with dexamethasone, a synthetic adrenal hormone, a fall in ACTH is observed some time later. This bears witness to the braking effect exerted by the adrenal hormone on its own command nerve centres. It is interesting to note that this negative feedback does not take place in people suffering from a severe nervous breakdown.

The nerve cell is also rapidly influenced by steroids which directly affect the membrane and the electrical excitability of the neurons (figure 21). Their exact role in interneuronal or neurohormonal communication is not yet known.

Peptide hormones are also found at work in the central nervous system.

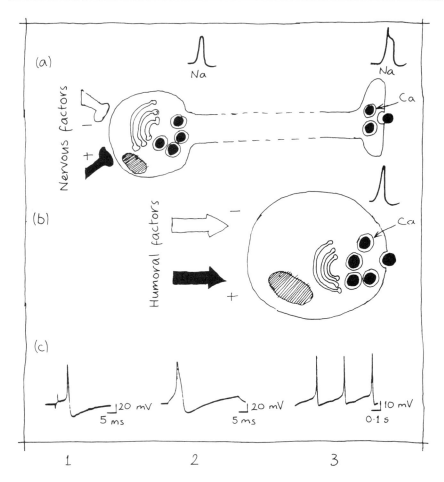

FIGURE 19   Comparison between (a) a neuron and (b) an endocrine cell. In both cases, the messenger-release stimuli are integrated in the form of action potentials which allow calcium (Ca) to enter the axonal terminal or the cell. The increase in internal calcium induces the release of the messenger (hormone or neurotransmitter) by exocytosis. A few examples of action potentials are shown in (c): 1, spinal cord neuron; 2, dorsal root ganglion neuron; 3, prolactin hypophyseal cell. It should be noted that the time-scale is different in 3 and that the action potential of the endocrine cell, being almost exclusively composed of a calcium influx, is much slower than those of 1 and 2.

Where do they come from since they do not cross the haemato-encephalic barrier? We have already seen in our evolutionary examples that most systemic hormones are also synthesized and released in the brain, whether they be digestive hormones (gastrin, cholecystokinin (CCK), vasoactive intestinal peptide (VIP or substance P)), tissue hormones (angiotensin,

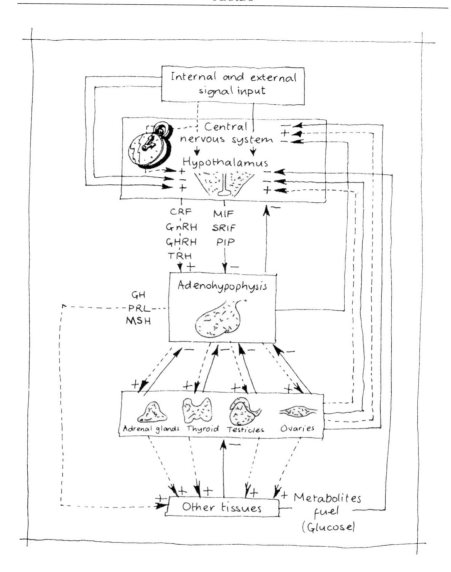

FIGURE 20 General view of feedback constituting the conceptual basis for neuroendocrine systems. The actions or feedback can sometimes be positive (+) and sometimes negative (−). Some hormones, such as oestradiol, can have either a positive or a negative effect depending on their level in the blood and the length of their action.

bradykinin) or hypophyseal hormones. What are the functions and the modes of action of the endocerebral peptide hormones? It is not enough to say that these hormones can act as neurotransmitters or modulators since this does not explain why the same substances are to be found in the brain and the peripheral circulation. The case of angiotensin clearly illustrates the problem. We have already noted the multiple effects of this hormone. Angiotensin, which is released into the bloodstream each time the blood volume diminishes, also works in the brain, where we saw that it induces a desire to drink, a rise in blood pressure and a release of vasopressin, three effects which combine to restore the blood volume. As the angiotensin in the bloodstream does not cross the haemato-encephalic barrier, the existence of an endogenous angiotensin in the brain must be admitted, and has indeed been found by immunocytologists.[9] The peripheral hormone and the cerebral neurohumour contribute to the same homeostasis, as if a central

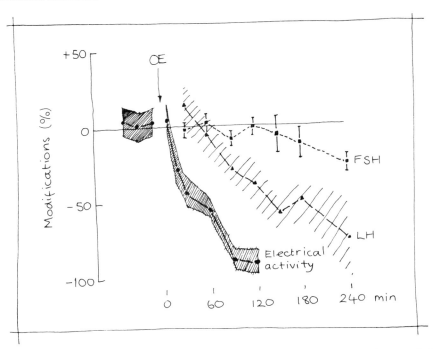

FIGURE 21   Negative feedback of oestradiol. A systemic injection of oestradiol (OE) rapidly inhibits the release of luteinizing hormone (LH) and follicle-stimulating hormone (FSH), the gonadotropic hormones. This negative feedback is interpreted as a direct action of oestradiol on the hypothalamic neurons, an example of which can be seen in the figure. The fall in the electrical activity of the cell is due to a membranous action of oestradiol. This action induces a fall in luliberin secretion followed by a fall in the secretion of LH and FSH. (After Dufy et al., 'Effects of oestrogen on the electrical activity of identified and unidentified hypothalamic units', *Neuroendocrinology*, 22, 38–47, 1976.)

nervous regulation using the same chemical agents were being used to back up the systemic hormonal regulation, adding the adaptive precision of the central complex. The same can be said for vasopressin. Immunocytologists have clearly shown the existence of vasopressin in the brain. The same osmotic and circulatory stimuli that release vasopressin into the blood trigger its release in the brain. We can therefore advance the hypothesis that the central vasopressin takes part in the same homeostatic regulations as the systemic vasopressin.

Hormonal communication

First, it should not be forgotten that the distinction between neurotransmitters and hormones does not entirely correspond to the facts.

Spatially, messengers of neuronal origin act at a distance from their emission site. The substance released spreads outside the synaptic space and addresses itself to neighbouring neurons which have no synaptic links with the emitting neuron. This case is observed in the sympathetic ganglia, where a luliberin-type peptide exerts an action of this kind. The messenger can also be released at scattered and multiple terminal branchings which present no synaptic differentiation. Certain neurons spray their messengers over a large area in the cortex without establishing a real connection with the neurons there. The information transmitted by such messengers concerns large parts of the brain which they help to regulate.[10] They may be responsible for a sort of localized homeostasis, controlling the microenvironment of certain neuronal groups. These regulations may possibly be linked to the emotions, humours and everything which constitutes the 'instinctive' functions. This hazy brain, responsible for the emotional and passionate side of the individual, may be superimposed, as it were, on the wired brain responsible for the sensorimotor, cognitive and rational functions.

Operationally, a strictly neurotransmitter action consists in the passive opening of ionic canals induced by an electrical signal. The final integration of this signal allows the neuron to emit an impulse in its turn. Certain messengers of nervous origin can exert a hormonal-type action through a second messenger which spreads the information throughout the receptor cell and modifies its energy properties or its excitability.

Furthermore, a single messenger can reach the receptor membrane at different concentrations depending on whether it follows the synaptic pathway (high concentration) or the hormonal pathway (low concentration). Its action differs accordingly (figure 19). As for the cell, it has receptors of varying sensitivity for the same substance![11]

Conclusion

We have shown that alongside the neuronal brain, a computer of unheard-of complexity, there exists a true hormonal brain. The latter unceasingly and extensively modifies the functioning of the former. Our approach to the passionate individual is based on this duality, as you may have guessed. If you start with a spiritless brain, you end up with a bodiless spirit or a marvellous computer in search of a programmer. But before dealing with this autonomous brain reconciled with its bodily humours, we must settle the account of a certain number of unmarried machines.

Notes

1   J.T. Fitzsimons, *The Physiology of Thirst and Sodium Appetite*, Cambridge, 1979.
2   C.A. Pedersen et al., 'Oxytocin induces maternal behavior in virgin female rats', *Science*, 216, 648–9, 1982.
3   C.F. Ferris et al., 'Vasopressin injected into the hypothalamus triggers a stereotypic behavior in golden hamsters', *Science*, 224, 521–3, 1984.
4   E.A. Kravitz et al., 'Neurohormones and lobsters: biochemistry to behavior', *Trends Neurosci*, 6, 345–9, 1983.
5   There is a great deal of information about peptides in the brain in D.T. Krieger, 'Brain peptides: what, where and why', *Science*, 222, 975–85, 1983.
6   R.H. Scheller et al., 'A family of genes that codes for ELH, a neuropeptide eliciting a stereotyped pattern of behavior in aplysia', *Cell*, 28, 707–19, 1982.
7   On the concept of neurons and paraneurons belonging to the endocrine cell family, see T. Fujita et al., 'Secretory aspect of neurons and paraneurons', *Biomed. Res.*, 5 (Suppl.), 1–8, 1984.
8   J.M. Lundberg and T. Hökfelt, 'Coexistence of peptides and classical neuro-transmitters', *Trends Neurosci.*, 6, 325–32, 1983.
9   G. Simonnet et al., 'Angiotensin II in the central nervous system in the rat', *J. Physiol.*, Paris, 79, 453–60, 1984.
10 See the special issue on neurotransmitters in *Trends Neurosci.*, 6 (8), 1983.
11 P. Legendre et al., 'Electrophysiological effects of angiotensin II on cultured mouse spinal cord neurons', *Brain Res.*, 293, 287–96, 1984; J.D. Vincent and J.L. Barker, 'Substance P: evidence for diverse roles in neuronal function from cultured mouse spinal neurons', *Science*, 205, 1409–11, 1979.

PART II
Unmarried Machines

'The Large Glass'

What is an unmarried machine? It is a surrealistic creature sprung from the brain of the joker Marcel Duchamp, and it is as out of place in a scientific work as a sewing-machine on a dissecting table.[1] It is a machine constructed from elements of the real, but which is not supposed to work as such. It is a myth producer.[2] It is unmarried, solitary and onanistic, because it contributes only to the joy of the person who made it or to the jubilation of those who have borrowed it. *The Large Glass* in the Philadelphia Museum (figure 22) is the prototype of the unmarried machine: *The Bride Stripped Bare by her Bachelors, Even*. *The Large Glass* cannot be dealt with in a few lines: its execution gave us the capital work (in the sense of capital punishment) of twentieth-century art. It is a textual painting with the text rubbed out, but it can only function with a text. Let us take as an example the ninety-four documents, reproductions and manuscripts which served in its execution and which we find gathered in *La Boîte verte*,[3] or the abundant literature devoted to the work.[4] According to Octavio Paz, *The Large Glass*

> mocks the grotesque process in which it is impossible to distinguish between desire and a combustion engine, love and petrol or sperm and gunpowder . . . *The Large Glass* is a devilish and clownish portrayal of modern love, or more exactly of what modern man has turned love into. To turn the human body into a machine, even if the machine is a computer capable of creating symbols, is worse than a degradation. Eroticism is at the frontier between the sacred and the damned. The body is erotic but sacred. The two categories are inseparable: if the body is nothing but sex and animal heat, eroticism is lost in the monotonous functionality of reproduction.[5]

Neurobiology offers us a certain number of models drawn from studies of the real which can explain the mechanisms of desire, pleasure, hunger, thirst or sex. We invite the reader to consider them as unmarried machines, i.e. not as plans of robots which are supposed to work, but rather as workshops for the imagination. It is in no way downgrading for the researcher to have his inventions compared with Poe's pendulum or the feeding machine in Chaplin's *Modern Times*. But at least the scientist has been granted a licence for occasional gratuitousness and humour, without depriving him of his reputation for serious work. Nobody doubts the usefulness of research. All we are asking for is the right to be ironic from time to time!

Notes

1   Comte de Lautréamont, *Les Chants de Maldoror*, Paris, 1868.
2   M. Carrouges, *Les Machines célibataires*, Paris, 1976.
3   From 1913 on Duchamp gave up painting in the classical sense (he had had enough of the smell of turpentine) to devote himself to 'idea-painting' or painting

FIGURE 22 Marcel Duchamp, *The Large Glass* or *The Bride Stripped Bare by her Bachelors, Even* (1915–1923), Philadelphia Museum.

without paint. *The Large Glass* is the most perfectly unfinished example of this activity. This work of 'absence' has caused a lot of perplexity, aggravated by the documents used in its making. They have been left to us in *La Boîte verte* (1934), which includes the preparatory material, photographs, drawings and calculations which went into the composition of *The Large Glass* and which, according to Duchamp himself, 'resembles a kind of Army and Navy Stores catalogue'.

4   R. Lebel, *Sur Marcel Duchamp*, Paris, 1959.
5   O. Paz, *Deux transparents: Marcel Duchamp et Lévi-Strauss*, Paris, 1970.

6

The Spying Fly and the Neuron Box

Why has not man a microscopic eye?
For this plain reason, man is not a fly.
Alexander Pope, *Essay on Man*

In this chapter, we give examples of simple or simplified living models which illustrate the marvels of nerve wirings and underline the advantages and dangers of 'reductionism'.

Eye, said the fly

It is astonishing that a fly does not lose its head when flying in all directions or walking on the ceiling. It is even more astonishing that a male fly can follow to the millimetre the capricious flight of a female. The organization of the nerve cells in the visual system of the fly explains such performances. The solutions are different from those adopted in vertebrates, but there are similarities which allow us to perceive general laws for the organization and functioning of visual systems.

Seeing in a moving world

What can a fly do? Fly all over the place, walk on the ceiling (better than the most skilful poet) and witness the death of poor Cock Robin. But how can it keep a stable picture of the world despite the endless acrobatics which are its main pastime (figure 23)?

The fly flies, but for its eye it is the world that moves. The apparent rotations in the environment are translated by the nervous system into twisting movements along the different axes of the body: the head rolls, moves up and down, moves forwards and backwards, and tips over, and all

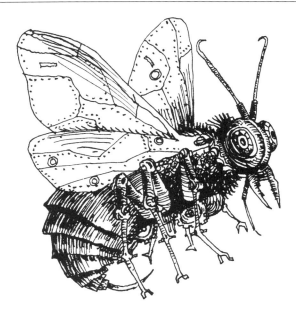

FIGURE 23   The mechanical fly (François Durkheim).

this is visio-motor coordination which minimizes the rotation of the fly relative to the environment, helping to stabilize its course.[1] In the brain a mere few dozen giant neurons integrate the information on the moving space picked up by the cells on the retina. Each neuron is specialized in reading a movement along a vertical, horizontal or head-to-tail axis. Here we have the example of a neuron realizing an abstraction, the idea of movement, from a raw image of the world formed on the retina. This identical neuron, named and numbered according to the spatial direction it processes (H1, H2, V1 etc.), is to be found in the same place in the brain of every fly. The fixity of the system is remarkable when you compare it with the mix-up of movement-sensitive neurons in the visual cortex of a vertebrate.[2]

We shall note that it is possible to draw up an almost complete plan of the wiring of the visual system of the fly, as could be done for an electronic machine. It is true that we do not know exactly how the components work, but 350,000 neurons are nothing alongside the thousand million neurons in the visual brain of man.

The compound eye

The fly has a panoramic vision covering a hemisphere for each of the two eyes. The eye is composed of three thousand juxtaposed facets or ommatidia. This mosaic structure is to be found in each of the three optical ganglia which progressively analyse the various visual messages: shapes, colours, movements and light polarization.

Each ommatidium is a true miniature eye with its own cornea, a 30 micron convex lens and its own retinula which contains eight photo-receptor cells. These have a lateral refringent stem or rhabdomere which contains the visual pigment and functions as an optical waveguide. Their mouths, measuring from 1 to 2 microns, and so hardly longer than the light wavelength, are precisely situated in the internal focal plane of each cornea. It will be seen in figure 24 that the photoreceptor cells occupy a very special position in each ommatidium. Six large cells, numbered 1 to 6, surround two central cells (7 and 8) with perfectly superimposed rhabdomeres. The light which reaches rhabdomere 8 is the light which has not been absorbed by rhabdomere 7. Lastly, each ommatidium has seven rhabdomere mouths, each exploring a limited visual space in a given direction.

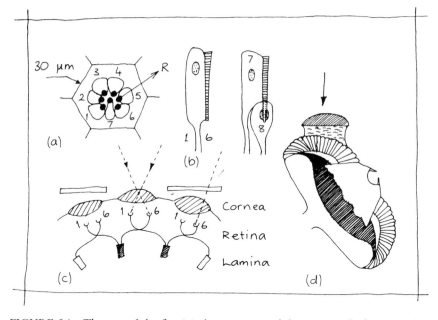

FIGURE 24   The eye of the fly: (a) elementary module composed of six peripheral receptor cells R_1-R_6 and two central cells R_7 and R_8 which overlap; (b) longitudinal section of receptor cells; (c) longitudinal section through three ommatidia (cells 1 and 6 of neighbouring ommatidia which 'look' in the same direction send their axons towards the same neuro-ommatidium where they synapse with a second neuron); (d) fluoroscopy, a method for visualizing rhabdomeres *in vivo* on a large number of ommatidia, consists in optically neutralizing the cornea with a drop of water and observing the top of the receptors with a fluorescence microscope. (After N. Franceschini, 'Chromatic organization and sexual dimorphism', in Borselliero and Cervetto (eds), *Photoreceptors*, Plenum, New York, 1984.)

Beyond the retinal receptor, the eye of the fly, like that of man, possesses three ganglionic relays. In the first ganglia or lamina, the three thousand ommatidia give way to the thousand neuro-ommatidia which gather the nerve extensions from the retina in a very special way. A brief description is sufficient to give an idea of the 'ingenuity of nature'.

Structurally, there is a remarkable identity between the angle of the axes of two neighbouring ommatidia and the angle of divergence of two neighbouring rhabdomeres. Therefore cells belonging to neighbouring ommatidia look in the same direction. For any given direction, we can find six peripheral cells (1–6) from six different ommatidia, and a group of central cells (7 and 8) which all correspond to one mouth. Connectivity is such that the six peripheral cells from the six neighbouring ommatidia send their extension towards the same neuro-ommatidium of the lamina where they make a synaptic connection (figure 24).

The six electrical signals arriving in the same neuro-ommatidium result in a factor of 6 improvement in the light signal, and so heighten the absolute sensitivity of the system.[3] A special fate is reserved for the central cells 7 and 8: instead of sending their axon to the neuro-ommatidium corresponding to their direction, they send it directly to the corresponding column in the second ganglionic relay or medulla.

Franceschini has put forward the hypothesis that the eye of the fly is composed of two coaxial visual subsystems.[4] The first system, with its input from the six peripheral cells 1–6 and their axons converging on a single neuro-ommatidium, has a high absolute sensitivity and is responsible for vision in dull light. The second system, with its input from the two central cells 7 and 8, transmits contrast better but to the detriment of its absolute sensitivity; it could be specialized in colour perception.

The spectral sensitivity of these two systems is different. Cells 1–6 in the scotopic system have a common sensitivity with two peaks, one in the blue and the other near the ultraviolet. The homogeneity of the 1–6 population over the whole retina contrasts with the heterogeneity of the 7–8 population. Thanks to the fluoroscopic method developed by Franceschini, most of the rhabdomeres are seen to be fluorescent in the living animal. While rhabdomeres 1–6 all present the same emission (red under blue excitation), rhabdomere 7 appears green, red or black (no fluorescence) according to the ommatidium. A microscope equipped with a precision goniometer can be used to map the ommatidia according to the type of fluorescence of their rhabdomere 7. This map is different in the male and female fly.

Flights of fancy

Is desire in the eye of the fly? Here we describe the mechanical courtship of the housefly (*Musca domestica*).

The male fly chases the female. But there is no passion in love-struck flies. Only the cold stem of the multifaceted glance unites them. A cine-camera records the love chase (figure 25). The two courses flown at the same speed

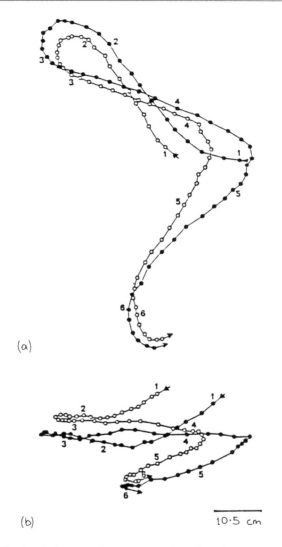

(a)

(b)   _____
                                 10·5 cm

FIGURE 25   Chasing behaviour between two flies filmed simultaneously from (a) above and (b) the side. The corresponding points are shown by the same number on the two trajectories. (After C. Wehrhahn, 'Sex-specific differences in the chasing behaviour of the flying houseflies *Musca*', *Biol. Cybernet*, 32, 239–41, 1979.)

(1–4 metres per second) are almost parallel, as if the male was attached to the female by some invisible thread.

Let us use fluoroscopy to examine the retina of the male (figure 26). The number 7 rhabdomeres in a dorsofrontal zone emit a red fluorescence that makes them indistinguishable from the neighbouring rhabdomeres

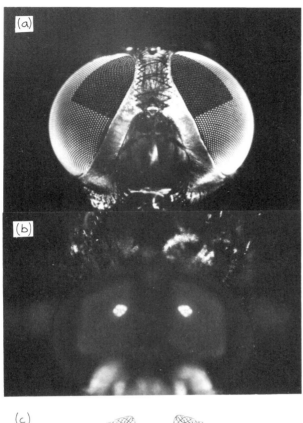

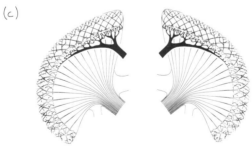

FIGURE 26 (a) Head of a male fly photographed by N. Franceschini using a microscope (the dark region outlines the part of the eye where the male R_7 receptors are to be found); (b) two deep pseudo-pupils (see N. Franceschini, in A.W. Snyder and R. Menzel (eds), *Photoreceptors Optics*, Springer, Berlin, 1975); (c) third optical ganglion of each eye showing the giant number 1 neuron, the dendritic tree of which is superimposed (in black) on the ramifications of the other neurons (this neuron is found only in the male). These pictures are meant to show the complexity of a simple system. (After K. Hausen and N. Strausfeld, 'Sexually dimorphic interneuronal arrangements in the fly visual system', *Proc. R. Soc. London, Ser. B*, 208, 57–71, 1980.)

1–6. The ultrastructural study of the red fluorescence number 7 cells in the dorsofrontal zone shows that they terminate in the neuro-ommatidia of the first ganglion as with the other number 7 cells of the retina. Therefore the neuro-ommatidia of the dorsofrontal part of the male eye receive not six axons, but seven, all from cells with the same spectral sensitivity. The principle of nervous superimposition can help us understand the biological usefulness of the phenomenon. By integrating seven signals instead of six in a particular part of the retina, the male eye improves its contrast discrimination (a kind of sexually oriented fovea). The small moving black smudge that is the female is seen from underneath through the dorsal spy-hole of the retina of the male, who perfectly shadows the flight of the female.[5] Other anatomical traits, such as the existence of collateral branches leaving axon 7 before it penetrates the neuro-ommatidium, improve contrast by lateral inhibition.[6] Everything, even the loss of colour vision, seems to contribute to making the dorsofrontal zone of the male retina the obstinate detector of a minute mobile black smudge – the female of the species!

This example shows how structure, mechanisms and function can be inextricably linked in a single cell and underlines the usefulness of studying them simultaneously. As Franceschini says, 'the unusual connection of red fluorescence number 7 cells in a neuro-ommatidium of the first optical ganglion would have seemed quite incomprehensible to us if we had had neither the behavioural context, nor the information relative to the spectral sensitivity of the cells.'[7]

The number 7 cells of the dorsofrontal zone of the male retina are genetically programmed to resemble their neighbours, and this constitutes an example of genetic rigour in establishing sexual dimorphism. When we compare the male and female brains, we find other disparities such as the presence of an exclusively male giant neuron, MLG 1, in the third optical ganglion which receives information from the sexual fovea on the retina.

Fly to fly

The brain of the male fly is different from the brain of the female fly. Its body and behaviour are also different. These differences are genetically programmed. Drosophila offers incomparable laboratory material for the study of the genetic determinism of behaviour patterns and their relations with nervous structures.

Play it again, gene

The fly is not flighty. The female offers herself once and once only. The male, in order to seduce her, observes the sequence of courtship actions like the verses of a recorded song: first comes the chase, then the contact, a tap of the legs, followed by a tune from the beating wings. Then the male licks the sex of the female, folds his abdomen under her and accomplishes penetration for twenty minutes or so. The passive female spreads her ovipositor to make penetration easier. She would hurl it at the head of any fly who attempted re-entry.[8] Such is the unchanging sequence of events in a long-standing scenario where action follows action in response to ever-identical trigger signals. The brain, like a phonograph, rolls out the motor programmes recorded in the neuron grooves by the chromosomal matrix.[9]

Every ten days, a generation of *Drosophila* offer a mutational treasure for observation: for one altered gene, we may obtain a wing growing instead of an antenna or a behaviour pattern which disappears etc. Taking the jigsaw apart enables a structure, function or act to be linked to a given gene. Mitotic recombinations carried out in the larva produce mosaics in which a fragment of the adult individual has a different genetic make-up from the rest of the animal.[10] There exist sexual mosaics, composite animals in which certain cells are genetically female and others male. The sexual genotype of the cell is identifiable by means of enzyme markers.[11] Parts of the brain must be genetically male for the different series of male behaviour patterns to take place: the dorsal part for the preliminaries, the thoracic ganglion for the love song. Certain mosaics court virgin females with the male parts of their brain and are themselves courted by males on account of the female cells of their abdomen.[12]

Judging from these results, we would be justified in concluding that the sexual behaviour patterns of the male and the female are governed by the difference in the brain, which is itself determined by genes. This is a very different situation from that observed in vertebrates, as we shall see.[13] Nevertheless we must be wary of attributing such an absolute power to genes.

Hot cross flies

A mutation on the transformer 2 gene produces flies with the female genotype XX and, when bred at an ambient temperature of 16°C, they look and behave like females. However, when bred at a temperature of 29°C, they look and behave like males. What is more surprising is that such flies, bred at 16°C and having developed into fertile adult females, behave like males when placed at 29°C and try to court females with their female abdomen, which takes some doing.[14]

A combination of alleles from the sex lethal gene produces flies of female genotype XX which look like males. The transformation is total: the sexual apparatus is that of a male, and produces sperm.[15] However, the behaviour is that of the female, even to the point of using its male apparatus as an ovipositor. Some individuals carry the ambivalence so far that they court females.

The male and female structures may coexist in the brain of either sex, in which case every *Drosophila* brain may contain the circuits responsible for male and female behaviour, with the circuits for the appropriate sex being permanently blocked.[16] This solution is not too distant from that adopted by vertebrates, as we shall see.

Remembrance of flies past

The love-making of flies may not be the encounter of two egos, the independent, complementary and parallel accomplishment of automatic actions. The chase, courtship and copulation express a permanent circulation of information between the lovers. The exchange is not limited to a sequence trigger signal but associates a considerable number of auditory, olfactory and visual signs sent out by each partner. Mutants that are blind, deaf and have no sense of smell can help us appreciate the relative importance of these different signals.[17]

The female accepts the male once only. After copulation, the male goes through a few hours of depression. While she is still a virgin, the female secretes a powerful aphrodisiac which attracts the male, but the seminal fluid is transformed into an anti-aphrodisiac in the abdomen of the female, and this discourages the male from trying again.[18]

Merely being exposed to this anti-aphrodisiac, however, is not enough to induce a depression in sexual activity. For this to happen, exposure to the extract must be associated with the sighting of another fly.[19] The postcopulatory sexual depression in the male seems to depend on an apprenticeship which implies the presence of the partner. It is to be observed that mutants suffering from amnesia (a strain of flies incapable of learning) do not suffer from this depression. Since he forgets that he has just copulated, the amnesia-suffering mutant never stops. In this light, depression appears as a true cognitive process.[20]

This last remark brings us full circle: if memory and complex associations of signals are capable of modulating what seemed unchangeable, what is the validity of mechanical and stereotyped behaviour models for invertebrates?

Advantages and drawbacks of being an invertebrate

A common trait of invertebrate behaviour patterns is their clear outline, even if, little by little, the details reveal a complexity one believed was reserved for the higher animals. We can dream of knowing one day all the workings of the machine, with each circuit of the nervous system, built from the plans provided by the genes, corresponding to a behaviour pattern triggered by a specific signal. However, it is not long before we notice that the intervention of such and such a circuit depends on multiple variables both inside and outside the animal.

A male cricket knows six songs of love and war: a song which announces his presence, a song which beckons the female, a song of seduction, a song calling the parting female back, a song to warn off rivals and a song after love-making. It is as if each song were recorded on a cassette and taken up again, without a single change, in response to a given situation: the presence of a rival or the distance separating the male from the female, but also the hormonal state of the partner.

The male fly and the male cricket seem to share the same certainty about their females and the way to behave in their presence. In contrast, knowledge leading to choice and uncertainty seems to be exclusive to the higher animals. This is not in fact the case, and certain invertebrate behaviour patterns can be described in terms of what Tolman has called 'cognitive processes'. In short, the sign is linked by a behaviour pattern to what is signified. The sign, if responded to in a certain way, leads to what was signified. The latter provides a confirmation of what was expected. This allows the animal to choose later. The postcopulatory depression of the male fly is an example of such a learning process.

Perhaps because the neuronal aspect is more important than the hormonal, the mechanisms of invertebrates are easier to study in depth than are those of vertebrates. Indeed, the importance of the wiring system reveals itself in all its magnificence when we try to link a behaviour pattern to the workings of isolated groups of nerve cells. The example of the giant cell of the optical ganglion of the fly showed us how the abstract idea of movement, an idea which made poor Zeno lose his head, was treated by a single neuron.[21] The simplicity of a nervous system makes cell spotting easier, and allows us to study its basic mechanisms: short-term memory (minutes) or long-term memory (days), familiarization etc.[22] The relative contributions of knowledge acquired by experience and hereditary innate knowledge can be appreciated because of the frequency of successive generations and the detailed knowledge of genetic stock, as with *Drosophila*.

The very advantages of invertebrates, however, limit their usefulness. Their simplicity and stereotyped behaviour are of no help in taking on the complex strategies observed in the higher vertebrates. Even if they were, the evolutionary solutions found in certain invertebrates are not necessarily applicable to man. In the cephalopod, for example, the eye is made of skin and seeks light, whereas in insects and other invertebrates, the eye is an expansion of the brain and avoids light.[23] Evolution is opportunistic, and has chosen various solutions. Man cannot be considered as a higher insect, even if both have certain basic mechanisms in common.[24]

What characterizes invertebrates is how precise their mechanisms are, how marvellously and fatally adapted to the environment they are, to the point of dying out if the environment changes. Man is great because he is uncertain, versatile and adaptable to the point of overrunning the whole planet: he is not about to disappear.

We must be excused for quoting at this point a fable made up by a butterfly collector during his afternoon nap:

> God, who had studied as an engineer, manufactured the invertebrates. Each day he marvelled at their astonishing mechanical precision. But God finally tired of the monotonous repetitiveness of their existence, and He created man. But God, who had studied as an engineer, was shocked by man's changing and uncertain moods, and threw him out.

Neuron culture

Another way of obtaining simplified models of nervous systems is the in vitro *method in which nerve cells are cultivated outside the animal. The cells in question are either transformed cells which have acquired the possibility of multiplying indefinitely outside the organism (neuroblastomas) or non-transformed cells removed from the living organism and artificially cultivated in the appropriate nutritive element.*

By using *in vitro* methods simplified preparations can be obtained, either containing a single type of cell or realizing groups from a single part of the nervous system or a single layer of cells.

Neuroblastomas are cells of tumoral origin which have consequently acquired the property of dividing and reproducing themselves indefinitely in a nutritive element. These cells allow the elementary properties of the nerve cell to be studied. Certain kinds possess odd characteristics (such as the capacity to secrete a neurotransmitter or the presence of receptors, enzymes or ionic canals) which make them interesting tools for study. As they produce homogeneous populations of identical cells, neuroblastomas are particularly suited to research in molecular biology and biochemistry, even if from a biological point of view they remain freaks, capable as they are of acquiring properties which normal cells do not have or of shedding certain basic characteristics.

Normal nerve cells obviously do not reproduce *in vitro* like tumoral cells, the characteristic of a neuron being its incapacity to divide. Neurons *in vitro* keep or acquire a number of the properties of neurons *in vivo*. According to the problem to be dealt with, different techniques can be used.

One of these methods consists in preparing slices of nervous systems or explants and keeping entire pieces of brain alive for several hours after having removed them from the animal and transferred them to a suitably oxygenated and nutritive liquid environment. This technique respects the structure and connections of the region under study. It allows the neurons to be approached more easily by means of microelectrodes which record the electrical properties and the contacts which are established between different neurons. It is also possible to measure the substances released by the neurons into the liquid in response to various chemical stimulations.

Quite unlike this technique which respects the architecture of the brain, there exist primary cultures of dissociated cells. These are generally developed from nervous systems removed from embryos. The cells, after being separated mechanically or by enzymatic digestion, are dispersed on the bottom of a container, covered with a suitable liquid and placed in incubators where the temperature and atmosphere are controlled. After a few days, the cells which have adhered to the bottom become larger and begin to grow like a plant. Each surviving neuron sends out extensions in the direction of other neurons and establishes synaptic contacts with them.

In a few days, a network-type organization can be seen on a single cellular layer, which makes direct observation under a microscope relatively easy (figures 27 and 28).

In addition to allowing the basic properties of certain kinds of neurons to be studied, these methods also enable us to study factors of differentiation

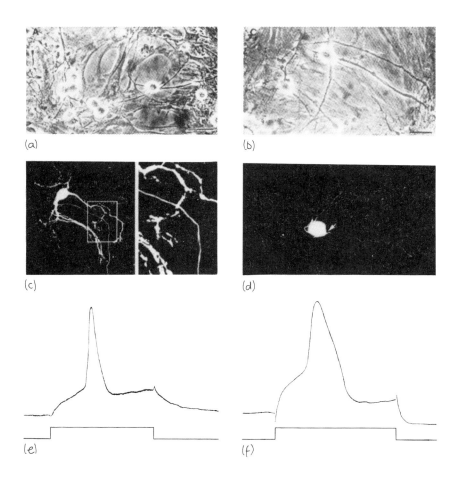

FIGURE 27   Spinal cord neurons and dorsal root ganglia from fourteen-day mouse embryos, kept in culture for twenty-eight days. In (a) and (b) the cells are viewed in phase contrast. Extensions can be observed which have grown from the cellular bodies and developed on the bottom of the dish, creating synaptic connections. In (c) and (d), a spinal cord cell (c) and a dorsal root ganglion cell (d) were recorded using a glass microelectrode inserted into the neuron. At the end of the recordings, the injection of a fluorescent dye allowed the cellular body and its extensions to be marked. In (e) and (f), examples are given of action potentials measured in neurons (c) and (d) respectively. (After P. Legendre, U.176, INSERM.)

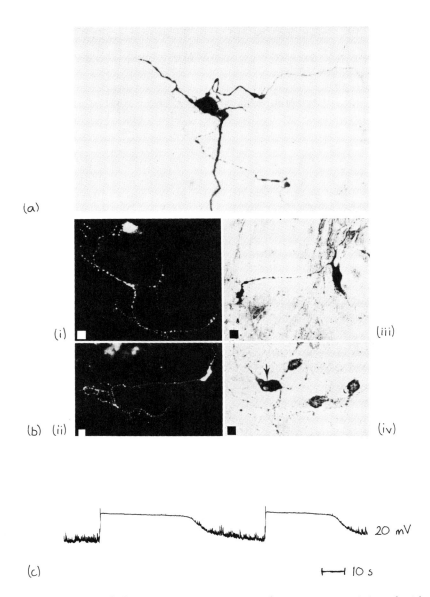

(a)

(b) (i) (ii)   (iii) (iv)

(c)   20 mV

⊢⊣ 10 s

FIGURE 28 Hypothalamic neurons in primary culture: (a) neuron injected with a contrasting product (peroxydase); (b) the culture has been treated with an immunoserum directed against vasopressin (the immunoprecipitate made visible by the fluorescein in (i) and (ii) and by the peroxydase in (iii) and (iv) allows the cellular body and its extensions to be observed); (c) the neuron was recorded by microelectrode before being revealed by the immunoserum and shows the 'plateau'-type electrical activity characteristic of vasopressin cells. (After P. Legendre et al., 'Regenerative responses of long duration recorded intracellularly from dispersed cell cultures of fetal mouse hypothalamus', *J. Neurophysiol.*, 48, 1121–41, 1982; D.T. Théodosis et al., *Science*, 221, 1052–4, 1983.)

which give each neuronal type its morphological characteristics and functional properties.[25]

In the first example given here (figure 27), we can see cells obtained from the spinal cords of foetal mice. After three weeks, different types of neuron can be recognized. One has the characteristics of neurons from the spinal ganglion, and the other those of a spinal cord neuron. By means of intracellular microelectrodes, their electrical activity can be observed, as well as action potentials and synaptic potentials which demonstrate the functional nature of these neurons and the junctions established between them.

Another example is that of neurons obtained from the hypothalamus of foetal mice (figure 28). After some weeks, the microscope shows us large nerve cells containing vasopressin, a hormone manufactured *in vivo* by the hypothalamus. The very special electrical activity of these cells allows us to understand the electrical phenomena observed *in vivo*.

We must not extrapolate carelessly from the properties of a layer of neurons grown on the bottom of a plastic dish to the complexities of a spinal cord or hypothalamus, even if they are those of a mouse. But it is quite out of place to worship *in vivo* research alone, as many properties are preserved *in vitro*. Nevertheless it is absurd, in behavioural terms, to speak of the love-life of a Petri dish.

An interesting development in neuron culture is to grow neurons previously cultivated *in vitro* inside an *in vivo* nervous system. There have been some spectacularly successful brain grafts in this field. A strain of mice which congenitally lacked luliberin-manufacturing neurons in the brain, received a graft of *in vitro* cultivated neurons in the hypothalamus. The animals had not previously been able to ovulate, and the graft remedied that problem.[26]

Oversimple conclusion

There are two kinds of reductionism. The first is the practical reductionism of the researcher, who uses simple or artificially simplified preparations to try to understand how more complicated organisms work, for example by extracting laws which can be exported from the model to the original. The second, triumphant and sectarian, reduces everything to the sum of its parts. The first admits that all knowledge is useful, provided that it can be checked. The second claims that each parcel of truth contains the whole truth. The second is vain while the first is modest. Who gives whom a bad reputation?

Notes

1 K. Hausen, 'The lobula complex of the fly: structure, function and significance in visual behavior', in M.A. Ali (ed.), *Photo Reception and Vision in Invertebrates*, New York, 1984.

2 D.H. Hubel and T.N. Wiesel, 'Brain mechanisms of vision', *Sci. Am.*, 241, 150–62, 1979.

3 J. Scholes, 'The electrical responses of the retinal receptors and the lamina in the visual system of the fly *Musca*', *Kybernetik*, 6, 149–62, 1969.

4 N. Franceschini, 'Sampling of the visual environment by the compound eye of the fly: fundamentals and applications', in A.W. Snyder and R. Menzel (eds), *Photoreceptors Optics*, Berlin, 1975.

5 See N. Franceschini et al., 'Sexual dimorphism in a photoreceptor', *Nature, Lond.*, 291, 241–4, 1981.

6 The lateral inhibition of the sensory systems has been described by E. Mach (1964). A zone of sensation produced by a local stimulus is surrounded by an inhibition zone which increases the contrast and focalization of the stimulus.

7 N. Franceschini, 'Aspects du traitement de l'information dans l'oeil composé d'un insecte', in *Bilan et perspectives des neurosciences*, Paris, 1980.

8 H.T. Spies, 'Courtship behavior in *Drosophila*, *Ann. Rev. Entomol.*, 19, 385–405, 1974.

9 G. Hoyle, 'Exploration of neural mechanisms underlying behavior in insects', in R.F. Reiss (ed.), *Neural Theory and Modeling*, Palo Alto, CA, 1964.

10 J.C. Hall et al., 'Mosaic systems', in M. Ashburner and E. Novitski (eds), *Genetics and Biology of Drosophila*, New York, 1976.

11 D.R. Kankel and J.C. Hall, 'Fate mapping of nervous system and other internal tissues in genetic mosaics of *Drosophila melanogaster*', *Develop. Biol.*, 48, 1–24, 1976.

12 J.C. Hall, 'Control of male reproductive behavior by the central nervous system of *Drosophila*: dissection of a courtship pathway by genetic mosaics', *Genetics*, 92, 437–57, 1979.

13 N.J. MacLusky and F. Naftolin, 'Sexual differentiation of the central nervous system', *Science*, 211, 1294–1302, 1981.

14 J.M. Belote and B.S. Baker, 'Sex determination in *Drosophila melanogaster*: analysis of transformer-2, a sex-transforming locus', *Proc. Natl. Acad. Sci. USA*, 79, 1568–72, 1982.

15 T.W. Cline, 'Positive selection methods for the isolation and fine-structure mapping of *cis*-acting, homeotic mutation at the sex lethal (Sxl) locus of *D. melanogaster*', *Genetics*, 97, 323, 1981.

16 In this model inappropriate sexual behaviour is potentially possible but permanently blocked. It is interesting to recall here the male sexual behaviour of the praying mantis which is inhibited by the cephalic nervous system, only decapitation allowing it to take place. It would be dangerous to draw conclusions about man based on the example of hangings. Man's sexual behaviour has no need of a decapitation, even a symbolic one, to express itself! (See chapter 11.)

17 W.G. Quinn and R.J. Greenspan, 'Learning and courtship in *Drosophila*: two stories with mutants', *Ann. Rev. Neurosci.*, 4, 67–93, 1984.

18 J.M. Jallon et al., 'Un anti-aphrodisiaque produit par les mâles de *Drosophila*

melanogaster et transféré aux femelles lors de la copulation', *C.R. Acad. Sci., Sér. III*, 292, 1147–9, 1981.

19 L. Tompkins et al., 'Conditioned courtship in *Drosophila* and its mediation by association of chemical cues', *Behav. Genet.*, 13, 565–78, 1983.

20 R.W. Siegel and J.C. Hall, 'Conditioned responses in courtship behavior of normal and mutant *Drosophila*', *Proc. Natl. Acad. Sci. USA*, 76, 3430–4, 1979.

21 Zeno (fifth century BC) is one of the main representatives of the Eleatic school. According to this school, if things seem to move, it is because our senses deceive us. Zeno uses the argument of Achilles and the tortoise to show the non-existence of movement. 'A slow mover can never be caught by a more rapid pursuer, for this pursuer must always arrive at the point occupied by the former, and when he does so, the slow mover is no longer there' (Aristotle, *Physics*, VI, 9).

22 E.R. Kandel, *Cellular Basis of Behavior: An Introduction to Behavioral Neurobiology*, San Francisco, CA, 1976.

23 C.G. Simpson, *The Meaning of Evolution*, New Haven, CT, 1949.

24 W. Hodos and C.B.G. Campbell, '*Scala naturae*: why there is no theory in comparative psychology', *Psychol. Rev.*, 76, 337–50, 1969.

25 A. Tixier-Vidal et al., 'Primary cultures of dispersed fetal hypothalamic cell. Ultrastructural and functional features of differentiation', in J.D. Vincent and C. Kordon (eds), *Biologie cellulaire des processus neurosécrétoires hypothalamiques*, Paris, 1978.

26 M.J. Gibson and D.T. Krieger, 'Neuroendocrine brain grafts in mutant mice', *Trends Neurosci.*, 8, 331–4, 1985.

7

The Three Brains

When imprisoned
For a singular duel
Farther from the sun
Than the Holy Ghost,
Cry threedom!

Huw Johns, *Trinity*

A piece of fly and a ladle of neuron soup cannot possibly furnish us with the necessary material for an overall understanding of the brain, above all in the higher vertebrates in general and man in particular. We must now study the organic unity of the nervous system and its integrative activity. The observations of partial lesions of the central nervous system have shown that certain regions have a specialized role. Various descriptions have been suggested in an attempt to show how the different structures are spatially arranged to ensure functional harmony. The global structure which produces this harmony, according to the different theories, performs solo, as a duet or as a trio. The latter theory suggests the existence of three brains in one.

The damaged brain

Here we shall relate the story of Phineas P. Gage as told by Colin Blakemore.[1] The original accident took place at half-past four in the afternoon on 15 September 1848, near the small town of Cavendish, Vermont.

Phineas P. Gage, a friendly energetic twenty-five-year-old foreman, was working with his men on the construction of a new railroad track between Burlington and Rutland. There was a large rock in the way which had to be blasted. A hole had to be made in the rock and then filled with explosive powder. Phineas decided to carry out this delicate operation himself. He had almost finished ramming the charge into the hole with a metal rod when the ramming action of the rod against the stone produced a spark which ignited the powder. The metal rod was blasted back out like a shot from a gun and pierced the foreman's forehead, making an enormous hole in it, before falling 40 yards behind him.

Strange as it may seem, this was not the end of Phineas P. Gage. He had been thrown to the ground by the tremendous force of the blow, and his arms and legs twitched convulsively for a short time. Five minutes later, however, he had come to, was speaking and could even stand up, albeit shakily. His workmates took him to a hotel in town. Phineas got out of the cart by himself and walked upstairs to his room to await the arrival of the doctors. They could not believe what had happened to Phineas before seeing with their own eyes the gaping hole in the middle of his forehead.

At ten in the evening, although the wound was still bleeding, Phineas had recovered sufficiently to say to his workmen that he would be back on the job in a few days. Nevertheless there was not the slightest doubt that a metal rod several centimetres wide had pierced the anterior part of his brain without apparently affecting in the slightest his senses, language or memory.

The following days were difficult. The wound became infected, and Phineas became anaemic and delirious. However, as a result of the application of large quantities of calomel, rhubarb and castor oil, he recovered little by little. Three weeks later, he asked for his trousers and was impatient to get up. By mid-November, he was strolling in the town and making plans for the future. This is the turning-point in the story: Phineas had a different future in front of him, for he was no longer the same man. The hard-working foreman who had been well thought of by his employers and well liked by his men no longer existed. The brave and friendly Phineas Gage was dead. In his place was a depraved child as strong as a bull.

A few years later, John Harlow, one of the doctors who had examined Phineas after the accident, wrote that he was in good health and seemed to have recovered, but that the balance between his intellectual faculties and animal tendencies seemed to have been destroyed. He wrote that Phineas was capricious, lacking in respect and utterly vulgar (which had not been the case before the accident). He was impatient when contradicted, and changed his opinions and plans at the drop of a hat. From this point of view, Harlow wrote, Phineas had completely changed, and his friends and acquaintances said that he was 'no longer the Gage they had known'.

The new Phineas, rejected by his employers, began to travel all over the United States, earning his living as a fairground attraction, carrying with him the metal rod responsible for his metamorphosis. He died in San Francisco, but his skull and the rod are in the medical school museum at Harvard.

The story of Phineas P. Gage took place in the middle of the nineteenth century when Gall's theory of the brain was in fashion.[2] His theory was that the different mental faculties were situated in different parts of the brain. The exceptional clinical example of Gage showed that the brain was not only master of our movements and sensations, but also of our sentiments and passions: the brain was the seat of our personality.

After Broca's description (1865) of a narrow region of the left cerebral hemisphere responsible for language activity, and after experiments on the electrical stimulation and ablation of partial zones of the cerebral cortex carried out on dogs by Fritsch and Hitzig (1871) and on monkeys by Ferrier (1873), research focused on the cerebral localization of the sensorimotor functions. However, it was not before the work of Papez (1937) that it became acceptable to suggest that certain regions of the brain, forming what would later be called the 'limbic system' (MacLean 1949), were in charge of the emotional aspects of life.

At about this time (1939), Phineas P. Gage was emulated by monkeys through the surgical talent of H. Kluver and P.C. Bucy.[3] Monkeys whose temporal lobes had been removed showed spectacular changes in their social and emotional behaviour. These previously wild animals had become gentle and tame, and they were no longer afraid of a human presence. They were submissive and did not react when attacked by other monkeys. Their sexual and feeding behaviour was caricatural, excessive and inappropriate, as they sought to eat anything within reach, whether edible or not, and showed an incongruous sexual inclination for the most unlikely objects. This condition was called 'psychic blindness', as the monkeys were incapable of interpreting visual stimuli correctly. Poor Phineas and the monkeys show us that there are regions of the brain which govern our sentiments and emotional relations with the world, just as there are others which deal with perceptions and movements. If the sensorimotor nervous system can easily be dismantled, there is no reason why we should not try to do the same for the emotions and conceive of nerve mechanisms producing our desires and woes.

The cogs of these 'sentimental machines' have the appearance of nuclei containing neurons, and pathways serving to communicate both internally and with the input and output systems. We shall not describe the complex anatomy of the nervous system. Figure 29 gives a simple diagram of the main subdivisions.

We could imagine nerve impulses following a signposted course, coming and going from one region to another, dealing with memories in one place, weighing the pros and cons in another and making plans for the future in yet another, only to end up by deciding to have a lie-in. With a little updated Leibniz seasoned with complexity and in secret worship of the lost algorithm, we could even manufacture a bit of 'mind' with the help of a positron camera.[4] Our project is more modest: we shall briefly present a functional architecture of the nervous system, the plans it seems to have been built from, the general organization of its different parts and the distribution of the tasks without which the individual could not navigate in the world about him. Without deliberately contradicting ourselves, we shall

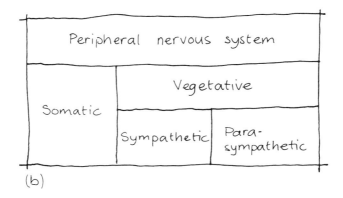

Central nervous system			
Brain			Spinal cord
The brain itself	Telencephalon	Neocortex	
		Striatum	
		Limbic system	
	Diencephalon	Thalamus	
		Hypothalamus	
Brainstem	Mesencephalon		
	Rhombencephalon		
	Bulb		

(a)

Peripheral nervous system		
Somatic	Vegetative	
	Sympathetic	Para-sympathetic

(b)

FIGURE 29   The main subdivisions of the nervous system in mammals.

envisage different approaches to the nervous system considered as one unit, or as being divided into two or three parts.

One

The reticular system is catholic, i.e. one and universal. Like the central column of a flamboyant vault, it rises in the brainstem towards the brain where it branches out and seems to uphold the vault of the cortex (figure 30). In the brainstem, the reticular formation forms a tight mass of neurons (which occupy the space left free by the nuclei and nodes).

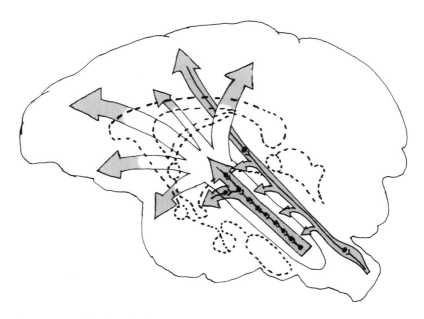

FIGURE 30 Sketch of the reticular substance of the brainstem forming an ascending activating system supplied by sensory pathways and projecting itself onto the different regions of the brain. (After H.W. Magoun, 'The ascending reticular system and wakefulness', in J.F. Delafresnage (ed.), *Brain Mechanisms and Consciousness*, Charles C. Thomas, Springfield, MI, 1954.)

While stimulating the reticular formation by means of electrodes placed in the brainstem of an anaesthetized cat, Magoun and Moruzzi (1949) observe a general reaction of wakefulness, accompanied by an acceleration in the rhythm of the electroencephalogram. When the region is destroyed, however, the electroencephalogram slows permanently and it is impossible to wake the animal. When only the ascending paths which transport the sense impulses to the brain are interrupted, such effects are not observed.

According to Magoun and Moruzzi, the reticular formation both integrates and activates. The subject is wakeful because his brain is activated. The pictures and the sound, the sensations at the surface and inside the body, cause and maintain this activation, which is not produced directly by sense perceptions but indirectly through the reticular formation. The sensory pathways which ascend to the cortex delegate to the reticular formation, by means of collateral branches, a sample of all the impulses travelling along them, and the reticular formation, by means of its ascending projections, distributes to the cerebral structures the sum total of the excitation it receives. The sensory information, upon entering the reticular system, loses its original specificity (visual, tactile, auditory etc.) and serves only to maintain a reticular tone which in its turn keeps the brain awake. In order to fulfil this function the reticular neuron is both a pole of convergence, grouping sense perceptions of various origins, and a site of divergence, which by means of long axons projects itself over a range of cerebral regions.

Comparing the cerebral edifice with a Gothic church is useful not only architecturally, but historically. According to the ideas developed in the nineteenth century by J.H. Jackson, the brain, in the developing individual as well as during the evolution of the species, is built up by the addition of successive and increasingly complex layers, so that each new stratum covers and integrates the underlying structure.[5]

Just as the modest old Roman church can spring back up out of the grandiose Gothic cathedral which has absorbed and hidden it when certain parts collapse, so certain normally inhibited elementary reflexes can sometimes reappear in the case of brain damage. For example, when brain damage paralyses the limbs, scratching the skin can induce bending reflexes which are normally absent when the brain is intact.

The reticular system no longer has the universal status it was accorded a few decades ago. Far from being a uniform and undifferentiated structure, it appears to be made up of anatomically defined and strictly hierarchical subsystems. However, the concept of activation has lost none of its value (see chapter 8). Nevertheless it should be dissociated from the banal function of wakefulness, and be associated with the animal passions, the expression of the singularity of the individual.

Two

Structures and functions often go two by two in the nervous system. This binary distribution is valid for the peripheral nerves and for the central nervous system. It is also to be found in the functional dualism based on the confrontation of excitor and inhibitor 'centres'.

The central nervous system and the sensorimotor system

The brain, brainstem and spinal cord are connected to the rest of the body by a peripheral nervous system composed of two main elements: the autonomous or vegetative system and the skeletal sensorimotor system.

The vegetative system is responsible for the working of the organs, heart, liver, lungs, digestive tube and glands. It is divided into two subsystems, the orthosympathetic and parasympathetic. The orthosympathetic system controls the responses of the organism which consume energy and enable it to confront emergencies. The parasympathetic system, in contrast, contributes to the maintenance and economic functions. In short, the vegetative nervous system is a two-faced administrator: the orthosympathetic system spends, while the parasympathetic saves. In general, each organ receives a double orthosympathetic and parasympathetic innervation, and these opposite actions result in a balance which is adapted to the surrounding conditions.

Alongside the motor innervation of the organs, there exists an internal sensitivity (interoception) which gathers information for the brain about everything that takes place inside the body. Specialized receptors record variations in blood pressure, blood volume, osmotic pressure, chemical composition of the blood – in short, everything that is a homeostatic constant. Generally, we do not feel what goes on inside us, so occupied are we with the outside world. However, in certain circumstances (illness or emotional shock for example) our internal world becomes extremely noisy and reveals the existence of a visceral sensitivity.

The somatic sensorimotor system gathers the extensions of the motoneurons and sense neurons in the nerves. The motoneurons lodged in the anterior horns of the spinal cord send out their axons to all the skeletal muscles. The sense neurons, lodged in the spinal ganglia, connect the skin and muscles to the posterior horns of the spinal cord (figure 11). The motoneurons make the muscles contract. The sense neurons provide the brain with a representation of the outside world (exteroception) and of the subject in that world (proprioception).

The pantry and the parlour

The old precept of separating the wheat from the chaff could have served as a guide for the distribution of tasks in the central nervous system, with the hypothalamus being put in charge of maintenance and subsistence, and the upper floors looking after the noble functions of personal relations.

The hypothalamus is a small funnel-shaped region at the base of the brain which, given its narrowness, is astonishing for the number of functions it carries out and for the number of physiologists vying for elbow-room there. It has a tradesman's entrance, through which it receives information from different viscera. It is directly sensitive to changes in the internal milieu (pressure, volume, temperature, chemical composition) as a result of specific receptors. The hypothalamus can also act on the organism through the endocrine system and the orthosympathetic and parasympathetic vegetative nervous system (figure 31). All the visceral regulations concerning the homeostasis of the body are grouped in the hypothalamus. In short, the hypothalamus is the brain of the internal milieu.

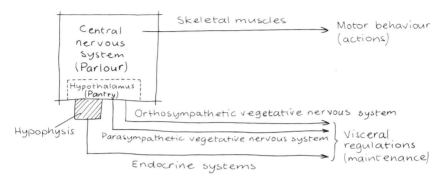

FIGURE 31   The pantry and the parlour. The brain controls, on the one hand, behavioural responses (actions) in the external environment and, on the other, the homeostatic regulations of the internal milieu (maintenance). (After G.J. Mogenson, *The Neurobiology of Behavior: an Introduction*, LEA, Hillsdale, 1977.)

The other brain is responsible for acting on the outside, whether it be the wiggling of a toe or the delivery of a world-shattering speech. These motor functions are inconceivable if the brain receives no information about the outside world. At each level of the central nervous system, interaction takes place between the motor messages descending to the motoneurons and the sensory messages ascending to the cortex (figure 32).

The separation between a visceral brain and a brain responsible for actions covers another division suggested by Konorski (1967) in which a cognitive brain is opposed to an emotive brain. According to Konorski, on the one hand the cognitive system uses specific divisions of the brain with more or less strict localizations of the pathways leading from the receptors to the centres and from the centres to the receptors according to tightly hierarchical groups such as the specific nuclei of the thalamus and the associative and projectional cortical areas; on the other hand, the emotive system uses non-specific divisions with looser topographical distribution and includes the reticular system, the non-specific thalamus, the hypothalamus and the rhinencephalon.[6] We have already given a definition of what we mean by 'cognitive'. This term is sometimes thought to mean 'higher mental activity', the product of the growing complexity of the brain, culminating in man with the appearance of language. We should remember that cognitive activity concerns relations of a propositional kind (x is y) which suppose knowledge of the goal to be reached and verification of the results. The emotive brain, in contrast, appears to use relations based on

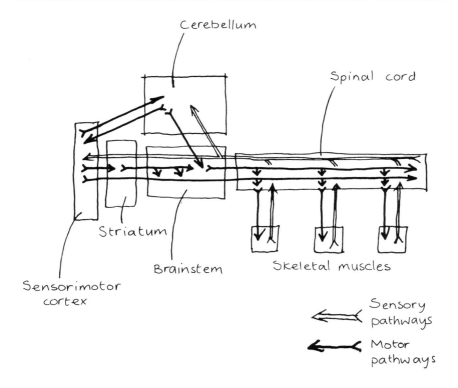

FIGURE 32   The sensorimotor system. The basic mechanism is represented by a closed loop in which nerve impulses from a given muscle are reflected in the motoneurons which control the same muscle (myotatic reflexes). Pathways descending from the cortex and brainstem also control motoneuron activity. The striatum takes part in controlling the activity of these motor pathways. The cerebellum, which simultaneously receives sensory and motor information, coordinates the functioning of the whole system. (After E. Henneman, 'Organization of the motor systems: a review', in V.B. Mountcastle (ed.), *Medical Physiology*, C.V. Mosby, St Louis, MO, 1974.)

contiguity which only allow stimulus–response type links to be established. But the same behaviour pattern can be explained differently according to the point of view. In Hull's associative theory, the satisfaction of a need (hunger, for example) reinforces the behavioural stimulus–response link.[7] In the cognitive theory, the presence of food becomes an object of knowledge confirming the expectation which led the animal to behave in a certain way.

The binary division of the brain proposed by Konorski should not be mixed up with our attempt to oppose a wired and vague brain which is not based on a territorialization of the brain, but covers all the cerebral structures and related activities.

By separating a cognitive brain capable of judgement from an emotive brain blindly serving bodily imperatives, it seems to us that some people are placing man in front of an impossible dilemma. According to Riley and Furedy, by choosing the former man runs the risk of burying himself in his own thought and being unable to act, while choosing the latter makes of the animal a self-centred machine, exclusively attached to the satisfaction of its own needs.[8]

We shall try to show in the third part of this book that higher mental activity is never absent from elementary behaviour patterns such as eating, drinking or love-making, and that far from belonging to two separate brains, the emotional and the cognitive are always coextensive.

Functional dualism

When analysing the nerve mechanisms of the passions, we shall see that two centres, one an inhibitor and the other an excitor, are almost always involved in controlling the same function. This dualistic conception is in the tradition of both Claude Bernard and Sherrington. The former has taught us that the centres come into play each time the internal milieu records an abnormal value, and the latter that these centres are linked by the principle of reciprocal innervation. An example of this is the nervous control of breathing. Breathing out results from the action of an excitor centre which itself inhibits a breathing-in centre, in the same way that a bending movement is always the result of the contraction of a flexor and the simultaneous relaxation of an extensor. The nervous control of eating behaviour illustrates this mechanism perfectly, when the hunger centre is inhibited by the satiety centre (figure 33).

An entire theory of paired centres could be built on the hypothalamus. Besides the centres of hunger and satiety, we find those of pleasure and aversion, approach and retreat, a parasympathetic region opposed to the orthosympathetic etc. This anatomical and functional Manicheism goes beyond the hypothalamus to other structures, especially the limbic system and the amygdala where facilitating and inhibiting areas confront each other for each of the passions. Concerning these passions, we shall see that, however complex the dialectic between the centres may be, they are incapable of explaining the extraordinary flexibility of behaviour patterns.

Right and left

It will not be necessary in this discussion of the binary divisions of the brain to spend too much time on the distinction between a left-hand and a right-hand brain, as it has received much recent publicity and strongly impressed our imagination.

Suffice it to say that, since the work of Sperry, we attribute different properties to the two cerebral hemispheres.[9] The left-hand or dominant hemisphere is responsible for speech, writing, calculation and logical and

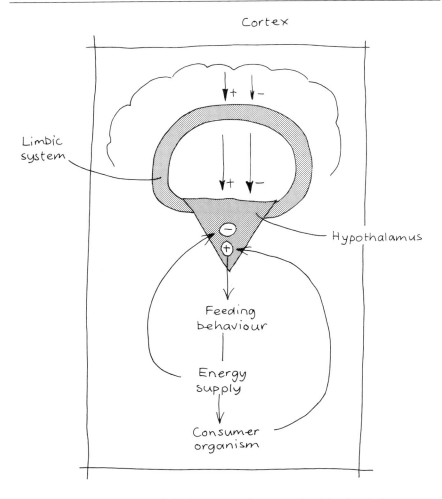

FIGURE 33   Functional dualism using the example of feeding behaviour.

serial thought. The right-hand hemisphere has a more spatial, global and intuitive apprehension of the world: it recognizes shapes and faces, and it appreciates music and poetry. It would be too easy to oppose a passionate and mystic right-hand hemisphere to a cold and calculating left-hand hemisphere. Can we imagine the right-hand brain dying of hunger while the left-hand brain counts the pieces of cake? Like any other dismantling of the brain, this one has its limits, if only because the functions of the two hemispheres are always revealed in animals or patients whose two brains have been surgically separated (split-brain). In the normal individual, several million fibres link the two brains, so that nothing that happens in one can escape the other.

Three

MacLean is the inventor of the brain in three parts (figure 34). According to him, during evolution the brain of primates has developed according to three main patterns which can be called reptilian, palaeomammalian, and neomammalian. There is a remarkable association between the three cerebrotypes which are radically different in chemistry and structure and which are, in an evolutionary sense, independent aeons. There exists a hierarchy of three brains in one, or what MacLean calls a triune brain. We can deduce from this that each cerebrotype has its own form of intelligence, its own specialized memory and its own motor functions. Although the three brains are tightly interconnected and functionally dependent on each other, says MacLean, it is a fact that each is capable of operating independently of the other two.[10]

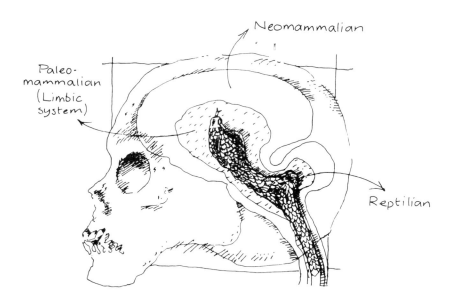

FIGURE 34   The three brains.

The reptilian brain includes the reticular formation and the striate cortex. It is the seat of the survival behaviour patterns of the individual and the species. The behaviour it commands is automatic and invariable. It offers no possibility of adapting to changes in the environment. The second brain (palaeomammalian) corresponds to what MacLean calls the limbic system. It is the seat of motives and emotions. It is capable of responding to present information in the light of memories of past information. The third brain (neomammalian) is represented by the neocortex. Because of its frontal part in particular, it is the brain of anticipation, capable of choosing the response to a stimulus according to what the result will be and also in the light of the past. Obviously, this is the most highly evolved brain, the intelligent brain of the higher vertebrates. It gives the individual an extra degree of adaptability and therefore affords him more freedom.

The snake and the archetype

The reptilian brain is mainly composed of striated bodies or the striate cortex which plays an important role in motivity. Damage to this part of the brain in man results in motor problems such as those that can be observed in cases of chorea or Parkinson's disease.[11] The striate cortex reaches downwards into the brainstem, and especially the substantia nigra, and maintains relations upwards with the other brains, the neocortex and limbic system which envelop it like a mould. The action of these different parts in the control of motivity cannot be summarized in a few lines. It is responsible for what has been called extrapyramidal motivity, which uses curled neuronal circuits, as opposed to pyramidal motivity which uses descending pathways linking the cortex more or less directly to the motoneurons of the spinal cord.

According to MacLean, the striatal complex participates in the character-istic behaviour patterns of the species, from posture to action: choosing a territory, hunting, making a nest, defending young etc.[12] The striate cortex also apparently helps in imitational behaviour and the recognition of signals which are important for the survival of the species. Thus, if we present an animal with a specific stimulus, even if it is a partial one in the form of a crude decoy for example, the striate cortex is responsible for a stereotyped response: the animal attacks a prey, and flees from a predator. This reptilian brain consequently appears to be the repository of the ancestral–archetypal actions and passions of the species. This is why a child who fearlessly touches an electric wire will run horrified from the harmless grass snake that it meets for the first time.

The sentimental brain

The term 'limbic system' comes from Paul Broca's description (1878) of the great limbic lobe which groups the structures situated on the internal face of the hemispheres. It is sometimes called the rhinencephalon to show that these regions of the brain derived in the course of evolution from structures previously associated with the sense of smell. The fact that the rhinencephalon is highly developed in animals like the dolphin and man, where the sense of smell is non-existent or extremely limited, shows that it participates in other activities.

We shall retain only its key-ring structure opening upwards towards the neocortex and downwards towards the brainstem (figure 35). To orient ourselves a little, we shall point out the hypothalamus at the base, the

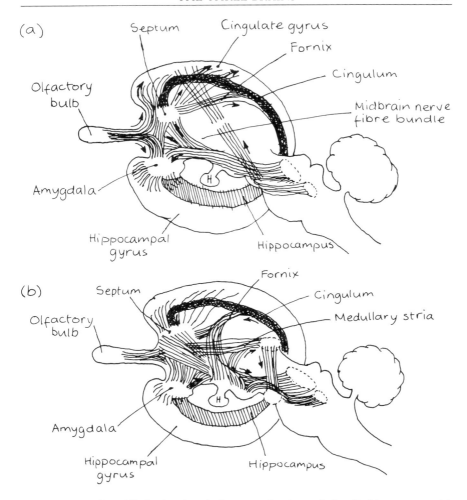

FIGURE 35 Simplified sketch of the organization of the limbic system: (a) the projections on the limbic system from the olfactory bulb and brainstem; (b) the pathways out of the system. The region round the septum is above all linked to the survival of the species, according to MacLean, whereas the region round the amygdala is concerned with the survival of the individual. (After P.D. MacLean, 'The limbic system with respect to self-preservation and the preservation of the species', *J. Nerv. Ment. Dis.*, 127, 1–11, 1958.)

septum and amygdala at the front, and the habenula and interpeduncular nuclei to the rear. The cingulum, the hippocampus and their neighbouring cortices, the fornix and the medullary stria, link these regions together in concentric circles.

Like the limbo of Christian mythology the limbic system is the intermediary between the neocortical heaven and the reptilian hell.

The representations of the outside world and the internal milieu are superimposed there. All the sensory information about the perceiver's environment are inscribed in the neuronal network of the limbic cortex, the hippocampus and the amygdala. The vegetative, nervous and humoral functions which contribute to homeostasis are represented simultaneously in the limbic system.

Nothing illustrates the function of the limbic system better than the description of epileptic fits. An epileptic fit is the paroxystic firing, whether spontaneous or induced, of the electrical activity of the nerve cells in a given region or in the whole of the brain. Unlike the fits concerning the neocortex, limbic epilepsy is often characterized by sensations of an emotional nature: feelings of *déja vu*, strangeness, depersonalization etc. These vague feelings are often accompanied by visceral factors: nausea, palpitations and unusual sensations of taste, smell and vision. The fit also frequently includes motor activity with automatic well-coordinated movements bearing no relation to the environment. Thus, in the course of a fit, we can observe the three components of what we shall define later as the fluctuating central state: the extracorporeal and sensorimotor components and the temporal component.

If you record the electrical activity of the different regions of the brain during a limbic fit you will see that the firing generally remains circumscribed within the system, as if the wave of paroxystic shocks, caught up in a round, cannot escape from the limbic circuits. The neocortex is excluded from the torment which agitates the palaeomammalian brain. This observation leads MacLean to speak of a 'schizophysiology' of the limbic system and the neocortex which may possibly create conflicts between what our neomammalian brain knows and what our palaeomammalian brain feels.

The apple and the neocortex

The neocortex maketh man, with the extraordinary development of regions specialized in the reception of messages from the outside world and the ordering of movements. On the one hand we have the primary and secondary receptor areas linked to the sense organs and various bodily receptors, and on the other the main and supplementary motor areas with their keyboard corresponding to the movements of different parts of the body.

This modern cortex results from the ever-accelerating process of encephalization throughout evolution. The older underlying structures have tended to be replaced or dominated. A monkey with no occipital cortex is blind; in contrast, if a shrew, a direct ancestor of the primates, is deprived of its visual cortex, it is still able to recognize shapes, visually situate objects in space and distinguish between vertical and horizontal stripes.[13]

Electrophysiology allows us to record the electrical signals of a single neuron in relation to a given type of peripheral information or movement.

Therefore we can observe neurons situated in the main motor areas with an electrical activity linked to the execution of a movement, and other neurons in the so-called somatic sensory areas activated by sensory information from a special part of the body. In the visual areas, we can observe neurons with an activity which is sensitive to outlines of shapes, or to their contrast or colour, or to the movement of a target through space. It is as if each abstract piece of information were materialized in a given neuron possessing the subjectivity of a Leibnizian monad.[14] It is clear, however, that an isolated neuron loses all specificity, except for certain morphological and biochemical properties, and that its functional value derives from the connections which link it to other neurons and thereby to the whole organism.

The neocortex cannot be reduced to the juxtaposition of motor and receptor regions. Alongside the primary and secondary areas there exist so-called 'associative' areas, whose name suggests that they can only function in association with the others.

The prefrontal cortex is the most recent of neocortical developments, and reaches its highest degree in man. Phineas P. Gage is an example of a man with no frontal cortex. The frontal cortex participates in all motor and sensory activities but is indispensable to none. It is connected not only to the other neocortical areas, but also to the subcortical structures, especially the striate cortex. Damage to this cortex causes cognitive and emotional problems. The prefrontal cortex would seem to participate in the temporal organization of behaviour, with a retrospective and anticipatory function allowing a movement to be planned in the light of past experience. The prefrontal cortex would also seem to suppress undue external or internal influences which might interfere with normal behaviour.[15]

In the neighbourhood of the receptor areas other associative areas are to be found. In the parietal lobe, near the somatic sensory areas, there exist neurons which would seem to play a part in decision-taking, probably in the light of the perceptive data provided by the receptor areas.[16] Similarly, certain regions in the temporal lobe apparently help to endow visual signals with emotional meaning.[17]

Let us illustrate these different workings of the neocortex. There is an apple on the table. My occipital cortex sees it. My associative temporal cortex says, 'It looks good'. My associative parietal cortex concludes, 'I'm going to eat it'. My prefrontal cortex then says, 'I'm going to put it in my mouth and bite it'. My motor cortex accomplishes this under the strict control of my somatic sensory cortex, and my whole brain is absolutely delighted!

This dismantling of the brain has allowed us to get to know the anatomy of the nervous system of the higher mammals. We shall find these different sites at work when we study the animal passions. In presenting several different physiologically oriented anatomical combinations, we wished to underline their slightly overtheoretical bias. They are undoubtedly helpful in understanding the pathological disorders which hinder man in his relations with the outside world, but they are incapable of accounting for the whole human being. They present us with a divided man, whose right-hand brain gets upset about what the left-hand brain is doing, or whose hungry hypothalamus keeps its eyes open for enemies under the haughty supervision of a neocortex preoccupied by intellectual problems. It is too much of a simplification to suggest that the reptilian brain marches off to war while the neomammalian brain gives speeches for peace. Why not just ascribe good and evil to different parts of the human brain, and have done with it? The trivial diagrams of the machine-makers also open dark doorways for the surgeons of the mind. Our aim in the last part of this book will be to avoid these traps by expounding the concept of a central state.

Notes

1   C. Blakemore, *Mechanics of the Mind*, Cambridge, 1977.
2   F.J. Gall, *Sur les fonctions du cerveau et sur celle de chacune de ses parties*, Paris, 1851.
3   H. Klüver and P.C. Bucy, 'Preliminary analysis of functions of the temporal lobes in monkeys', *Arch. Neurol. Psychiatry*, 42, 979–1000, 1939.
4   The activity of the human brain can be shown with the help of a positron camera which records local variations in blood flow or glucose consumption by the nerve cells. Maps can be obtained in this way, showing the level of activity in different regions at any given moment. Ingvar speaks of 'ideography', relating the differences in regional blood flow to mental activity. See J.P. Changeux, *Neuronal Man*, New York, 1985; D.H. Ingvar, 'L'idéogramme cérébral', *Encéphale*, 3, 5–53, 1977.
5   M. Jeannerod, *Le Cerveau-machine*, Paris, 1983.
6   J. Konorski, *Integrative Activity of the Brain*, University of Chicago Press, Chicago, IL, 1967.
7   C.L. Hull, *Principles of Behavior*, New York, 1943.
8   D.M. Riley and J.J. Furedy, 'Psychological and physiological systems, modes of operation and interaction', in S.R. Burchfield (ed.), *Stress. Psychological and Physiological Interactions*, Washington, DC, 1981.
9   R.W. Sperry, 'Mental unity following surgical disconnection of the cerebral hemisphere', *Harvey Lectures Series*, 62, 293–323, 1968.
10 P.D. MacLean, 'Sensory and perceptive factors in emotional functions of the triune brain', in L. Levi (ed.), *Emotions. Their Parameters and Measurement*, New York, 1975.
11 Parkinson's disease usually affects people over fifty years of age. It sets in progressively with permanent muscle contraction, slowing down of movement, which becomes rare, and trembling. Degeneration of the substantia nigra is the general rule, with destruction of the dopamine neurons. Treatment with L-dopa, the precursor of dopamine, brings transitory improvement. Huntington's chorea is a hereditary degenerative affection of the central nervous system. Clinically, it is characterized by progressive neurological disorder leading to involuntary abnormal movements and inevitably to dementia.

12 P.D. MacLean, 'A triune concept of the brain and behavior, Lecture 1. Man's reptilian and limbic inheritance', in T. Boag and D. Campbell (eds), *The Hincks Memorial Lectures*, University of Toronto Press, Toronto, 1973.

13 M. Snyder and I.T. Diamond, 'The reorganization and function of the visual cortex in the three shrew', *Brain Behav. Evol.*, 1, 244–88, 1968.

14 Leibniz defines as a 'monad' a simple, discrete, invisible, active, perceiving substance which is the ultimate element of things. Compare this to the notion of 'entelechy' which is the sufficiency which makes monads the source of their own internal actions. The Leibnizian system would seem to resemble certain modern views of neurobiology (see chapter 5).

15 J.M. Fuster, *The Prefrontal Cortex: Anatomy, Physiology and Neuropsychology of the Frontal Lobe*, New York, 1980.

16 J. Seal et al., 'Activity of neurons in area 5 during a simple arm movement in monkeys before and after deafferentation of the trained limb', *Brain Res.*, 250, 229–43, 1982.

17 Z. Weiskrantz, 'The interaction between occipital and temporal cortex in vision: an overview', in F.D. Schmitt and F.G. Worden (eds), *The Neurosciences Third Study Program*, Cambridge, MA, 1974.

PART III
The Animal Passions

Animal nature, which chemists call the animal kingdom, procures by instinct the three things which are necessary for it to perpetuate itself. These are three veritable needs. It has to feed itself, and for this not to be a chore, it possesses a sensation called appetite and takes pleasure in satisfying it. Secondly, it must preserve the species by procreation and would certainly not do its duty in this domain, whatever Saint Augustine may say, if there were no pleasure to be had therein. Thirdly, it has an overpowering tendency to destroy its enemies, and nothing is more reasonable, for in order to preserve the species, it must hate anything that brings about or desires its destruction . . . These three sensations, hunger, coital desire and hatred of the enemy are habitually satisfied in beasts, and we can dispense with calling them pleasures; they are self-centred, immediate and unreasoned. Only man is capable of feeling real pleasure, for he is gifted with the faculty of reason, and so foresees it, seeks it out, composes it and reasons upon it after the act . . . Man is like a beast if he satisfies these three penchants without exercising his reason. When our mind participates, these three satisfactions become pleasure, pleasure, pleasure, an inexplicable sensation which gives us a taste of happiness, which we cannot explain even though we feel it.

Casanova, *The Story of my Life*

8

Desire

Some desire is necessary to keep life in motion
Samuel Johnson, *Rasselas*

The word 'desire' is as pretty as it is vague. Its definition is a conceptual soup, a semantic stew which offers up a new and tasty morsel with each ladleful. So, is desire undefinable? The biologist, as a scientist, cannot tolerate this: he knows and measures. If we accept that desire expresses itself in the greater or lesser haste shown in the pursuit of an object, this haste can be measured in order to obtain one dimension of desire: the number of hedgehogs killed on country roads in spring is a measure of their desire to join the female. The speed with which a rat covers a certain distance to reach a piece of food is also an estimation of the relationship which links the behaviour of the animal to an incentive. Scientists who study behaviour speak of motivation. The term is perhaps valid for the laboratory rat, the motivated animal par excellence, which spends its professional life pushing levers, finding its way around mazes, eating bits of food and receiving electric shocks, but it will not do to describe animals or men in their natural environment, where the motive for action is not always clear even if the action itself is clear enough (figure 36). We prefer the word 'passion' to 'elementary behaviour' or 'emotion', and for the same reasons we shall speak of 'desire' instead of 'motivation' for the state underlying the passions. Whereas motivation presupposes the act, desire points to an internal state, a 'tendency' of the subject which does not necessarily lead him to action.

Did you say 'desire'?

Desire floats between pleasure and need, profit and loss. The satisfaction of a need leads to response reinforcement, and this is the basis of learning

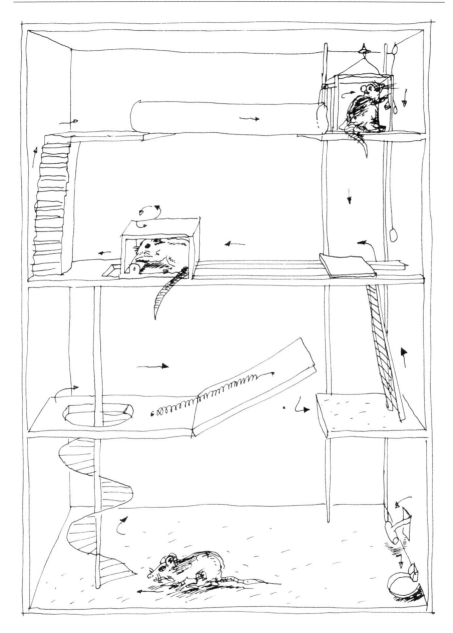

FIGURE 36   Rat working in a psychophysiological laboratory (François Durkheim).

theories. Desire is also central to Freudian psychology based on need and the experience of satisfaction. But more than need, it is perhaps a feeling of lack, which is an anticipation or stimulation of need, which underlies desire and gives it a temporal dimension.

Desire is first and foremost a desire for reward. This can consist in obtaining a profit for a job well done. The laboratory animal's job is to push levers and buttons. If this is done correctly, the animal will receive a reward, food for example. One of the rules of learning would seem to be that no gesture is learnt if it is not followed by some benefit for the animal (Thorndike's law).

One form of reward is pleasure. Desire, according to Rauh and Revault d'Allonnes is 'a natural will to pleasure'.[1] Georges Bataille clearly advances the profit–pleasure duality as a component of desire in man:

> In the beginning was work; work is the key to mankind. Through work, men progressively distanced themselves entirely from animality. In particular from a sexual point of view. In their work they first adapted their activity to the use they saw for it. The same process also took place in other fields, and their behaviour became totally goal-oriented . . . For the first men conscious of it, the aim of sexual activity was probably not to get children, but immediate pleasure . . . There are still archaic tribes who are ignorant of the necessary relationship between sexual intercourse and the birth of children. From a human point of view the coupling of lovers or husband and wife originally had only one cause: erotic desire. Eroticism is different from the sexual impulse in animals in that it is theoretically, like work, consciously goal-oriented, the goal here being pleasure . . .
> In a still valid primitive reaction, pleasure is the foreseeable result of erotic play. But the result of work is gain: work brings profit. If the result of eroticism is considered from the point of view of desire, independently of the possible birth of a child, we are faced with a loss which corresponds to the paradoxically valid expression *'petite mort'*. This 'miniature death' has little to do with the cold horror of death, but is the paradox out of place where eroticism is concerned?
> Man's consciousness of death does indeed differentiate him from the animal, but so does eroticism, because in man a willed, calculated seeking after pleasure has taken the place of the blind instinct of the organs.[2]

In addition to affirming the duality of profit and pleasure as the founding principles of desire, this text illustrates the confusion with which anthropomorphism can surround words like 'pleasure' and 'desire'. Neither desire nor pleasure are exclusive to man, whereas the linking of them is, as well as the knowledge of death. We shall see that the blind instinct of the organs is a component of desire, and that reciprocally the cognitive functions in animals and men allow them to distinguish between desire and instinct. A final risk would be to tie desire exclusively to sexuality. Nothing biological, at any rate, indicates the pre-eminence of sexuality over the other functions.

Therefore desire can apparently be defined by the goal to be reached, and justified by the reward obtained. It would also seem that the intensity of the act can be used to measure it.

Another component of desire is need. Need is experienced as an intolerable situation which must be brought to an end. This internal state that psychologists call motivation induces an overwhelming tendency (drive) to accomplish the act that will relieve it. The animal deprived of food for several hours will start looking for nourishment liable to relieve the unpleasant state developed by this lack. Furthermore, he rapidly learns any behaviour that will provide him with food. When the animal eats, hunger is reduced, and this lessens the need for food. The actions which make food accessible are reinforced. This means that they become more likely in the future in similar situations. The American behaviourist school has widely developed this theory, called the reduction drive theory, which links learning to needs. This school states that there is a primary need when one of the products or conditions necessary for the survival of the individual or species is lacking, or when they naturally deviate from an optimum.[3] We shall see later the furious criticism, often pronounced in the name of the freedom of the individual or higher anthropomorphism, which has made this theory fall from grace into the hell of paradigms lost. It is true that any claims to exhaustivity are countered by the fact that the theory explains nothing of the extreme variability of our actions compared with the scarcity of the needs vital to our survival. However, it is also true that the theory has the merit of linking actions to the internal state of the subject.

Despite a radically different interpretation and history, the notions of need and the experience of satisfaction are also at the origin of the concept of desire in Freudian psychology. As in reduction drive theory, there originally exists a state of internal tension linked to need which is satisfied by the 'specific action of the adequate object' (food, for example). There is a basic difference, however, in that desire cannot be identified with need. It consists in a renewal and reinvestment of the image of the satisfaction-giving object when the state of tension reappears. Therefore, except initially, what we have in this case is not a real but a hallucinatory satisfaction: 'The mnemic image of a certain perception remains associated with the mnemic trace of the excitation resulting from the need. As soon as this need recurs, the link which has been established will induce a psychic motion which will seek to reinvest the mnemic image of this perception and even evoke it; in other words there is an attempt to recreate the situation of the first perception. This motion is what we will call "desire"; the reappearance of the perception is the accomplishment of desire.'[4] Therefore desire accomplishes itself in the hallucinatory reproduction of perceptions which have become signs of satisfaction. The economics of fantasy replaces the economics of biology (sugar, salt, hormones), but association remains the basic mechanism, and in this respect Freud, like the reflexologists and behaviourists of his time, is a good disciple of Spencer. The associative game, the management of images, is played out inside the subject independently of input and output. The latter, in contrast, are the almost exclusive concern of the behaviourists.

The concept of need defined as a deviation from the norm locks behaviour into a kind of homeostatic cell where the only behavioural possibilities are consumption and regulation. The role of play in animal behaviour is enough to contradict this. And what about sexual 'needs'? Can we still consider desire as an end in itself? As the indispensable tiger in the tank? Lack and not need would seem to activate desire, lack becoming a simulation of need. And in this case it is need that is imagined, and not its satisfaction. Take lovers' desire. Crystallization, according to Stendhal, is only the ceaseless reactivation of desire through the simulated loss of the beloved: '. . . the sight of each moment of happiness she can give you and that you thought you would never experience ends with this heart-rending thought: I shall never be so deliciously happy again! and it's my fault if that happens . . . then and only then does the second crystallization appear and it is much stronger because of the element of fear.'[5] Stendhal has too good a sense of humour not to excuse us for quoting him, although our subject is mainly the rat. But just as a prolonged period of sexual abstinence cannot account for the writer's passion for Métilde, a fall in the amount of energy-giving substances available in a rodent's blood cannot totally explain the animal's sitting down to dinner. However, a visual or olfactory signal or simply a habitual timetable can renew a virtual primary deficit or stimulate desire. But neither is desire only an expectation of pleasure. Otherwise, it would have no reason to cease, and the event-centred character of behaviour could not be explained.

Finally, in the eternal triangle composed of desire, pleasure and need, each partner plays a double game and in each primary behaviour pattern it is difficult to say whether pleasure comes from the satisfaction of a need or is an end in itself.

Behaviour patterns

Before trying to understand how desire takes part in those reactions of an organism which are grouped under the general word 'behaviour', we shall suggest a classification based on a growing degree of complexity.

We shall distinguish between three basic types of behaviour. An old experiment by Bard clearly shows what the distinction is. If you touch the sexual organs of a female cat with a small stick, the animal will react differently according to whether or not it is in heat. The castrated or sexually restful female cat brushes the nuisance aside; the cat in heat or having received hormones, in contrast, accepts the approaches of the experimenter by raising its behind and moving up and down on its hind legs with its tail to one side. If you separate the spinal cord from the brain by severing the brainstem, the animal responds to each vaginal stimulation as if it were in heat, whatever its actual internal state. This is a reflex. Things are different if the nervous system is severed in such a way as to leave the spinal cord and the lower brain in contact. The response to the vaginal stimulation depends on the internal state of the animal, i.e. on the presence of sex hormones in the blood. There is no active response in a castrated animal until hormones are injected. This is instinct at work. In order for it to be triggered, a particular internal state must be able to influence a nervous centre. Finally, if we consider a female cat untouched by the vivisector's hand, we observe that at certain times of year she will forget her domestic duty and overcome the greatest obstacles to place herself in a position of sexual invitation for some anonymous alley cat on some unattractive gutter: this is desire-driven behaviour. We can see in this example that the same behaviour can be classed as reflex, instinct or desire-driven in the range of possible responses to a sexual stimulus.

What is a reflex?

In classical parlance, a reflex describes a stereotyped reproducible action which is inevitably linked to the stimulus which caused it. The concept of the reflex action has been widely developed by the American behaviourist school and the Russian reflexological school. Watson suggests that in a totally established psychological system, if the response is known, the stimulus can be deduced, and if the stimulus is known, the response is perfectly predictable. The principle of learning by association is at the root of everything. All the behavioural possibilities of an individual depend on his associative capacity, whether it be for associating different stimuli (classical conditioned reflex) or for associating behavioural responses and stimuli (instrumental conditioning).[6] The reflex action may be the basic structure which links the animal to its environment, but alone it cannot account for the organization of complex behavioural patterns. An animal in action is not just an answering machine; it also acts spontaneously or responds only inconsistently according to its desire or instinct. Spontaneity and inconsistency are here considered as the expression of the variability of the internal state of the animal at the time of the act.

What is an instinct?

The word 'instinct', tainted by finalistic usage (preservation instinct), has been refurbished by the ethologists (Tinbergen, Lorenz).[7] It is an act or series of acts which does not change when repeated (fixed-action pattern). Instinct is essentially innate, but can be modified by learning which generally tones up or improves performance: the quality of flight for a bird, of teating for a young rat, in the choice of prey for a young squid etc. Far from explaining the diversity of individual behaviour, learning ensures instinctive behaviour in perfect harmony with the model defined for the species. Here, learning is a factor which makes every individual resemble every other, whereas desire-driven behaviour allows each individual to derive his difference from his learning. Instinct appears to be fascist and desire democratic. Lorenz mistakenly speaks of a 'parliament of instincts'; rather, it is a closed battlefield where unequal forces fight it out. It is fashionable to wonder at the intelligence and perfection of animal instincts. It would sometimes be more reasonable to show surprise at the stupidity and absurdity of instinct. What distinguishes instinct from desire-driven behaviour is the blindness of the former, oblivious to its goal. Instinct drives the moth into the candleflame. Instinct tells the greylap goose to roll an impossible square egg with its beak instead of using its feet as intelligence would have it. In this egg-recovering behaviour, well described by Lorenz, a distinction can be drawn between reflex-type behaviour, commanded by peripheral information, and instinctive behaviour. First, the goose places its beak behind the egg and moves its head laterally to centre its beak. Second, it withdraws its head into its body in such a way as to roll the egg under its breast. If the egg is exchanged for another, the goose adjusts its lateral centring movements according to the size and shape of the new egg. However, the head is always withdrawn in exactly the same way, whatever the shape of the egg and despite a poor result. The first stage is a reflex; the second is instinctive. It is logical to suppose that something as stereotyped as an instinct corresponds to a pre-established group of structures and nervous connections brought into play by what may be called a central programme. Here, there is no need for peripheral or internal information, and, once triggered, the sequence of actions is carried through unchangingly to the very end.

What is desire-driven behaviour?

Since Craig's work in this field, it is common to distinguish between an appetitive phase in all behaviour patterns, consisting in movements of orientation, agitation and seeking which demonstrate the exaltation of desire, and a consummatory phase which ends when the desire is satisfied.[8]

The first characteristic of desire-driven behaviour is individualization, which expresses itself in the difference in behavioural patterns from one animal to the next according to their acquired experience and abilities. Desire translates the particular genius of each man or rat and is thus what differentiates individuals.

The second characteristic of desire is the faculty of anticipation which is totally lacking in instinctive behaviour. An experiment performed by Schneirla illustrates this difference.[9] A rat and an ant are both capable of learning their way around a maze. Taken separately, we can observe a difference in their learning processes. The ant approaches the problem slowly and successively integrates each correct choice, step by step. However, at each stage the rat anticipates the stages to come. Furthermore, the rat learns how to learn and improves its performance from one maze to the next. The rat rushes all the faster towards a goal as he knows from past experience that he will find more food there. This expectation so typical of desire can be seen in the electrical activity of the brain. On the electro-encephalograph a negative wave can be seen in the frontal region of a man in the period preceding the action (negative contingent variation). By recording the electrical activity of the cells inside the central nervous system, it can be shown that certain regions are particularly active in this preparatory phase. The last characteristic of desire-driven behaviour is to be found in an affective component which is associated with the anticipation and unfolding of the action. It consists of visceral reactions and hormonal secretions which offer a true somatic translation of the emotion. The emotional countryside which surrounds a behavioural pattern is the proof of desire. It is very different from the emotional desert which typifies instinct.

The fluctuating central state

Is the source of desire to be found in the internal state? The internal state creates a tendency or drive by a deviation in the norm which defines the conditions of equilibrium for the milieu. But a living organism is in a permanent state of disequilibrium and it would be more accurate to speak of a fluctuating central state than of the constancy of the internal milieu. We shall define the three dimensions (corporal, extracorporal and temporal) of the fluctuating central state which represent the total living being.

Desire and the internal state

A space for desire (the inner space, Michaux would say): that is what we find with the lungs which breathe, the heart which beats and the vessels more or less swollen with blood transporting hormones and active principles. This is the internal milieu, the constancy of which, as we have seen, is the fundamental dogma. Homeostasis ensures this constancy and certain behaviour patterns contribute to its mechanisms (eating, drinking). But the inner space is also the subjective knowledge I have of my internal state, what my brain knows about my body. Hunger, thirst, and more generally, pleasure or aversion, are particular signs of this state. Language gives man but a meagre advantage over the animals in the knowledge of his internal state: *Ich weiss nicht was soll es bedeuten dass ich so traurig bin.*[10] The abundance of words is equalled only by their inaccuracy in describing what is actually just the encounter of our fancy with the state of our viscera. We can appreciate only indirectly the same phenomena in animals, but the combination of somatic and visceral signs can indicate the state: speeding up or slowing down of the heartbeat and breathing rhythms, variations in blood pressure, changes in the temperature of all or parts of the body, posture and facial expression, movements of parts of the body (neck, tail, ears etc.). The animal capable of desire-driven behaviour offers, then, a wide range of signs which show its internal state. A wordless language which man sometimes uses when in doubt about the internal state of his partner. After all, is there a better way for a woman to allay her doubts about her lover's desire for her than to observe the state of his penis? An erection is more eloquent than any speech. Come, come, you exclaim, what a trivial way of dealing with man's desire! Quite so. The condition is sufficient but not necessary. There are forms of lovers' desire which do not result in the slightest movement of the body.

The homeostatic order

According to the theory of homeostasis, an animal is a stable representation of the world around it. Desire is the response to an interruption of this balance, an expression of the elastic force which tends to bring the organism back to its normal level. The internal state is the place where this desire expresses itself in the form of a drive. A drive is not the stimulus which triggers the behavioural response, but the internal force behind it. It is not the sight of an object that produces desire, but a particular internal state which makes the object desirable and transforms it into a stimulus. So it is not the presence of food which makes an animal eat, but its internal state, subjectively identified as hunger . . . We may as well say immediately that we cannot accept such an excessive proposition. An appetizing dish is often enough in itself to trigger feeding behaviour. For a lover, the sight of his love is enough to stimulate his ardour independently of the state of his hormones or the activity of his blood. What can be said is that the stimulus which causes desire does so because it has been associated in the past with an internal state which has invested it with a special power.

A drive is induced by a deviation from the norm, the constants of the internal milieu. The concept of homeostasis, however, also applies to the external environment in the form of emotional and relational homeostasis. When the state of the world differs from the subject's usual idea of it, this also engenders a drive and behaviour which tends to reduce this difference: the black sheep comes back to the fold; the citizen eliminates any seemingly non-conformist traits which could lead to his rejection. A drive would consequently seem to be linked to any deficit in general, whether it be a deficit in water or a relational deficit. Any behaviour which tends to reduce the deficit has a greater chance of occurring again (it is reinforced) and its repetition leads to learning. It is not our aim to discuss whether the associations take place on the output side (response reinforcement) or on the input side (classical conditioned reflex).[11] That is an interesting argument for specialists in the field, but not for us. For a biologist, the drive concept is useful because it draws attention to what happens between the stimulus and the act in the little black box for associations, in other words the brain. The drive concept has allowed us to introduce measurable variables between the stimuli and behavioural responses. The sugar, amino acid and hormone content of the blood are such variables, as well as diverse physicochemical data. The problem for the physiologist is no longer to establish the operational reality of the drive but to give it an anatomical support. The flowering of hunger, thirst and other drive 'centres' all over the hypothalamus and brain bears witness to the risks of this task. The drive theory is nevertheless efficient in its simplicity. An animal deprived of food overcomes obstacles more quickly and learns faster how to avoid traps and carry out the gestures which will provide it with food. Its drive is proportional to its hunger and resulting inner state. Conversely, its degree of hunger can be deduced from its higher level of performance. One last advantage of drive theory is that it avoids the distinction between acquired and innate knowledge. Whether a behaviour pattern is learned or centrally programmed, it none the less depends on a special internal state which will define the drive.

It would nevertheless be naive and dishonest to try to use drive theory to explain all kinds of behaviour. We must not forget that the value of the concept is only operational. If sexual desire arose only out of need, what would be the use of all that sexy advertising for almost any product under the sun? In this connection, fancy is a realm unknown to the animal, of course, but even in typically homeostatic animal behaviour like eating and drinking, a drive, in the classical sense of the term, is not always responsible for the action. The time of day can be a determining factor which has nothing to do with the internal state of the animal in triggering eating behaviour.[12] The hunger which originally makes a rat run an obstacle race to obtain food can be long satisfied, but the animal goes on. A blood transfusion from a well-fed animal into a hungry one who pushes levers to obtain food will stop it eating but will not stop it pushing the levers. Is this action for action's sake or simple spontaneity that no homeostatic goal can explain?

The fact that both men and animals accomplish gratuitous acts with no apparent aim cannot be ignored. The goose normally feeds by filtering mud through its beak to extract what is edible. A goose which has just banqueted on grain continues to filter mud without feeding. It goes through the actions of eating in order to filter and no longer filters in order to eat. A baby fed with a bottle which is too easy to suck subsequently uses up its reserve of sucking movements on air or on substitute objects. The sexual behaviour of animals and men also offers numerous examples of activity which is not strictly goal oriented, and we can all remember personal experience of this if we try hard enough. It is as if there existed, alongside need-driven and goal-oriented activity, a veritable need for behaviour in itself, an inner pressure that brings certain motor sequences to the surface out of all meaningful context.

The inconstancy of the internal milieu

Inconstancy can be considered as a virtue. Desire springs from inconstancy and there is no learning without an associated desire. So desire, as it now appears to us, is the opposite of a drive, which is just a gloomy prefect supervising homeostatic morality. It is in no way an insult to the memory of Claude Bernard to suggest that the constancy of the internal milieu, which helped set up physiology as a science, is today no more than a cumbersome fossilized concept of no heuristic value. N.H. Spector speaks of a fluctuating central state defined by two propositions. First, any living organism, from birth to death, is in a state of non-equilibrium. Second, the reaction of an organism to a stimulus is dependent on and modulated by a central state defined as the total reactive condition, at a given moment, of a neuron, a functional group of cells, a subcellular element inside the nervous system or the nervous system itself as a whole.[13] By definition, this central state fluctuates. It changes with the time of day, the time of year and the time of life, not to mention the thousands of events which make up everyday life. It is simultaneously the whole and the part. What changes is what traditionally maintained the constancy of the internal milieu: not only the materials transported by the blood, as well as hormones, ions, acidity, temperature, antibodies, germs and toxins, and the nutritional state of the cells, organs and tissues, but also the information which inundates the brain, the position of the body, the memories which spring up out of the past and the sediments deposited by the passing of time. This infinity of moving, changing data means that the subject, whether praying mantis or praying nun, grasshopper or grace-hoper, will never be the same from one moment to the next.

The central state, which is an image of the world, is a projection with three dimensions: corporal, extracorporal and temporal. The corporal dimension is defined by the physico-chemical composition of the inner space (internal milieu and cerebral environment), in addition to the state of different parts, muscles, tissues and organs which make up the organism. The extracorporal dimension concerns the individual's image of the world, the sensory space perceived by the sense organs and the moving space perceived by specialized receptors which indicate the position of different limbs, the tenseness of different muscles, the angle of different joints etc. The temporal dimension is occupied by the traces accumulated during the development of the individual, from birth to death. It includes both genetic determinism, which sets up the central programmes and controls maturing and ageing, and historical contingency, which integrates all the experiences of life, in short, everything which contributes to making us what we are.

Three dimensions for an organism whose central state governs its existence in the world – its global reactivity, its orchestrating image and its action.[14] The central state deals with the input and output. It controls the selective aspect of perception and it directs action towards its goal. Here, we must not forget the attributes of desire, attention and intention. Attention is related to perception as intention is to action.

In order to materialize this central state, we shall call upon the vague brain, or the humours, hormones and mediators at work in the nervous system. Do I hear you calling for other metaphors? Very well, then, it will be the tree with innumerable branches of biogen amine neurons, an unknown lush vegetation dripping with neuropeptides, a flower tapestry of synapses. The central state is both the tree and the forest. Rather than cut a path through the undergrowth, we shall try to use one of its elements, the dopaminergic system (the best-known system of neurotransmission in the brain), to represent the whole.[15]

Dopamine

Using the example of dopamine, a substance manufactured by the brain, we shall try to show desire at work in the functioning of the central nervous system.

The substance and the place

Attention and intention are the two attributes of desire. Are they produced by dopamine and, if so, where does this amine lodge in the brain?

There was a time when neurologists and physiologists tried to find a centre of law and order in the brain for every function of the body and mind. There is an explanation for such an attitude. As is often the case, the development of a scientific concept is linked to that of the methods used, here, progress in stereotaxis, which allows a part of the brain to be destroyed or stimulated, the progressively richer anatomical observation of brains after death and the clinical inventory of symptoms.[16] Globally, the results of these observations are still valid. We can consequently say that the prefrontal part of the cerebral cortex is important for our attention, as the analysis of cognitive tests in men and animals with a damaged prefrontal cortex shows. Lesions of deeper parts of the brain, the basal ganglia, show that these structures participate in motor initiative, where a gesture can be triggered 'from inside' (intention) without the presence of an outside stimulus. You have only to watch a patient with this kind of damage to realize what the loss of motor initiative means. The patient is not paralysed and he can make most movements in a reflex way, but he has become akinetic. Spontaneous movements surface slowly, almost regretfully. Attention and intention, then, are examples of functions associated with certain places in the brain. If we accumulate such marriages, however, certain parts of the brain run the risk of being overcrowded. The frontal cortex and the hypothalamus have a dickens of a time trying to find room for all the functions attributed to them, and could come to resemble old curiosity shops stuffed with dusty concepts . . .

The rise of biochemistry and neuropharmacology has overthrown place and crowned substance. Anatomical centralism has been replaced by biochemical centralism. Catecholamines in general and dopamine in particular have thus been given a role in many functions. Besides playing a role in attention and intention (to which we shall return later), dopamine also helps to control motricity. The motor problems of sufferers from Parkinson's disease are appreciably improved by the use of medicine which provides the brain with dopamine. Dopamine is also to be found at work in pleasure, in sexual behaviour, in interpersonal relations and social behaviour, in mental illness, in reproduction and lactation, and, more generally, in the control mechanisms of the hormonal expression of the brain.[17]

Despite the variety of their expression, dopamine neurons are concentrated in a narrow part of the brain. Except for the neurons isolated in the hypothalamus, all the dopamine in the brain comes from a small group of cells bunched in the mesencephalus at the point where it opens out into two symmetrical expansions, the hemispheres. In the mesencephalus the dopamine cells stretch uninterruptedly from the edges (substantia nigra) to the middle (figure 37). The prolongations of these neurons gather in the lateral walls of the hypothalamus, forming a symmetrical trunk which climbs up to the homolateral structures of the brain. The cellular bodies and trunk are bunched, but the terminal branchings of the dopamine tree are cast extremely wide. The three brains, the neocortex, the limbic system and the striatum, receive a dopaminergic innervation (figure 38). The continuity of the cellular bodies is mirrored by a continuity of the projections. The central neurons send their terminals onto the prefrontal cortex and median striatum. The neurons of the more lateral region extend to the limbic system and striatolimbic system where the nucleus accumbens is to be found. The lateral neurons of the substantia nigra reach out to the lateral striatum. This anatomical continuum is echoed by a functional continuum from perception

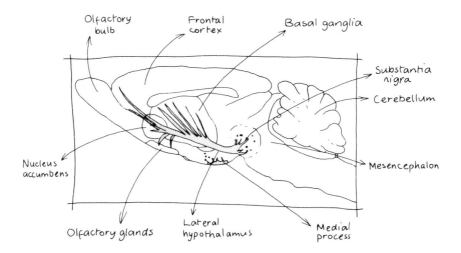

FIGURE 37   Neurons and dopaminergic pathways in the central nervous system of the rat. (After U. Ungerstedt, 'Stereotaxic mapping'.)

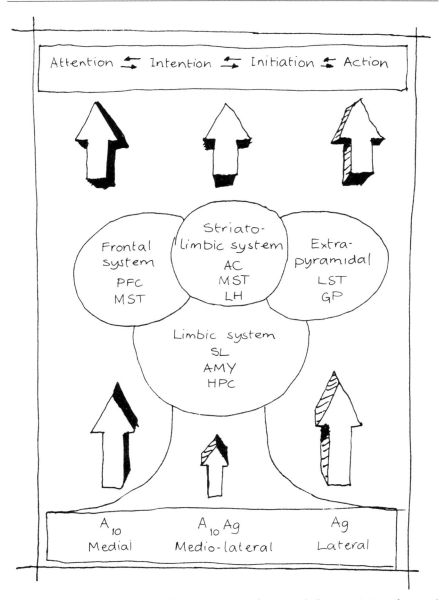

FIGURE 38 Synthetic view of some anatomo-functional characteristics of ventral mesencephalon dopaminergic neurons. This diagram shows the variety and homogeneity of the anatomo-functional organization of these neurons: AC, accumbens; AMY, amygdala; GP, globus pallidus; LH, lateral neuron of the habenula; HPC, hippocampus; PFC, prefrontal cortex; SL, lateral neuron of the septum; mST, medial striatum; LST, lateral striatum. (After H. Simon, *Les neurones dopaminergiques.*)

through intention to action. Furthermore, these nerve terminals do not establish precise synaptic contacts in the structures they innervate, but spread out everywhere in diffuse branchings which secrete dopamine. Dopamine thus seems to sketch functional groupings with vague frontiers within the unclear limits of anatomical structures. Here again, the term vague brain seems particularly fitting.

The absent-minded rat and the indifferent rat

The neurobiologist can today reconcile place and substance by using false transmitters in his experiments. A chemical agent, 6-hydroxy-dopamine for example, replaces the real transmitter inside the neuron and destroys it. Therefore, by injecting this agent into a region of the brain we can selectively destroy the dopaminergic terminals while leaving the structure intact.

What do we notice when we eliminate the dopaminergic terminals in the prefrontal cortex of a rat? Nothing spectacular at first sight. However, if we submit the rat to behavioural tests, like the delayed alternation experiments in a T-shaped maze, we discover that it is incapable of finding a signal which could guide it into one or other of the branches where the reward is alternatively placed. On the way the animal dallies, retraces its steps, looks all around and, in short, does not possess the frank determination of a normal rat hurrying towards its reward. It can be concluded that the frontal cortex, when deprived of dopamine, does not fulfil its function of selective attention. A. Rougeul has recorded rapid electrical rhythms in the prefrontal cortex which appear only when the animal is attentive. If you show a cat a mouse, these rhythms can reach 40 hertz. If dopamine antagonists such as neuroleptics are injected, these rhythms disappear; they reappear in the presence of a dopamine agonist.[18]

When the dopaminergic terminals are destroyed in the nucleus accumbens of a rat, a different kind of disorder can be observed. The rat constantly visits the same part of the maze, the one where it was rewarded first. Confronted with a new situation it is incapable of modifying its behaviour. When it should go from one compartment to another in order to maintain a certain level of reward, the animal is incapable of making the intentional effort which would allow it to pass the barrier. It has lost its flexibility, its adaptability, and no longer shows the exploratory enthusiasm of the typical laboratory rat. The frontal rat becomes absent-minded, and the accumbens rat indifferent! However, neither of them has lost its motor possibilities, and both are still able to learn and remember. They may be absent-minded or indifferent, but they are not paralysed or stupid.

The prefrontal cortex and the nucleus accumbens are two central structures which play complementary roles in action, but these do not coincide. Biochemical studies have none the less shown that there is a remarkable balance between the dopamine of the accumbens and that of the prefrontal cortex. When dopamine is destroyed in one of these structures, it is massively released in the other.[19] The release of dopamine seems to fluctuate from one structure to the other according to the animal's worldly occupations. Dopamine is omnipresent in this continuum of functions superimposed on a continuum of structures. Should we conclude that it plays a different role in each structure? Or is it rather a single supporting role necessary to the working of each? In this case, the substance would seem to serve the function without defining it. Dopamine, being distributed like a local hormone over the different regions of the brain by the dopaminergic branchings, would seem to count more by its mere presence than by precise connectivity. This might explain the efficiency of certain kinds of medicine which correct certain partial sensorimotor disorders of the Parkinson type through their general action on the dopaminergic systems. The successful grafting of dopaminergic cells in different nervous structures of the rat to replace previously damaged terminals shows that the mere presence of dopamine released locally by the graft is enough to re-establish normal functioning of the structure.[20] In these last two cases there is no connectivity, and so it is not the neuronal brain which is in action but the hormonal brain. H. Simon has summarized the general character of dopaminergic action in the central nervous system very well: 'Dopamine can modulate behavioural response at different stages, from the perception and integration of internal and external sensory information to the triggering and carrying out of the appropriate action. This modulating influence could be that of a catalyser of functional reactions.'[21]

Dopamine thus appears to be a non-specific central activator. It has been spoken of as an agent in behavioural wakefulness, the expression of desire at an elementary level. This leads us to discuss the general concept of activation as a basic spring of desire.

Aspecific activation

Aspecific activation is the name we give to the general phenomenon which activates all sorts of behaviour without, however, controlling them. It is desire, considered as the basis of spontaneity. For desire to be fully effective, it must reach an optimal level beyond which its action becomes harmful.

The concept of activation

In the mid-1950s Hebb introduced the term 'activation' for psychologists to be able to name the general phenomenon which provides the necessary energy for behaviour without actually directing it.[22] This theory is inseparable from the discovery at the same period of the role of the reticular substance in the central nervous system. We have already seen that the flux of corporal and extracorporal stimulations converges in this median region of the brainstem. An activation is then communicated to the cerebral structures by ascending pathways. Wakefulness and behaviour consequently depend on the activity of the reticular substance which is a true spring of spontaneity. The more stimulations of the reticular substance there are, the more wakeful and open the subject is to the world. This chain reaction will work in reverse when sleep comes, as a result of a progressive cutting-off of the activation spring.

Behaviour is extremely varied, but there would appear to be only one reticular activation, the general source of desire. In the light of present knowledge it would be more correct to say that the reticular system actually includes a hierarchy and juxtaposition of systems. We have seen that the reticular substance is not a uniform structure but a mosaic of nuclei where dopaminergic neurons are to be found.

When we use bilateral surgery to interrupt the nervous pathways (including a lot of dopaminergic fibres) which climb the lateral walls of the hypothalamus and link the anterior brain to the nuclei of the reticular substance, the animal not only stops eating and drinking, but falls into a state of akinesia and catalepsy. We shall say that the animal has lost all spontaneity; it has reached desire degree zero. It no longer moves, and remains in the unnatural positions into which the experimenter forces it (figure 39). This does not mean that all activation has disappeared. On the contrary, an exaggeration of the posture and balance reflexes is observed.[23] The animal opposes a kind of negativism to any attempt at movement. It is no longer anything except a machine struggling against gravity, and a fragile one at that, for if the external stimulus is suppressed, the animal collapses. It

FIGURE 39   Catatonic rat (François Durkheim). For several hours, the rat stays in the totally abnormal position which has been imposed upon it. (After Y.F. Jacquet, 'β-endorphin and ACTH optiate peptides with coordinated roles in the regulation of behavior', *Trends Neurosci.*, 10, 140–5, 1979.)

is tempting but surely mistaken to compare this state with the negativistic and catatonic symptoms observed in schizophrenics for whom a disorder of the dopaminergic systems has been suspected.

If we destroy the lateral hypothalamus of an animal and yet allow it to survive by feeding and caring for it, the sources of activation progressively return, but their undifferentiated character should be noted. Pain induced by tail-pinching is enough to bring the cataleptic posture to an end. If the animal is placed in water heated to body temperature, it sinks without reacting. When placed in icy water which stimulates it, it swims energetically to escape. After a few days, the animal moves spontaneously and is attracted towards food. If it is well fed, however, it immediately collapses and relapses into catalepsy, as if food had eliminated a source of activation from the empty stomach. The nature of the stimulus is of little importance. Pinching the tail of the aphagic animal is enough to make it eat. Cold water or a few electric shocks would have had the same effect. This activating effect can also be observed in normal rats. Feeding behaviour is not the only sort to be activated. The same tail-pinching or a series of painful electric shocks transform an indifferent male rat into an active sexual partner for the female, or a bad mother into one that starts caring for its young.[24]

Hunger, maternal behaviour and sexual desire have nothing in common. Nevertheless they can all be induced by stimulations which apparently are irrelevant to them. The activation theory allows us to interpret this phenomenon if we accept that behaviour can take place only when the general level of activation is high enough. Teitelbaum suggests that this could explain why some people inflict pain on themselves to increase their sexual desire. Rather than call upon the austere and inevitable Krafft-Ebing to illustrate our point, we prefer to quote a nice little Lithuanian nursery rhyme:

> Come on Nancy, whip my back,
> Don't you stop, just crack, crack, crack!

Tail-pinching may be enough to arouse the sexual desire of a rat, but man disposes of other means of increasing his level of activation, since Nancy can also tickle his fancy!

This non-specific activation is also called arousal. Anything which helps arousal helps performance. We have already seen that dopamine is a major arousal agent. The use of neuroleptics to block the action of dopamine can be compensated for by greater stimulation of the animal. We can, for example, condition an animal to obtain a reward by pushing a lever. A neuroleptic injection will reduce the number of times the lever is pushed. This deficit can be marked if we use a lever which disappears each time it is used, thus demanding a higher level of participation, and consequently activation, on the part of the animal. Similarly, the effect of the neuroleptics can be masked by solicitations and manipulations of the animal.

Optimal level of activation

Too much activation is as harmful to action as not enough. An excess of desire paralyses the lover. In an attack, only 20 per cent of soldiers fire their rifles! When defining the concept of activation, Hebb also introduced the notion of an optimal level. The performance of a subject according to his level of activation, represented by his cardiac rhythm for example, describes a bell-shaped curve. The level of response in a behavioural test first increases proportionally to the activation, and then decreases after a peak which corresponds to the optimal level of activation (figure 40). This can explain the paradoxical effect of tranquillizers which improve the performance of an overexcited driver, whereas they normally induce a dangerous drop in reflexes.

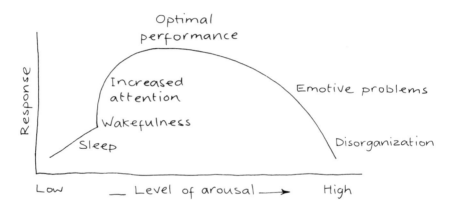

FIGURE 40 Rections to external stimuli. They depend on the degree of wakefulness of the subject. When this level is too low or, in contrast, too high, performance quality suffers. (After D.O. Hebb, *A Textbook of Psychology*, Saunders, Philadelphia, PA, 2nd edn, 1966.)

Nothing differentiates Hebb's level of activation from our concept of the central state. The effects of drugs and medicine can be used to check the fluctuating nature of this central state. Amphetamines are known to have an anoretic effect, for example, and are sometimes used to make people lose their appetite during crash diets. Interestingly, a dose of the very amphetamine that blocks feeding behaviour in a normal rat will produce feeding behaviour in a rat that has been made anorexic by hypothalamus lesion or injection of neuroleptics. Therefore diametrically opposite effects can be observed with the same drug according to the internal state of the animal.

This is an important point for doctors. The same medicine can have opposite effects because of the central state of the subject. It is only apparently paradoxical to use an amphetamine (normally a stimulant) to calm children suffering from a hyperkinetic syndrome which makes them overactive and aggressive. Their agitation may be caused by a catecholamine deficit in the central state, which the amphetamine may help to make up. If given in strong doses, however, so that the patient goes beyond the state of equilibrium, the amphetamine will accentuate the character disorder. We find the same paradoxical situation for anaesthetics, which in strong doses and at certain stages of their action can cause agitation and overexcitement. Alcohol excites or sedates according to the state of the subject and the amount absorbed. It can in certain cases be a marvellous stimulant which improves the performance of the drinker, and in others a powerful sleep inducer. Both uses are extremely frequent, and the same drink can be used for Dutch courage or as a nightcap. As the level of activation or the internal state are impossible to control, and as it is extremely difficult to adapt the dose required to the situation in hand, alcohol is of doubtful help in questions of desire.

Chemistry and the hour-glass

The central state is not just the protean and fluctuating expression of dopamine; all the neurohumours are concerned. Neither can it be reduced to interest and lack of interest as there is a whole series of manifestations oscillating between two poles. Here, time introduces a basic dimension which makes the living being, at each instant, an image of his own past.

The multiplicity of the central state

Up to this point we have for practical reasons more or less led you to believe that dopamine, the central state and desire are one and the same thing. The time has come to clear up a possible misunderstanding. Dopamine is not the central state any more than it is the hormone of desire. The central state is the multiple and fluctuating expression of all the neurohumours. In the continuum between interest and lack of interest, other substances are at work. Their variety can be observed by recording the electrical activity of the brain of a cat in a state of wakefulness. When a cat stares at a mouse placed behind a transparent barrier, the 40 hertz rhythms we have already mentioned invade its frontal cortex, and dopamine certainly contributes to this. But when the cat is waiting for an as yet invisible prey in front of a mousehole (many biologists seem to suffer from a Tom and Jerry complex), 14 hertz rhythms are recorded on the parietal regions of the cortex, which are specialized in the reception of sensory messages. And those rhythms are no longer controlled by dopamine but by a noradrenergic system. The noradrenaline is blocked by an antagonist. When the animal finally tears itself away from the environmental stimulus, slow 8 hertz rhythms are recorded in the same region. These rhythms depend on a serotonin system. So, for three substances, we have three different thythms corresponding to three different aspects of the fluctuating central state.

The fluctuating central state cannot be exclusively reduced to the interest –lack of interest continuum. A continuum is also to be found between such poles as sleep and wakefulness, hunger and satiety, calm and anxiety within the central state which consequently includes all the regulating mechanisms which modulate the input and output of the central nervous system. It is sometimes possible to record some of the activity of some of the mechanisms at work in the central system by means of electrodes placed in the brain. For example, when an animal watches a target, this produces signals on its visual cortex which are perceptible as variations in potential which stand out to a greater or lesser extent against the background noise of electrical activity. An increased spontaneous wakefulness or the electrical stimulation of the noradrenaline neurons situated in the small part of the brainstem, the locus coeruleus, increases the amplitude of the signals relative to the background noise.[25] Noradrenaline is therefore capable of locally amplifying the reception of a signal from the visual environment of the subject. Neurons from this same locus coeruleus increase the response of the hippocampus cells. Would you like some more noradrenaline? Well, a noradrenergic pathway would seem to help the brain of a female rat to accept the homage of a male.

The catalogue of substances which play a role in the central state is far from being a mere list of amines. Luliberin, along with male hormones, changes a shy male hamster who is intimidated by his aggressive female into a willing and intrepid lover.[26] Acetylcholine modulates the activity of the prefrontal cortex and limbic brain.[27] Morphinic peptides have many receptors in the cortex and regulate the level of sensory input.[28] Neuropeptides are also on the list. All these substances, and the list is constantly increasing, are the often mysterious ingredients of our central state.

The number of substances at work is not the only factor of complexity. Neither are the innumerable wide-spreading criss-crossing nerve terminals the end of the story. We have already seen that one terminal can release more than one substance: dopamine and cholecystokinin, for example, with the latter amine also being released near the cellular bodies. Dopamine controls its own release etc.

Proust and rats

We have already defined the central state as an image of the subject's corporal and extracorporal space. An object, smell or sound in the environment can be ignored if the central state does not invest them with a particular value. An extra dimension of this state – time – has not yet been mentioned, but will be discussed in detail for each of the passions. Desire is not only the result of the fusion of body and environment, but is also a product of personal history, expressed by the plasticity of the brain and the fluctuations of the humours.

Is there a more beautiful example of the working of the central state with its three spatial and temporal components than the famous tea and cake episode in Proust? Marcel gives a description of an internal state that is as pleasant as it is vague:

> A delectable feeling of well-being had come over me, cutting me off from the others, without my knowing why. It had immediately made me feel indifferent to life's ups and downs, its trivial catastrophes, its derisory shortness, in the same way that love does by filling me with a precious essence: but rather should I say that this essence was not *in* me, it *was* me.[29]

The author realizes the cause: the taste of the piece of cake dipped in the lime tea re-actualizes a former internal state, echoes a past stimulus and creates a feeling of unspeakable happiness by resuscitating the extracorporal space associated with it, namely the old grey house overlooking the street and Aunt Leonie's bedroom.

Remembrance of things past is not always synonymous with a feeling of well-being. Without going so far as to call it a Proustian experience, a rat can be conditioned to feel aversion. The experiment consists in making a rat eat food with a new taste and then giving it an injection of a toxic substance such as lithium chloride, for example. This injection makes the animal sick shortly afterwards.[30] Subsequently, the rat avoids that food. Similarly, a rat which has survived poisoning will never return to the place where it was poisoned. This is not a classical conditioned reflex because only one food–sickness association was necessary for the aversion to be created, and furthermore, however surprising it may seem for conditioning theorists, the feeding behaviour and the sickness were several hours apart. This must be an important phenomenon in the forming of our tastes and habits, in so far as one association between an internal state and a stimulus is enough to give the latter a definitive value.

A song of Kong's

> *Desire, my dear desire, are you but a witches' brew,*
> *With not much more spice than a rat-humour stew?*
> *My eyes are drawn to you, Nancy, by dopamine and serotonin;*
> *It's for you that the luliberin in my hypothalamus is groanin'.*

This little pastiche of a schoolboy's love poem is just to illustrate the weakness of any theory which tries to reduce desire to the action of a few cerebral amines.

But an all too perfectly wired brain functioning exclusively in a logical mode would not leave any room for desire, either. The fluctuating central state which mixes soup and spaghetti seems to us to be a concept which avoids both extremes.

Notes

1 Quoted by A. Lalande, in *Vocabulaire technique et critique de la philosophie*, 13th edn, Paris, 1980.
2 G. Bataille, *Les Larmes d'Eros*, Paris, 1964.
3 C.L. Hull, *Principles of Behavior*, New York, 1943.
4 S. Freud, *The Interpretation of Dreams*, London, 1900.
5 Stendhal, *On Love*, London, 1957.
6 R.J. Herrnstein and E.G. Boring, *A Source Book in the History of Psychology*, Cambridge, 1965, contains a selection of texts concerning reflex activity and learning. Watson gave a synthesis of behaviourist theories in J.B. Watson, *Behaviorism*, New York, 1930.
7 K. Lorenz and N. Tinbergen, 'Taxis und Instinkt Handlung in der Eirollbewegung der Graugans', *Z. Tierspychol.*, 2, 1–29, 1938.
8 W. Craig, 'Appetites and aversions as constituents of instincts', *Biol. Bull.*, 34, 91–107, 1918.
9 T.C. Schneirla, 'The process and mechanism of ant learning. The combination problem and the successive–presentation problem'. *J. Comp. Psychol.*, 17, 309–28, 1934.
10 Heinrich Heine, 'Lorelei', *Buch der Lieder*, 1827.
11 On reinforcement and associations, see the original text by B.F. Skinner, 'The Generic Nature of the Concepts of Stimulus and Response', *J. Gen. Psychol.*, 12, 40–65, 1935. Brinda has attempted a synthesis of cognitive and ethological approaches for understanding behavioural responses. See D. Brinda, 'How adaptive behavior is produced: a perceptual-motivational alternative to response-reinforcement', *Behav. Brain. Sci.*, 1, 41–91, 1978.
12 See the criticism of the drive concept in M.J. Morgan, 'The concept of drive', *Trends Neurosci.*, 2, 240–4, 1979.
13 N.H. Spector, 'The central state of the hypothalamus in health and disease. Old and new concepts', in P.J. Morgane and J. Panksepp (eds), *Handbook of the Hypothalamus*, New York, 1980.
14 On representation and action, see the chapter 'Représentation programme' in M. Jeannerod, *Le Cerveau-machine*, Paris, 1983.
15 U. Ungerstedt, 'Stereotaxic mapping of mono-amine pathways in the rat brain', *Acta Physiol. Scand.*, 82 (suppl. 367), 1–48, 1971.
16 Stereotaxis is a technique which allows an electrode to be implanted in a given region of the brain, to stimulate or destroy. One must have an atlas divided into vertical and horizontal coordinates showing the main structures of a given frontal plane. The head of the subject (animal or man) is immobilized in a frame permitting precise spatial localization. The atlas is used to determine where the electrode will be inserted.
17 J.J. Schildkraut, 'Current status of the catecholamine hypothesis of affective disorders', in M.A. Lipton, A. Di Mascio and K.F. Kilam (eds), *Psycho-pharmacology: A Generation of Progress*, New York, 1978.
18 On dopaminergic neurons, see J. Glowinski et al., 'The mesocortico – prefrontal dopaminergic neurons', *Trends Neurosci.*, 7, 415–18, 1984; H.

Simon and M. Le Moal, 'Mesencephalic dopaminergic neurons: functional role', in E. Usdin, A. Carlsson, A. Dahlström and J. Engels (eds), *Catecholamines. Part B: Neuropharmacology and Central Nervous System: Theoretical Aspects. Neurology and Neurobiology*, vol. VIII, New York, 1984, pp. 293–307.

19 G. Blanc et al., 'Response to stress of mesocortico-frontal dopaminergic neurons in rats after long-term isolation', *Nature, Lond.*, 284, 265–7, 1980.

20 J.P. Hermnan et al., 'Pharmacological and behavioral analysis of dopaminergic grafts placed into the nucleus accumbens', in A. Bjorklund and U. Stenevi (eds), *Neural Grafting in the Mammalian CNS*, Elsevier, Amsterdam, 1985, pp. 519–27.

21 H. Simon, 'Les neurones dopaminergiques du tegmentum mésencéphalique ventral. Etude anatomique et comportementale chez le rat', Thesis, Bordeaux II University, 1982.

22 D.O. Hebb, *The Organization of Behaviour*, London, 1949.

23 P. Teitelbaum et al., 'Sources of spontaneity in motivated behavior', in E. Satinoff and P. Teitelbaum (eds), *Handbook of Behavioral Neurobiology*, vol. VI: *Motivation*, New York, 1983.

24 H. Szechtman et al., 'Tail-pinch facilitates onset of maternal behavior in rats', *Physiol. Behav.*, 19, 807–9, 1977.

25 For information on behavioural states, see P. Karli, 'Complex dynamic interrelations between sensorimotor activities and so-called behavioral states', in *Modulation of Sensorimotor Activity during Alterations in Behavioral States*, New York, 1984.

26 H.S. Phillips et al., 'Immunocytochemical localization of LH-RH in the central olfactory pathways of hamster', *Brain Res.*, 193, 574–9, 1980.

27 On the role of acetylcholine in the cortex and its possible involvement in dementia, see Y. Lamour and P. Davous, 'Démences de type Alzheimer: données récentes', *Presse Médic.*, 12, 1415–20, 1983.

28 M.E. Lewis et al., 'Opiate receptor gradients in monkey cerebral cortex: correspondence with sensory processing hierarchies', *Science*, 211, 1166–9, 1981.

29 M. Proust, *A la recherche du temps perdu*, vol. 1: *Du côté de chez Swann*, Paris, 1913.

30 J. Garcia et al., 'Biological constraints on conditioning', in A.H. Black and W.F. Prokasy (eds), *Classical Conditioning II. Current Research and Theory*, New York, 1972; J. Garcia et al., 'Behavioral regulation of the *milieu intérieur* in man and rat', *Science*, 185, 824–31, 1974.

9

Pleasure and Pain

There are said to be two feelings experienced by all living beings: pleasure and pain. Pleasure is natural, pain is not. Therefore, we can use these feelings to distinguish between what is desirable and what is to be avoided.

Diogenes

Pleasure

Pleasure is an obscure concept but a luminous feeling and should be thought of as both state and act, inseparable as it is from the behaviour which gives rise to it. Pleasure is a reward for the individual, a motor element in his learning and in the evolution of the species. Only man can express his pleasure through language, but when we observe animals in action we can sometimes conclude that they too feel pleasure, though the state is easier to experience than to define.[1]

Pleasure and the prawn

'Joy is a pleasant emotion of the soul which consists in enjoying something good which the brain represents as its own.'[2] According to Descartes, joy, the passionate extension of pleasure, is born in the brain. Of course, pleasure is moralistically presented as the enjoyment of what is good. What is good is pleasurable, and anything evil is painful. The highly moral notion that anything which is a pleasure is good is often preferred to the aphoristic 'Doing good is a pleasure'. The choice between pleasure for pleasure's sake and pleasure in the good deed is resolved when we recognize the pre-eminence of pleasure itself.

A physiologist could not care less about good and evil when he observes animal behaviour. An exclusively biological description of pleasure would include a description of the state of the viscera and secretions: 'a sweet and moderate warmth which flows into the limbs, making them tingle and glow', according to Cureau de la Chambre.³ No matter how precise the instruments we use, a mere catalogue of physiological data is not enough to characterize such a subjective state as pleasure. We cannot speak of pleasure without introducing an intellectual element which some pedants will call 'cognitive'. It is true that an emotional state such as pleasure is connected with a certain organic movement, but it is also true that this state draws its meaning from the subject's knowledge of it. The whole experience constitutes what Maisonneuve calls a 'unit' which is integrated in what we have called the fluctuating central state.⁴

Pleasure falls into the category of feelings described by Max Scheler.⁵ It is not just a passive state of organic origin, but always has a certain meaning which is expressed in an intention. Pleasure considered from the point of view of emotional interest is thus both state and act, which brings us back to the notions of tendency and desire.

In its homeostatic version, pleasure does not seem to be of primordial importance. 'We must eat in order to live and not live in order to eat', as homeostatic morality tells us. The tendency satisfies the need, and pleasure is secondary. On the contrary, we believe that pleasure is a basic need of the higher animals and that the more evolved the species, the greater the demand, 'Man was born for pleasure and he knows it; no proof is needed.'⁶

Freudian metapsychology is not far from the homeostatic models and introduces the pleasure principle. Psychic processes result from the circulation and spread of energy inside a psychic apparatus that is subdivided into structures or systems that can be localized. Respecting the laws relative to the preservation and transformation of physical energy, the psychic apparatus tends to maintain the amount of excitation it contains as constant as possible (principle of constancy). Anything which increases tension by deviating from this constancy leads to displeasure. Anything which releases this tension by discharging the accumulation of excess energy is pleasurable. The ultimate goal of psychic activity is therefore not just to avoid displeasure and seek pleasure (pleasure principle), but to maintain a basic balance. We shall not hereafter discuss psychoanalytical theory in much detail, which may seem surprising in the light of everything contemporary psychoanalysts have to say about desire and pleasure. There are several reasons for this reticence, the first of which is our own ignorance and the fact that it is very difficult for an outsider to find his way about in the maze of psychoanalytical literature. But it is Freud's system itself which is the main problem. The description of the psychic apparatus as subdivided into systems with different functions may seem to echo what we have said about the brain and its systems. However, this is not the case at all. As Reuchlin emphasizes, Freud's psychic apparatus is an abstraction, a fiction, and the spatial terms used to describe it are pure metaphors.⁷ Lacan confirms our refusal of this analogical language: 'Both the self and the prawn, when they moult, quickly recover a thick skin; is this any reason to consider my self as just a prawn in the game?'[8] Our language is that of a biologist, and since we have little access to man, we shall often have to make do with prawns and rats.

We must come back to desire in order to say that for Spinoza it does not precede pleasure but evolves parallel to pleasure and pain, the primordial feelings. Desire is no different from appetite,

> except that desire generally concerns men in so far as they are conscious of their appetite and that is why we can give the following definition: desire is appetite which is conscious of itself . . . We do not strive towards anything, want anything or tend towards anything out of appetite or desire because we judge it to be good: we judge a thing to be good because we strive towards it, want it and tend towards it out of appetite or desire.[9]

In the fluctuating central state, it similarly appears that approach or avoiding behaviour cannot be dissociated from the feeling of pleasure or aversion: the act is inseparable from the state. Pleasure and pain are therefore primordial feelings which give our body strength to act. The famous definition '*Laetitia est hominis transitio a minore ad majorem perfectionem*' affirms the dynamic character of pleasure.[10] In animals, we describe a continuum of approach and avoiding behaviour which is the motor equivalent of the affective continuum of pleasure and aversion. Pleasure attracts, whereas pain repulses. If pleasure cannot be dissociated from an individual's action, it must also play a role in the evolution of the species which has produced that individual.

I do a stately pleasure-dome decree

Such could be the motto of the species which have survived in the course of evolution. Alexander Bain and Herbert Spencer, contemporaries of Darwin, attribute a key role to pleasure in how the species adapts to natural selection. Spontaneous bursts of nervous energy cause diffuse muscular activities; the pleasurable movements are selectively reinforced whereas those which are unpleasant progressively disappear. This choice helps the species to adapt. What is good for it causes pleasure and what is bad causes displeasure. A pleasurable stimulus sends a considerable amount of energy to the muscles in action, making the motor canals more permeable, whereas the unpleasant stimuli progressively close off the corresponding motor canals. Even the behaviourist school, which is more concerned with learning than evolution, leans in the same direction when it establishes that a behavioural response is reinforced only if it is followed by a reward: there is no reward which is not a pleasure and vice versa.[11]

If, within the framework of classical conditioned reflexes, we consider only the associations of stimuli instead of behavioural response, it is just as true that a stimulus will be perceived as positive only if it comes along with a perceptual situation which suggests pleasure.[12] Whatever theory is put forward to explain the formation of the neuronal assemblies which underlie behaviour, pleasure can be said to be at the heart of associative processes. It is an essentially dynamic principle which allows the plasticity of the nervous system to express itself.

All this does not tell us much about the nature of pleasure. As a subjective phenomenon, it can only be discussed relative to man. To illustrate this, let us take Neal Miller's work on rats.[13] Rats become compulsive eaters when their ventral hypothalamus is damaged. They eat so much that their weight goes up to 2 or 3 kilograms. When quinine is added to their food these monsters obstinately refuse to eat and starve to death. Normal rats in the same situation eat in order to survive, even though the food is bitter. Should we draw the conclusion that our fat rats eat without feeling hungry just for the sake of the pleasure it gives them? When the food tastes bad, pleasure disappears and so does the eating behaviour. If we ask them to make an instrumental effort to obtain food, they refuse. The moral of the story is that rats with no ventromedian hypothalamus not only become compulsive gluttons but also become extremely lazy.[14] Serious behaviourists will no doubt be up in arms about this facile interpretation. It is used here simply to show how difficult it is to describe affective states in animals, when only the act is measurable. Thus pleasure, if it exists, is not separable from action. In man, however, pleasure can be described with words, and Marc Jeannerod has rightly underlined the relationship between language and action.[15]

'As we can say nothing about feeling, since there is no reason why it should be what it is rather than anything else, let us take action as our starting-point, as it is the faculty we have for changing things. This faculty is proved by our very consciousness, and all the power of the organized body seems to converge on it.'[16] Does quoting Bergson, who favours action, mean that we have abandoned the brain as image? On the contrary, the concept of the fluctuating central state means we can avoid the philosophical debate without denying its existence by turning the brain into an acting metaphor.

Pleasure as a quantifiable element in biology

It is possible to quantify pleasure in man by means of psychophysics. Experiments consist in the subject's making choices according to the pleasure and comfort he feels. Similar experiments can be carried out on animals by means of a direct intervention on the brain. Self-stimulation has brought pleasure into the field of physiology. Problems of interpretation can be raised here since the points of self-stimulation in the brain are regions where electrical stimulation also induces different types of elementary behaviour such as eating and drinking. The relationship between this behaviour and pleasure will be discussed. We shall also see that the stimulation of other cerebral structures seems to cause aversion.

Measure for pleasure

Shakespeare had a few ideas about pleasure, as we can see from the ambiguity of the title *As You Like It*, but psychophysics claims to be able to measure pleasure. A subject confronted with a given situation of stimulation is asked to evaluate what he feels on a scale which ranges from the pleasant positive to the unpleasant negative.

The merit of these methods is that they establish scientifically what sometimes seem to be stunningly banal conclusions. Thus it is proved that a sensation reflects the central state and that the same stimulus can consequently seem delicious or disgusting. A drink of sugary water is judged positively by a hungry, thirsty subject, and negatively by the same subject if he has just absorbed a large amount of sugar. This alliesthetic phenomenon does not only concern the short-term physiological state of the subject, but also his long-term state.[17]

Certain volunteers agree to put on weight thanks to a high-calorie diet. When they are given a sugary solution which they previously judged as neutral, they find it frankly unpleasant and give it a negative mark. A few months later, when our volunteers have regained a sylph-like figure after a slimming diet, they give a very positive mark to the same sugary solution. In these experiments the appetizing quality of the food is not directly linked to the immediate homeostatic requirements of the individual. He may be fat or thin, but the test is always carried out at a moment of nutritive balance. What is at play is body-weight, for example, which involves the individual as a whole and the central state in its three dimensions as we have previously defined them. The term 'ponderostat', introduced by Cabanac to define the reference weight of an individual around which the incitation value of food oscillates, is a good example of one aspect of the fluctuating central state, as is the previously mentioned level of activation.

An indirect way of discovering the pleasure felt by an individual is to offer him a choice. Take a volunteer and put him in a bath where the temperature of the water can range from very cold to very hot (figure 41). Take his temperature, and ask him to note the pleasure or discomfort he feels; you will notice that his judgement becomes negative as the temperatures approach the extremes. Give him a bowl of water to put his hand into. He must express the degree of pleasure he feels at the different temperatures of water in the bowl. Will you be surprised to learn that the man in the very cold bath finds the bowl of hot water delectable and that the man in the very hot bath takes most pleasure in the bowl of cold water? If you now let the individual get out of the bath and take a shower at the temperature of his choice, the man whose temperature has dropped will spontaneously choose a hot shower and he whose temperature has risen will choose a cold one. In these experiments on choice dictated by pleasure, we can see that homeostasis is being unambiguously served. Therefore even if we refuse to raise homeostasis to the level of a dogma, this does not mean that its laws do not apply under certain conditions to the fluctuations of the central state.

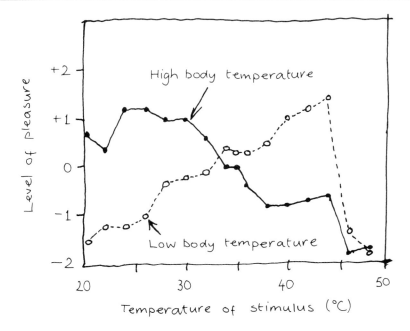

FIGURE 41 Pleasure and discomfort relative to the temperature of the water into which the subject plunges his hand (stimulus). When the subject is in a cold bath, he feels pleasure with a stimulus of over 35°C and displeasure with a cooler stimulus. Conversely, when he is in a hot bath and his body temperature is high, he feels pleasure with a cool stimulus and displeasure with a hot one. (After R.C. Hawkins, 'Human temperature regulation and the perception of thermal comfort', Ph.D. Thesis, University of Pennsylvania, 1975.)

Conflictual experiments give examples of men going beyond the desire for homeostatic balance. Scantily clad individuals are left in a room where the temperature can drop rapidly from 25°C to 5°C. They are made to walk on a moving belt with a slope varying from 0 to 25 per cent, which determines the intensity of the work which will permit them to fight against the cold. Therefore the choice is between discomfort due to cold and fatigue. Instruments measure the body and skin temperature as well as the energy metabolism of the individual, who must make a quantitative judgement on his state. When the slope is forced upon the individual, he can choose the room temperature. The more intense the work, the lower the temperature chosen. When a cold room temperature is forced upon the individual, he will choose to work harder to avoid a drop in body temperature. Beyond a certain point, however, the muscles have to work without oxygen, and this causes an unpleasant feeling of fatigue, which encourages the individual to prefer a drop in body temperature. Faced with unpleasant fatigue, thermal balance is thus sacrificed, and the desire for homeostasis overridden.[18]

Many examples can be found in man of the search for pleasure carrying all before it, even to the point of endangering the functional equilibrium of the individual. Moralists rejoice at these 'bad examples'. It remains to be seen how a moralist would behave on a moving belt: would he sacrifice his physical comfort to maintain his body temperature at a constant level . . .?

Experiments on choice are possible in animals and enable us to gain access to the brain.[19] A thermode is placed in the hypothalamus of a rat. This U-shaped tube can measure the local temperature of the brain and heat it up or cool it down by the circulation of hot and cold water. We thus obtain a kind of water-conditioned brain. The rat is placed in a cage where it can cool down or warm up its hypothalamus by pressing certain levers. The cage is equipped with a ventilator which blows hot or cold air on the body of the animal. The rat can choose the lever which controls this. To cut a long story short, when the hypothalamus is warmed up, the rat chooses the cold air, and vice versa. Similarly, if the rat is given no choice about the temperature of the air, it will choose to cool down or warm up its hypothalamus. The extracorporal space, represented by the thermal receptors on the skin, and the corporal space, represented by the thermal receptors in the hypothalamus, are thus equally important in behavioural choices. The example given is a perfect illustration of the integrating function of the brain within the central state.

It's a pleasure, Mr Rat

Let us say a little about the main character in our story: the rat. This fabulous creature has been the privileged muse of the creative imagination of psychoneurobiologists for more than fifty years. Whether it be reduced to the state of a membrane or submitted to tests which jeopardize its health, the rat is here, there and everywhere. It must be remembered that researchers created the laboratory rat. It is a calibrated, often white-coated animal whose strictly controlled pedigree would make many a duke or duchess green with envy. One of its favourite occupations is pressing levers to obtain a reward, generally food. It may also occasionally turn wheels, find its way through mazes, poke its nose into holes, make love, drink, eat, climb onto perches to avoid electric shocks, cross barriers, leave bright rooms for dark ones, sleep, wash, reproduce, feed its young, eat them, swim and jump (figure 42). What mere mortal can boast of having done as much at the end of his life?

Let us now observe this rat in a corner of its cage: it is obstinately pressing a lever, repeatedly, untiringly, oblivious to its surroundings, engrossed in its task. What is it doing? It is enjoying itself. The experiment was invented by Olds and Milner in 1954. The rat bears an electrode. Its point has been placed, by means of stereotaxis, in a precise region of the brain: the lateral hypothalamus. This electrode is linked to a stimulator which releases a current of variable frequency and intensity at the point of the electrode. It is the rat itself which briefly triggers the stimulator by pressing a lever. It

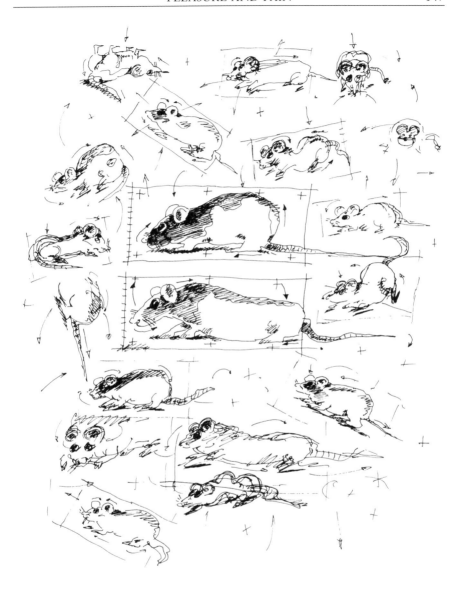

FIGURE 42   For ever and ever, our rat (François Durkheim).

learns very quickly. The rhythm of pressing actions is proportional to the intensity of the current it receives through the electrode. The rat is said to be practising self-stimulation (figure 43). It stops pressing the lever as soon as the current is cut off. The desire which dictates the pressing action is

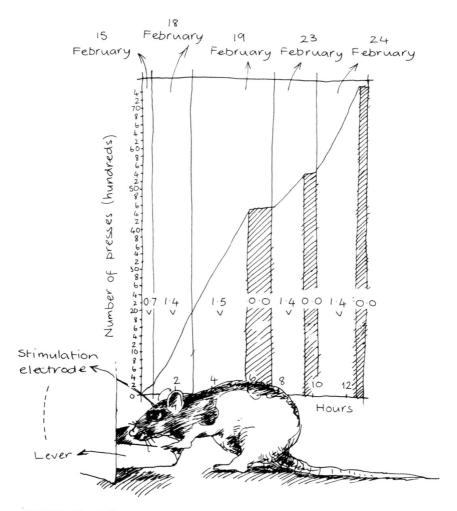

FIGURE 43 Self-stimulation experiment. By pressing a lever, the rat triggers an electric stimulator which sends a current to an electrode located in the lateral hypothalamus. The number of times that the rat presses the lever is shown on the curve. When the current is stronger, the rat presses the lever more often. When there is no current, the rat stops pressing. (After J. Olds and P. Milner, 'Positive reinforcement produced by electrical stimulation of septal area and other regions of the rat brain', *J. Comp. Physiol. Psychol.*, 47, 419–27, 1954.)

imperious since it is preferred to any other. A hungry animal which is given the choice between two levers, one distributing food and the other electrical stimulation of the lateral hypothalamus, will invariably choose self-stimulation, even if this means endangering its own survival. The rat is insatiable. But imperious and insatiable are two key words for the description of pleasure . . . Could the lateral hypothalamus be a 'pleasure centre'?[20] This idea is contradicted by the dispersion of cerebral sites for self-stimulation, roughly spread in the shape of a horseshoe open towards the front. However, the lateral hypothalamus does remain the main self-stimulation region; it is an avenue linking the anterior brain to the brainstem, traversed in both directions by nerve fibres, many of which use catecholamines to transmit their message.

Two theories have been put forward to explain self-stimulation. For Olds, self-stimulation produces a reward (pleasure).[21] This naturally reinforces behavioural response. The aim of desire is to obtain pleasure, and the behavioural choice is dictated by the pleasure it gives. For Deutsch, self-stimulation activates desire and pleasure in parallel.[22] It differs in this from normal behaviour in which desire corresponds to a homeostatic requirement: the natural satisfaction of a need gives pleasure, suppresses the desire and at the same time puts a stop to the corresponding behaviour. However, it is quite understandable that self-stimulation should be insatiable in so far as it drives desire along with pleasure. In the preceding chapter we saw arguments which refute both these theories a priori. We can nevertheless agree to say that self-stimulation gives rise to a central state called pleasure.

Pleasure and the act

Self-stimulation and the resulting pleasure will have a physiological meaning only if they cannot be related to a natural action. It can be seen that the electrical stimulation of all the self-stimulation sites produces all the different kinds of behaviour of which a rat is capable: sniffing, eating, drinking, washing, transporting and hoarding objects, digging, copulating, mouse-killing etc. Contrary to what was once believed, these actions are in harmony with the environment as the affective state is in tune with the situation: when stimulation of the lateral hypothalamus induces gnawing, the animal gnaws what is gnawable; when feeding is induced, the rat eats what is edible.

One cannot help thinking that neuronal circuits set out according to the plans furnished by the genome, revised and corrected by the learning experience, are responsible for these different behaviour patterns. For our purpose here, it is by no means necessary to know the extent of these neuronal complexes. Suffice it to say that the stimulation of the lateral hypothalamus can activate one circuit or another. The connections between the hypothalamic commands and the execution circuits are in no way rigid. A stimulated rat which does not encounter the object of the induced action does something else. If there is nothing to eat, it gnaws. It there is nothing to gnaw, it drinks. If there is nothing to drink, it runs about. The more intense the stimulation, the more easily interchangeable the behaviour. In the absence of an adequate object then, action for action's sake is what we observe. The vague brain is at work here. The stimulation of the lateral hypothalamus is not directly responsible for the reflex and muscular actions which carry out the behaviour pattern; it is more a kind of remote control which furnishes genetically pre-programmed nerve sequences that have been fine-tuned by experience with the possibility of expressing themselves through the ramifications of the stimulated system.[23] An illustration of this is given by the action of the adrenergic systems on the nerve circuits in the spinal cord which organize walking. Take a rat which is paralysed after its spinal cord has been severed. Give it an injection of clonidine, a substance which mimes the action of adrenaline and activates the adrenergic receptors. This induces the stereotyped repetitive movements characteristic of walking behaviour. Here is an example of hormonal action capable of activating the precabled circuits of the nervous system responsible for integrated behaviour: clonidine is a hormone which helps you put your best foot forward!

The behaviour patterns which are absolutely necessary for survival concern four things: sex, temperature, food and drink. Thermoregulatory behaviour consists in shivering and panting, sexual behaviour in moving the pelvis, eating and drinking in gnawing and swallowing movements of the mouth and throat. Without going so far as to speak of 'centres', a relative specialization of stimulation points from front to back can be observed along the lateral hypothalamus in the following order: temperature, sex, drink and food. These specialized regions are situated opposite medial zones where receptors are to be found which are sensitive to variations in the internal milieu concerning the relevant behaviour: heat and cold receptors for thermoregulation, oestrogen and androgen receptors for sex, osmoreceptors for drink and nutritive content receptors for food (figure 44).

Let us consider the point of stimulation which induces eating, for example. If the stimulator is triggered, the animal will devour any food within reach and presumably find pleasure in this activity. If the animal is given a choice, however, it will show total indifference to food and prefer self-stimulation. If its hunger is appeased by an injection of sugary serum or forced feeding, it will reduce its rhythm of self-stimulation. However, a hungry animal will self-stimulate more. Act and state are indissolubly linked. The observer now stimulates sexual activity, but, given the choice, the rat will again prefer self-stimulation, ignoring its partner. Castration diminishes the self-stimulation rate, whereas injections of testosterone increase it. These two examples show that the internal state influences the intensity of desire. Nevertheless it is difficult to say whether pleasure varies with the nature of a given act. Imagine asking someone if eating a good meal and making love give him different kinds of pleasure. His answer will probably reveal more about his habits and prejudices than about his internal

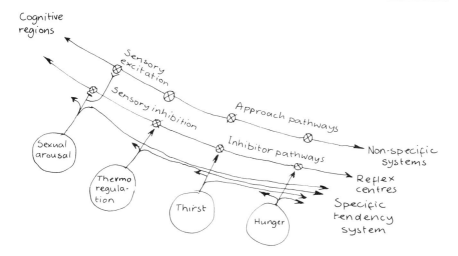

FIGURE 44   Simplified sketch of the interaction between receptors sensitive to various homeostatic parameters and transhypothalamic neuronal systems. (After J. Panksepp, 'Hypothalamic integration of behavior', in P.J. Morgane and J. Panksepp (eds), *Handbook of the Hypothalamus*, New York, Marcel Dekker, 1981.)

state. How can one compare an orgasm with a plate of caviar, even if the archives of English slang show that the word 'dish' has been used to describe a pretty woman? Pleasure and orgasm should be differentiated: the pleasure which precedes orgasm, like that of eating a good meal, reinforces the relevant behaviour. An orgasm, in contrast, acts more like a detergent and is responsible for eliminating desire. However, there is a definite specificity of internal states: the level of sex hormones has no effect on the self-stimulation rate in the activating sites of feeding behaviour. Conversely, the level of nutritive substances in the blood has no effect on the self-stimulation of the sexual sites. Being hungry does not increase sexual desire and a nice orgasm has never spoiled anyone's appetite.

Bull-flight

In 1954, while Olds and Milner were describing self-stimulation, Delgado showed that electrical stimulation of the medial regions of the hypothalamus made the animal run away.[24] Given the choice, the rat quickly learned to press the lever which stopped the stimulation. This same Delgado, doubtless spurred on by some national atavistic tendency, succeeded one day in stopping the charge of a rampaging bull and making it run away by electrically stimulating its medial hypothalamus.

All around the medial ventricle, and further back in the grey matter of the brainstem, there exist structures which seem to produce different effects from those associated with the lateral structures, namely aversion and avoidance instead of pleasure and approach. As in the case of the lateral hypothalamus, a site-by-site analysis shows great heterogeneity as to the behaviour induced. At certain points, the animal interrupts the stimulation and freezes before running away, or rears and springs about in all directions; at others, it tries to jump out of the cage in an attempt to escape, or engages in a frenzy of vertical leaps. This behaviour translates a state of aversion which the animal is trying to interrupt. The pleasure and aversion zones seem to be closely linked: the stimulation of the lateral hypothalamus lessens the aversion induced by medial stimulation and the latter reduces the lateral self-stimulation rate.

The chemistry of pleasure

Which neurohormones participate in the birth of pleasure? Which neuro-transmitters are involved in the self-stimulation phenomenon? Can they be considered as the chemical mediators of pleasure?

Catecholamines

We are back amongst old friends: catecholamines, and the prime suspect among them, noradrenaline. Fibres containing noradrenaline pass through the self-stimulation zone, and so the lateral hypothalamus is traversed by ascending noradrenergic pathways. If cocaine or amphetamine is used to encourage the synaptic release of noradrenaline, this increases the self-stimulation rate. If drugs like methyl-paratyrosine are used to inhibit its synthesis, self-stimulation stops. However, there are numerous arguments against an exclusively noradrenergic theory of self-stimulation.

Roy Wise champions dopamine as the chemical basis for self-stimulation. He unhesitatingly awards the exclusive title of pleasure neurotransmitter to this substance (figure 45). One of the best arguments in favour of this hypothesis is the fact that neuroleptics, which inhibit the action of dopamine as we have seen, suppress self-stimulation. However, it may be naive to substitute for the old idea of a pleasure centre the equally reductionist theory of a hedonistic synapse. Self-stimulation territory goes beyond the edges of the dopamine map of the brain. The destruction of dopamine neurons by 6-hydroxy-dopamine does not suppress the self-stimulation of certain centres, the nucleus accumbens for example.

Opioid peptides

Opium and its derivatives make you feel sleepy, and their immoderate use apparently affords immoderate pleasure. Use here leads inevitably to abuse and reminds us of the fanatical self-stimulating rat. Morphine favours self-stimulation after a transitory period of stupor which lasts about an hour (the time it takes for euphoria to appear in man). Naloxone, the antagonist

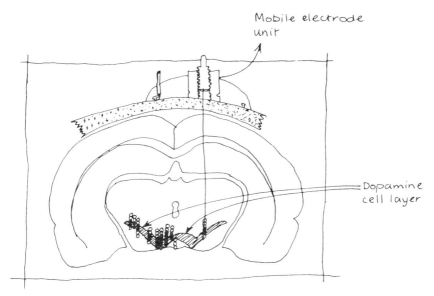

FIGURE 45   Frontal section of a rat brain showing the dopamine cells in the tegmental region of the brainstem. The mobile system which allows stimulation electrodes to be inserted into the brain is shown, as well as the series of successive points which were stimulated during the descent of the electrode. At the bottom, the positive stimulation points (inducing self-stimulation) are shown in black and the negative points in white. It will be seen that all the positive points are found in the dopamine cell layer. (After R.A. Wise, 'The dopamine synapse and the notion of "pleasure center" in the brain', *Trends Neurosci.*, 3, 91–4, 1980.)

of morphine, inhibits the favouring effect and in some cases even the self-stimulation. In so far as this effect requires the catecholaminergic system to function in an integrated way, it can be deduced that opioid receptors are playing a dominant favouring role. It has been suggested that self-stimulation is a good model for drug addiction. Would it be simplistic to say that the animal given to self-stimulation is addicted to its own natural morphines? And would it be an exaggeration to say that each time a man seeks pleasure too repetitively, his brain drugs itself with its opioids? Are the compulsive eater, the chocolate guzzler, the sex maniac and the jogging fanatic all addicts? The supermarket-rat experiment, in which the animal is given an extremely wide choice of delicious food, would tend to confirm this. The rat gobbles up far more than it needs. If naloxone is used to block the opiate system, the frenzied consumption stops dead.[25]

This interpretation is too hasty and does not account for the complexity of the system. We already know that there is no pleasure without pain and that aversive effects can counter pleasurable ones. γ-aminobutyric acid (GABA) and opioids are the brakes in the system; acetylcholine is the accelerator.[26]

Dopamine, noradrenaline, opioid peptides and GABA are omnipresent in acts where we assume pleasure to be involved. As with desire, we must define common functions of pleasure which will be differently expressed according to the circuits which are called upon.

The meaning of pleasure

Philosophical reflections can make a biological theory seem less serious. One is tempted to succumb to essentialism. Different interpretations will be put forward within a framework of objective data. They reconsider pleasure according to the three parameters of the fluctuating central state. The temporal dimension introduces the notion of opposed processes in which pleasure and suffering, a new pair, appear for the first time. Drug addiction will be used as an example.

Cerebral pleasure

Self-stimulation experiments have been carried out on man, but it is often impossible to quantify mere curiosity amongst the motives which make the individual stimulate himself.[27] What about pleasure? Sem-Jacobsen has made an assessment of the emotional states obtained in man using 2,852 stimulation points.[28] He finds nine categories of response: well-being and somnolence, euphoria, nervousness and anxiety, sadness and depression, fear, ambivalence, disgust, pain, orgasm. Imprecise verbal expression is the common trait here. Nor is there a really systematic mapping of points according to the kind of response. At best, we can only oppose a central aversive zone and lateral regions more associated with pleasure.

We have seen the role played by catecholamines in the neuronal traffic in the lateral hypothalamus. Consequently it is not surprising that drugs which act on the catecholamines should influence mood, bringing on depression and motivity-initiative loss in individuals treated with reserpine which eliminates the biogenic amines from the brain, or wakefulness and enhanced mental activity after treatment with amphetamine or cocaine which mobilize catecholamines.[29] The subjects studied were often suffering from pathological disorders which make the interpretation of the results a delicate matter. Far from throwing a new light on pleasure, experiments on man, which are always ideologically suspect, seem to us only to falsify the debate. Therefore let us come back to our animals, not because we are shamefully reductionist, but because we are cautious and modest.

Passion's slave

Pleasure! Pleasure and its opposite nestled in a narrow zone of the brain no bigger than a finger-nail. I can hear you sigh, 'Oh, no! Not the seat of the soul again!' No, no, rest assured; we are no longer concerned with the epiphyseal gland, the Cartesian well of animal spirits, but the pleasure-plying hypothalamus, essential to our behaviour. Aristotle, in *The Nicomachean Ethics*, criticizes Plato's doctrine according to which pleasure is born of the satisfaction of a need by suggesting that it is a natural concomitant of activity. Adopting an Aristotelian standpoint, Panksepp suggests that the lateral hypothalamus produces the impulse which triggers the act. He writes that the lateral hypothalamic system is isomorphic to the cerebral processes which activate the animal's investigations of its environment. Certain reservations should be made here concerning both the lateral hypothalamus as a 'centre' and the essential nature of its function.

The lateral hypothalamus is a crossroads which allows cerebral territories to communicate with one another through the branchings of the vague brain. It contains no cabled networks responsible for behaviour, no neuronal circuitry for eating, drinking or making love. Nor are there any traces of past experience here, and so none of the cognitive mapping produced by the learning process. The hypothalamus is open to the whole brain, but also to the internal milieu via the receptors it contains for the different bodily variables: temperature, blood pressure, hormone level etc. The hypothalamus reflects the different components of the fluctuating central state without compartmentalizing it into centres for this or that.

For Panksepp, the lateral hypothalamus is a goad without a goal. Once in the grip of desire, the goad urges all types of behaviour. The choice of behaviour is determined by the target present in the environment. Given adequate conditions in the internal milieu (hormones, blood etc), it is the sight and smell of a consenting female which will induce the animal to make love, or the presence of food which will trigger eating behaviour. When the lateral hypothalamus is stimulated electrically, the behavioural responses vary according to the motive present. The function of the hypothalamus would seem to be a kind of behavioural turning-on, dissociated from any particular goal. In a rat, one of the most spectacular signs of this turning-on is frantic sniffing. What does a normally wide-awake rat do? It sniffs. It is in this way that a rat expresses its awareness of the world. The more it sniffs, the greater the activation of its lateral hypothalamus, the more ardently it will approach the goals offered to it.

The activity of this system also corresponds to what is called exploratory impatience, which would seem to keep the brain turned on in anticipation of the goal to be reached, the choices being the domain of the cabled brain.[30]

The electrical activity of neurons in the lateral hypothalamus of a thirsty monkey lights up when the animal is presented with water. It stops as soon as drinking begins and long before its thirst is assuaged. If the water is taken away, the neurons become active again. The turning-on function is quite clear, and tends towards potential satisfaction of a need.

The tension reduction inherent here would seem to have a reinforcing role in the learning process. That self-stimulation should be insatiable is perfectly understandable, as is the fact that it plays no role in learning by secondary conditioning. There is no tension reduction, and so no reinforcing takes place. Here once again is the reduction drive theory so dear to behaviourists.[31]

The explanation remains theoretical, however. Dabbling in essentialism is fraught with risks. By talking of tension reduction, for example, one might encourage some people to take the hypothalamus for the Freudian psychic apparatus. An animal turned on by prolonged self-stimulation continues intense locomotive activity when the current is turned off, and this can be interpreted as a frustration effect. Such fraudulent analogies could be carried to the absurd lengths of locating the id in the hypothalamus.

Once again, what about pleasure? If we concede that it coincides with the activation of the lateral hypothalamus, we can establish that it appears when desire meets its object and thus anticipates the reduction in tension. At the dinner table, as in bed, pleasure is never directly linked to the satisfaction of a need. Indigestion and hot flushes are not pleasurable. However, let us consider desire contemplating its object: the eyes settle on a delicious-looking slice of smoked salmon hot (or rather, cold) from the Norwegian fiords . . . years of gastronomic experience etched on the cognitive maps of the cabled brain play a subtle duet with the vague brain from the lateral hypothalamus. The mouth closes on the delicacy and the waiting continues through the other senses which are solicited, the receptors on the tongue and palate keeping the pleasurable object at a distance (stop dribbling!). Once swallowed, however, the desired salmon is gone, the pleasure has vanished. As if expectation were all. Where is the lover who will dare say that he gets his pleasure from the satisfaction of a sexual need? Sad *post coitum*, reducing the delights and variations of coital assault to the terminal explosion, the mere powder-keg at the end of a winding smoking trail. Lovers' real pleasure is in waiting, manoeuvring and delaying. Michel Leiris uses a bull-fighting metaphor to evoke pleasure as the always possible but always deferred contact between the bull's horn and the matador's chest. Desire waves the red flannel cloth in front of the beast's blind gaze; the pleasure of the charge is ineffable faced with that defenceless body which sidesteps and deceives. The satisfaction of the desire in this case would be the death of the matador. Sexual desire has its own similar image of satisfaction in the post-coital drooping of the penis.[32]

We can avoid a too essentialistic definition of pleasure by introducing the notions of time and space. Neal Miller's model, inspired by Lewin, postulates that all kinds of behaviour, including cognitive dimensions, can be accounted for by opposed forces: approach and pleasure linked to the lateral hypothalamus, and avoidance and aversion linked to the medial structures.[33] The time dimension is to be found in the faculty of anticipation, an attribute of both systems.

The approach and avoidance coupling is present in Hess's classification of the effects of electrical stimulation of the brain (figure 46). The stimulation points are attributed to two systems according to the nature of the response. The trophotropic system, which corresponds to the lateral and anterior hypothalamus, would seem to support the activation of the parasympathetic

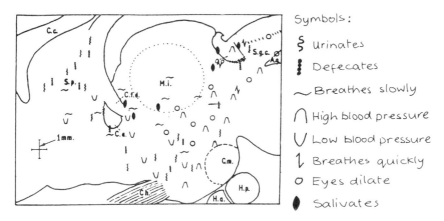

FIGURE 46 Parasagittal section of a cat brain, drawn by Hess, in which the various responses (obtained by electrical stimulation of the points indicated) are shown by symbols. (After W.R. Hess, *Diencephalon: Autonomic and Extra-pyramidal Functions*, New York, Grune and Stratton, 1954.)

nervous system: drop in blood pressure, slowing of pulse and breathing rates, salivation, contracting of the pupils, digestion, defecation, erection and sleep. These functions contribute on the whole to rest, assimilation and reproduction. The ergotropic system, in contrast, which corresponds to the medial and posterior structures, would seem to induce orthosympathetic activation: acceleration of pulse and breathing rates, high blood pressure, dilating of the pupils, horripilation, arousal, fear and anger. These are functions of exhaustion, destruction and attack. In other words a trophotropic Buddha and an ergotropic devil would seem to be cohabitants in the centre of the brain. We must admit that Hess does not indulge in any physiological Manicheism. Good and evil have no cerebral location. Such an idea is a dangerous fancy that nevertheless haunts certain minds, and the history of neurosurgery testifies to this.[34] We shall also leave Eros and Thanatos out of this, not in order to cast doubt on their theoretical usefulness (even Freud did not know how far he believed in them), but to avoid succumbing to the aforementioned delights of analogy.[35]

Pleasure is nothing without pain. This antagonistic couple must now be lodged in the fluctuating central state in order to escape the essentialistic smoke-screen.

Pleasure and the central state

We saw in the chapter on desire that the fluctuating central state expresses itself in three dimensions: extracorporal, corporal and temporal. The same three are relevant to pleasure.

The extracorporal dimension is represented by the objects of desire and disgust. The attraction and repulsion they exert on the subject are inseparable from the movements of the subject towards them. In speaking of the influence that the subject has on the action of the individual, it is equally valid to focus on the object of pleasure itself or on the attachment between it and the subject. A good example is the link between mother and suckling. H.F. and M.K. Harlow studied the behaviour of bottle-fed baby monkeys having no contact with their natural mother.[36] The young monkey is faced with two substitute mothers. One, made of wire netting, carries the bottle; the other, clothed in soft downy rags, has no bottle. The baby monkey spends its time on the second substitute and only approaches the other during brief feeding periods. The attachment to the downy decoy, evocative of the maternal fur, would seem to be innate. The basic need for food seems in this case to play no role in the choice of a substitute. Bowlby has shown that the child's attachment to the mother is programmed from birth.[37] Ethologists have found many examples of stimuli with a genetically determined affective value. This does not necessarily mean that the subject's extracorporal space is entirely programmed. It cannot be denied that secondary acquisitions associated with basic satisfactions can confer a hedonistic value on certain objects and the approach behaviour linking them to the subject. It is generally accepted that experience and learning correct, complete and fine-tune the central programmes.

The corporal dimension is represented by organ function and the composition of the internal milieu. The pleasure–aversion pairing is reflected by the workings of the parasympathetic and orthosympathetic systems. Pleasure can be accompanied by a drop in blood pressure, a slowing of the pulse and breathing rates, a contraction of the pupils, salivation and various hormonal secretions – in short, the general signs of activity of the parasympathetic system. For Halperin and Pfaff, parasympathetic activation and its vegetative translation would seem to form the organic basis of pleasure.[38] This is close to the theory of James and Lange according to which 'I feel pleasure because my breathing is calm, my pulse is beating slowly and my viscera are functioning at rest'. Self-stimulation would seem to give pleasure because it slows down the heart and lungs and creates a parasympathetic state. This debate on whether pleasure has a central or peripheral origin (I'm calm because I feel pleasure or I feel pleasure because I'm calm) is irrelevant within the conceptual framework of the fluctuating central state.

The temporal dimension brings us back to the role of learning in acquiring a personal stock of pleasurable objects. Pleasure and aversion are learned. The natural history of our preferences, which is based on a knowledge of the associative mechanisms of conditioning, lies outside the range of this book. We have already seen that aversion can be induced by the association of stimuli during a single experience. Other cases are linked to the repetition of a reinforcing stimulus without associative mechanisms. These affective states which have nothing to do with innate central programmes or acquired structures have been studied within the framework of the opponent-process theory developed by Solomon.[39] A striking example of these phenomena is the well-known story of the madman who, when asked why he keeps hitting himself on the head with a hammer, replies: 'It's so nice when I stop!' Take the case of the jogger who takes boundless pleasure in inflicting daily torture on his legs and lungs. We know that we often have to pay the price for enjoyment when it is over. The withdrawal symptoms of the drug addict are a dramatic example. Opposites coexist in our love-life and Romeo is not the only lover to find that parting is such sweet sorrow.

Besides withdrawal symptoms, two other phenomena are described in the opponent-process theory: affective contrast and addiction or affective habituation. As an example of the former we can point to the feeling of distress which appears when we abruptly deprive a subject of a source of pleasure: take away the baby's teddy-bear and see what happens! Affective habituation, in contrast, is the progressive disappearance of an affective state through repetition of the stimulus which gave rise to it. Repeated injections of morphine gradually lose their potency; a painful stimulus, if repeated several times, finally passes unnoticed. Affective contrast, affective habituation and withdrawal symptoms prove the existence of opponent processes. Any factor responsible for a given state, whether pleasurable or painful, seems also to create in the organism a process moving in the opposite direction, which gradually grows and tends to oppose the first factor. When the two factors cancel each other out, we would seem to have reached affective habituation. This process is all the more marked if the affective factor is intense and frequently repeated. When the stimulus is cut off, only the opponent effect remains, bringing on withdrawal symptoms (figure 47).

Addiction and abstinence immediately conjure up pictures of the world of drugs: opium and its derivatives morphine and heroin. When we think of the terrifying opponent effects that these drugs produce, we all too often forget the motive for taking them: pleasure. Opium is an exemplary drug for those studying the relationship between pleasure and suffering. The same drug suppresses pain and gives birth to pleasure . . .

The needle and the damage done

'Many years ago, if my memory serves me well, my life was an unending draught of outpouring hearts, of flowing wine . . .'[40] The drug addict is not the only guest at the banquet. Live now, pay later, is a commonly shared fate, and the piper will not often wait.

The drug addict's lot is not a simple one. The latest addition to the discussion comes from the biologist who has joined the priest and the policeman, the moralist and the pusher, at the debating table. He speaks out loud, claiming to have found in the brain natural morphines secreted by neurons. These endomorphines are henceforth the inevitable companions of any scientific study of pleasure. Margaret Mead once said during one of

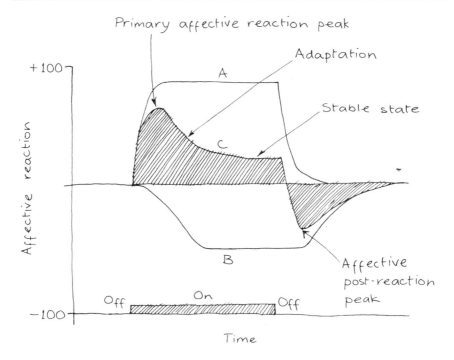

FIGURE 47   Explanatory diagram of the opponent process theory. An activating
stimulus produces two types of reaction: A, the primary reaction develops as soon as
the stimulus appears and stays at the same level until the stimulus disappears; B, the
opponent reaction develops more progressively and diminishes only slowly after the
stimulus disappears; C, the subject's affective reaction represents the algebraic sum
of the two reactions (A and B).

those innumerable special committee sessions on the drugs problem, which
are destined above all to ease the institution's bad conscience: 'Virtue is pain
followed by pleasure; vice is pleasure followed by pain.' One has only to
read the reports of those who care for drug addicts to realize the battle
which goes on between the memories of pleasure and the suffering caused
by withdrawal. It is a struggle in which the fluctuating central state tears and
strains, in which the fragile balance of opponent processes is destroyed. The
pain remains, meaningless pain which is an orphan of pleasure, abandoned
by morality. But suffering also sneaks up on 'normal' people during their
everyday activities and swings with pleasure on the pendulum of our central
state. A philosopher might say that it comes from the unbridgeable gap
between the cabled brain's reason and the vague brain's passions. Should we
follow Max Scheler in seeking the basis of morality in suffering or let
pleasure and pain get on with establishing a desperate homeostasis bent
only on survival?

We know that addiction to a drug leads to a gradual lessening of its effect. This goes hand in hand with a growing dependence which chains the addict to the drug and demands greater quantities, more often. Abstinence throws him into intolerable pain.[41] Some claim that it is the fear of this suffering which 'hooks' the addict. In fact, it seems that pleasure never totally disappears during the process of addiction and remains the main reason for drug-taking. The pharmacologist teaches us to observe dependence, addiction and abstinence in a length of guinea-pig intestine kept alive in a bath. The repeated application of opium derivatives leads to a gradual decrease in the contractile response of the intestinal muscles (addiction), whereas any interruption leads to a prolonged contraction (abstinence). Cellular and molecular mechanisms can be approached in the same way. We shall see the role of chemical messengers inside the cell: cyclic adenosine 3′,5′-monophosphate (cAMP), prostaglandins and membranous fats. The concentration of intracellular calcium rises during addiction and its role will also be examined. Certain neurotransmitters in the brain (acetylcholine, catecholamines) will be suspected of playing a role in the growth of addiction. Needless to say, no biologist seriously thinks that a bit of intestine or brain pulp behaves like an animal as regards drugs, and even less like a person. The advantage of these *in vitro* preparations is that they allow us to get to know the mechanisms of substances manufactured by the organism or by chemists, to study and classify the properties of their receptors and finally to understand at least how if not why we experience pain and pleasure.

Biology translates this association of pleasure and pain. It does not explain it, but formulates biochemically those opponent processes so far presented purely theoretically. Naloxone, the antagonist of morphine, suppresses in some cases the habituation to pain which results from repeated painful stimuli. This proves that endogenous morphines are at work in the brain during habituation. Opponent phenomena are also traceable through the injection of morphine into a region of the brain which is particularly sensitive to opiates: the peri-aqueductal grey matter. Within half an hour of the injection, the rat shows a turbulent state with vertical leaps and signs of distress which suggest the abstinence syndrome. Frozen stupor, accompanied by analgesia, follows this agitation. Jacquet thinks that two types of receptor are solicited in turn and that they have opposite effects. When the morphine supply is cut off, the action of the group of aversive-effect receptors is no longer in opposition with the other group. Dr Jekyll and Mr Hyde continue their struggle even inside the same endorphin molecule. It has recently been shown that a fragment of the β-endorphin molecule (one of the most active opioid peptides against pain) powerfully opposed the analgesic action of the whole molecule. Like pleasure, which contains the seeds of pain, here is a pleasure-giving molecule which contains its own antagonist.[42]

Pain

The special property of pain is that it is both an affection and a sensation. Receptors, nerves and pathways in the central nervous system which are specific to painful sensations can be described. These nervous pathways which ascend the successive levels of the spinal cord and brain set up their own inhibitory systems at each stage.

A sensational revelation

If we oppose pleasure to pain too systematically, we may forget a basic aspect of pain which makes it different from the other passions. It is not just an affection; it is also a sensation. As such, it has specific pathways and nervous centres and a social status the doctor ministers to.

Before leaving pleasure for pain, let us take an example which will illustrate the difference. A Turner sunset offers itself to my gaze. I take pleasure in this contemplation, but does the pleasure come from my cabled brain or my vague brain? From both. Neuronal and hormonal man walk hand in hand through the gallery. They have grown up together and are inseparable. The former has learnt to distinguish between good and evil, beauty and ugliness, but without the second it knows nothing. Such is my pleasure: a vague yet subtle product of my humours and reason. As I leave the gallery, I twist my ankle. In this case, I know where the pain comes from and which nervous pathways are transporting the distress signals.

There is also a significant difference in the attitude of biologists towards pleasure and pain. Research on pain has been directed since the nineteenth century by the notion of the existence of specific selective sensory canals. However, the recent idea of the existence of centres and nervous pathways for pleasure is having a hard time establishing itself.

The pathways of pain

The world and my body really do exist; this is proved by the fact that they gang up to make me suffer. There is no more personal manifestation of reality than pain. It is not in the least surprising that biologists since Descartes have rejected the essentially affective Aristotelian tradition in order to put pain under 'house arrest' in the body and dismantle its mechanisms. For Muller, every sensation is the product of specific energy transported to the brain by the nerves, and pain would seem to be no more than an exaggeration of the sense of touch. Von Frey modifies this doctrine by attributing to pain a specialized canal which links peripheral receptors to specialized nerve centres. This picture still prevails today. In the skin, muscles and viscera there are nerve elements which cause pain when activated. This pain signals to the brain anything which threatens the integrity of the body: burning, stinging, stretching, pinching, tearing, scratching, cutting etc. These sensations are grouped under the heading nociception. The behavioural reaction is a cry or a movement of the body away from the source of pain. We shall see that the subject acts on his own pain by various humoral and nervous means. As a manifestation of the central state, pain is no different from pleasure. Concerning pleasure, however, the sensory input has been neglected by scientists in favour of the mere affective aspect, whereas the opposite is true of pain. Pain remained an affective orphan, reduced to the status of a pure sensation, the object of strict traffic control in a specific cabled nervous network, until the work of the Melzack group restored to their rightful place the three basic factors in pain: the sensory, affective and cognitive aspects.[43] The first component refers to our ability to analyse the nature, the whereabouts, the intensity and the length of a painful stimulus. Its medium is the lateral columns of the spinal cord. The second component makes pain the antidote of pleasure. It is associated with the medial regions of the brainstem and brain in connection with the limbic structures. Operations such as leucotomy, which interrupt the limbic circuits, can in certain cases eliminate or attenuate this component. The last component, called the cognitive component, is involved in anticipation, suggestion, hypnosis etc. Pain is here the object of knowledge; the neocortex is at work.

'Does it tickle, or does it prickle?' Doctor Knock's question is, of course, one of the author's satirical weapons, but it can be answered. The physical qualities of pain can be described with a relatively accurate vocabulary explaining what the pain is like, where it is, whether it is spasmodic, sharp, throbbing, aching etc.

The pain sensation obeys laws studied in psychophysics, with a ceiling below which it does not exist (for example, 43°C is the temperature at which a sensation of burning replaces the mere feeling of heat) and an intensity which is proportional to the strength of the stimulus. Pain rings the alarm-bell when the body is attacked, and some people remark that God is a sadist because He made pain painful! Why should the signal be an unpleasant one? Is the pain sensation only an excuse for the pain passion which contrasts with pleasure and heightens it?

The pain receptors are known and catalogued. Their structure is extremely simple, consisting of fine free nerve terminations. Some (A delta) are covered in a fatty insulating sheath of myelin and pick up mechanical stimulations: they are generally specific to one kind of pain. The others (C) are finer and thinly myelinated and sensitive to various kinds of pain. However, they are cruder in the qualitative evaluation of the stimulus and slower to transmit the message. We do not know how these receptors are activated. On the periphery there is already both humoral and neuronal activity. The pain receptor is activated, and at the same time it is influenced by substances which are true local hormones, released by blood cells for example. Histamine, prostaglandins, peptides, bradykinin and substance P are to be found amongst these substances. The latter is the neurotransmitter which carries the painful impulse in the spinal cord, and it is also present at

the peripheral origin of the nerve where it dilates vessels and reinforces the
excitability of the nerve endings. All this activity in the skin or viscera
prefigures the neurohormonal interactions of the central nervous system.
These peripheral events are linked to psychophysical phenomena like the
radiation of pain. The sympathetic nervous system also influences pain
receptors which are sensitive to the action of adrenaline. Leriche even
suggested interrupting the system to calm certain kinds of pain. The brain
and the central state, then, can act on pain at the source.

Following a description of the pathways of pain is a little like reading a
recommended tour in a guide book: there is nothing more boring if you are
not on the spot. Nevertheless, let us enumerate the stages: the spinal cord,
the brainstem, the thalamus and the cortex.

The skin, viscera and muscles are the starting points on the periphery.
Every part of the body has pain receptors, although some sites are better
known than others: the pulp in tooth cavities which is famous for the pain
that no philosopher can endure patiently, or the joints which are frequently
the victims of rheumatism.

Nociceptive impulses are transmitted by fibres which reach the brainstem
and spinal cord through the cranial nerves and dorsal roots. The latter are
symmetrically paired, right and left, and capture sensations from different
regions of the body (figure 48). The pain-fibre cells are to be found in the
spinal ganglia.

First, at each different level, the pain fibres synapse with second-order
neurons in the dorsal horn. The first check takes place here. The painful
message is not passed on from the first neuron to the next without any
interference. All the peripheral information jockeying for position at the
entrance to the spinal cord along with that from the higher centres of the
brain contribute to a change in the painful message at the medullar stage.
Interneurons sort and disperse these various influences. We shall come back
to the chemical agents used in these transactions and note that substance P
helps to transmit the main message from the first neuron to the second. The
second neuron then enters the spinal cord after changing sides. A separation
between sensation and emotion can already be seen here. The sensory fibres
go direct to the lateral thalamus while the affective fibres lead to the medial
structures of the brainstem and thalamus. Stimulation of the lateral tract of
ascending fibres causes pain on the opposite side of the body, while their
destruction suppresses contralateral pain.

The second stage concerns the deep structures of the brain, the thalamus
and the brainstem. In the brainstem, the pathways of pain abandon
terminals which contribute to making up complex neuronal circuits.
The higher we climb up the central axis, the clearer the distinction
becomes between affective and sense-differentiation processes. In the lateral
thalamus, pain takes its third neuron, the one which leads to the cortex. In
the past, neurosurgeons had it in for the thalamus. Its role in pain had been
known since the nineteenth century because of the anatomical description of
the spinothalamic tract and the connection made between a painful

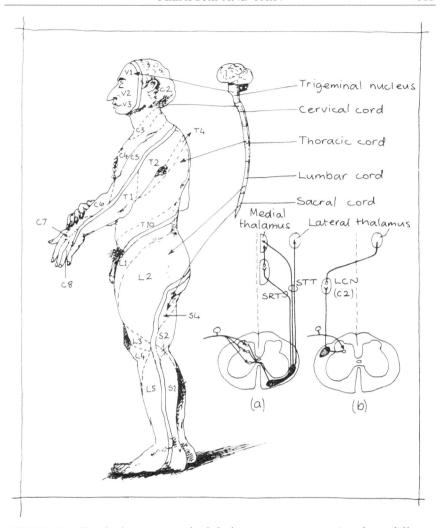

FIGURE 48   Sketch showing, on the left, how sensory perception from different parts of the surface of the body reaches different parts of the spinal cord, drawn separately. On the right, the pain pathways in the spinal cord: (a) spinoreticular tract (SRT) and spinothalamic tract (STT) in the anterolateral cord; (b) spinocervico-thalamic tract in the dorso-lateral cord, relaying in the lateral cervical nucleus (LCN). (After J.M. Besson et al., 'Physiologie de la nociception', *J. Physiol.*, *Paris*, 78, 7–107, 1982.)

syndrome described by Dejerine and certain thalamic lesions. As soon as stereotaxis made it possible to operate on a precise structure of the brain, neurosurgeons were off on the hunt for the nucleus responsible for the patient's pain in order to destroy it. The results of this empirically based assault were disappointing. Many neurosurgeons dropped the approach because of the often catastrophic results: the pain would reappear, much worse, after a few weeks or months.

As for the cortex, we know that electrical stimulation is not painful. However, there exist cortical neurons which are specialized in nociception, and this proves that it takes part in the painful sensation. But at this level it is difficult to separate the affective from the sensory.

'One pain is lessened . . .'

'. . . by another's anguish.' Many things help to soothe pain, even pain itself, as Shakespeare well knew. On its way, pain meets obstacles which attenuate it. First, in the spinal cord where the pain fibres end up in a mesh of local neurons, some of which inhibit the passage of the painful message. These inhibitor interneurons can be activated by impulses from large fibres which transport sensory information other than pain. Therefore the passage of the painful impulse can be temporarily blocked in the spinal cord. This explains the analgesic effect of peripheral electrical stimulation of the painful zone or the posterior roots. It is a technique used to soothe chronic pain.[44]

In the brainstem, the pathways of pain activate nerve structures with systems descending to the lower levels of the spinal cord. The exact role of these structures is uncertain. They are widely thought to have an analgesic function, inhibiting the passage of the painful information at the spinal relay stations through local neurons. Any painful stimulation can activate this descending control system. In a rat, stimulations as various as pinching the tail or immersing it in hot water, pinching its nose or giving it a painful visceral injection all inhibit the response of a nociceptive medullar neuron to the painful electrical stimulation of the rat's leg. Another hypothesis is that these descending pathways are there to stifle the hubbub of messages of all sorts bustling around at the medullar level. The inhibition concerns the signals not transporting pain. By attenuating the background noise, it makes the painful message clearer and more contrasted.[45]

The electrical stimulation of medial and periventricular regions of the brainstem (peri-aqueductal grey and raphe nuclei) has an analgesic effect on animals. However, we have already seen that the electrical stimulation of these regions causes aversion and avoidance behaviour. Thus it is difficult to distinguish between analgesia and emotional upheaval in the troubled central state. It is simplistic to say that pain inhibits pain, for there are many contradictory experimental results. Here are some more unmarried machines, working for the solitary pleasure of the scientist. An excitor neuron excites an inhibitor neuron which inhibits an inhibitor neuron, which will let a descending neuron be excited; this neuron excites an inhibitor neuron which will slow down the painful message in the spinal cord . . . (figure 49). This 'simplified' diagram shows why a rat does not feel its tail being pinched if its brainstem is stimulated at the same time. In any case, we can be sure that, given the choice, the rat would prefer to go and play some other game! However, new studies on animals which are free to come and go have clearly shown the presence of analgesic zones in the brainstem.

In short, there exist nerve structures in the spinal cord and brainstem which can inhibit pain. The discovery of endomorphines has thrown new light on this action of the nervous system.

The chemistry of pain

Has the discovery of endogenous morphines secreted by the brain changed what we know about pain? After a brief historical account of their discovery, we shall examine how they act and their role in certain paradoxical phenomena.

'Drowsed with the fume of poppies . . .'

'Our brain is a poppy which blossoms white and secretes an opium to ease our pains.' The discovery of the brain's ability to manufacture its own opium is a fascinating chapter in the history of science. At the end of the 1960s several dozen products of synthesis were available which imitated the action of morphine and other opiates but which had the same disadvantages: among other things, they were habit-forming. A powerful antagonist capable of blocking the effects of opiates had also been developed. This product, naloxone, turned out to be a marvellous research tool. Between 1968 and 1972, a group of researchers observed that electrical stimulation of the periventricular regions of the brainstem in the rat or the cat suppressed pain.[46] This analgesic stimulation was habit-forming, like opiates. In an animal already accustomed to morphine, the electrical stimulation had no effect. Reciprocally, the repetition of the electrical stimulation made the morphine ineffective. The conclusion drawn was that electrical stimulation of the brainstem and the administering of morphine had similar effects which could be cumulative and cross-addictive, and that their nerve mechanisms were probably the same. At the same time, it was shown that morphine linked with specific receptors in the nervous system. If there were receptors in the brain capable of linking substances of vegetable or synthetic origin, then the existence of endogenous substances capable of recognizing these same receptors could be suspected. In 1974, encephalin, a factor capable of fixing itself on morphine receptors, was extracted from the brain. Other substances of the same kind (opioid peptides), with an identical sequence of four amino acids and able to link with the same receptors as morphine, were soon isolated. This discovery, along with the analgesic effects of electrical stimulation of the brain, led to the conclusion that this stimulation brought a system of endogenous morphines (endomorphines) into play.

Today, numerous endomorphines have been identified (appendix 5).

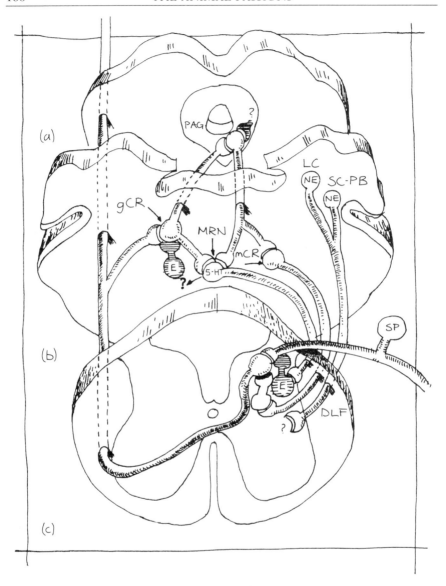

FIGURE 49 Analgesic effect of electrical stimulations of the brainstem and the self-analgesic action of painful messages. (After A.I. Basbaum and H.L. Fields, 'Endogenous pain control mechanisms: review and hypothesis', *Ann. Neurol.*, 4, 451–2, 1978.) (a) The electrical stimulation of the peri-aqueductal grey matter (PAG) and microinjections of small doses of morphine induce powerful analgesic effects; (b) at the bulbar level, the magnus raphe nucleus (MRN) and the magnocellular reticular nucleus (mCR), which are rich in serotoninergic cellular bodies, receive excitor messages from the PAG and send efferent impulses to the

They can be grouped in three families: encephalins, endorphins and dynorphins, with each family having at its head a precursor which is common to all its members. Immunology, chemistry and histology together allow us to locate these different substances in the neuronal fibres, control their concentration in the nerve structures and measure their release. Four classes of receptors can also be identified according to their affinity for different opiate derivatives. Faced with a mass of often contradictory information, we shall limit ourselves to a few generalizations.

Endomorphines are not found exclusively in the pathways of pain. They are also present in the physiology of the circulation, thermoregulation and digestion, in the secretion of hormones and in motivity. Pain is the tree which hides the wood.

Endomorphines are differently situated in the brain and spinal cord according to their nature. β-endorphin, which comes exclusively from the hypothalamus, travels far and, because of its long axons, descends into the brainstem and spinal cord. Its neuron is a tree with long branches. Encephalins and dynorphins, in contrast, are strictly limited to certain areas. Their neurons are bushes with short branches. The receptors are not only located at synapses, but are diffuse, which suggests hormonal-type activity in parallel with their neurotransmitter role.

The family relationship between endomorphines and morphine is spatial in structure rather than chemical, and explains their analgesic action. One level of intervention could be the spinal cord. Jessel and Iversen have studied the release of the pain messenger, substance P, in slices of spinal cord kept alive for the purpose. They noted that when encephalin was added to the perfusion liquid, less substance P was secreted. This would seem to be a so-called presynaptic inhibition, in which the encephalin blocks the release of the mediator at the level of the first nociceptive neuron. Other interventions are possible, as the encephalin neurons of the spinal cord can also act at the level of the second nociceptive neuron (postsynaptic effect), lessening its activity. The effects of naloxone give us further proof of the complexity of the system. As this substance blocks opioid action, we could expect naloxone to produce hyperalgesia. In fact, the opposite sometimes happens. There is an ingenious explanation for this paradox: encephalin

spinal cord by the dorsolateral tract; (c) the activation of the MRN and mCR fibres induces inhibiting effects on the nociceptive neurons located in layers I and V of the dorsal horn. These neurons, which receive messages transported by small-diameter fibres containing substance P, project towards the supra-spinal centres, indirectly activating the structures at the beginning of the descending systems (PAG–MRN) through the gigantocellular nucleus (gCR). The system as a whole thus possesses a negative feedback loop. Encephalinergic interneurons (E) are present at the medullary, bulbar and mid-brain levels. Furthermore, certain data indicate that the noradrenergic neurons (NE) of the locus coeruleus (LC) in the rat and the subcoeruleus parabrachialis nucleus in the cat (SC-PB) are also involved in modulator systems. (Commentary after Besson et al., 'Physiologie de la nociception'.)

neurons would seem to possess inhibitor autoreceptors and the encephalin released would seem to act on these, inhibiting its own further release; naloxone, blocking the autoreceptors first, consequently helps the release of encephalin.

These medullar encephalin neurons are probably the intermediaries which enable the descending pathways to exercise their inhibiting action on pain. Several neurotransmitters may be at work here, especially serotonin, which is perhaps to be found in the same descending fibre as substance P. Once again we find a peptide participating not only in the transmission of a message but also in its inhibition.

What is cabled and what is hormonal in this organization? How should we construe the analgesia induced by stress? We shall see later the various means of producing a state of stress in an animal, one of which is the electrical stimulation of its legs. Such aggressions on rats produce prolonged analgesia comparable with the indifference to pain shown by some wounded soldiers. Peripheral hormonal actions which are exerted through the blood are here conjugated with central nervous actions: the hypophysis and adrenal gland are responsible for the peripheral secretion of endomorphines, and, under stress, the brain secretes endomorphines. It is quite possible to induce a stress-conditioned reflex analgesia, which confirms the role of the nervous system. The rat becomes insensitive to other painful stimuli when it receives an electric shock from the ground. If the rat is put back on the same ground without being given an electric shock, it remains insensitive to pain. A comparable effect is produced by certain substances through the mere power of suggestion (placebo effect). The fact that these effects are blocked by naloxone would seem to suggest that cerebral endomorphines play a role in them. There could be a plausible explanation here for the influence of acupuncture on pain.

We should nevertheless soft-pedal this endomorphine piano concerto. These substances are present to such an extent, are so multiple and contradictory from the tip of the rat's whiskers to the tip of its tail, that it is easy to find a role for them in any circuit that explains a brain function. One researcher finds a rise in encephalin content in a structure during an experiment, and two others find a drop. The scientist's technique and honesty are not in question. It is quite simply impossible to master all the scientific parameters. This does not mean that we are certain of nothing. Experimental models are improving all the time. More precise immunological methods and release measurements prove the intervention of endomorphines in the brain during chronic or sharply painful episodes. Experimental situations close to physiology or pathology have recently been created in animals. Rats which have been made arthritic by injections allow us to study chronic pain, the sort of pain doctors are often concerned with. The spinal cord of these rats contains surplus encephalins which are no longer released and whose receptors become hypersensitive as they are no longer called upon. Progress in the struggle against pain is made possible, while addiction can be avoided. French researchers have scored one of the most spectacular successes of recent years in developing drugs which stop endomorphines being degraded by blocking the action of the enzymes which normally destroy them. The endomorphines then prolong and amplify their analgesic action by accumulation. The therapeutic principle is simple: instead of administering addictive opiates to the patient, his own morphine count is raised by preventing its destruction.

Pain and passion

The sensation makes us forget the passion attached to pain. Pain is an integral part of the person in that it is a manifestation of the fluctuating central state.

Knowledge of pain

Even if we speak of pain mainly in terms of networks of nervous pathways or as a specific sensation, we should not forget to mention it in the context of feelings and passions.

At the level of the medial structures of the brainstem or the thalamus, pain already mixes indistinguishably with aversion. The fact that endomorphines are more often neurohormones than neurotransmitters helps us to drown pain in the swamp of the humours. We cannot follow the biological track and pass from physical to moral pain without uttering cretinous generalities. The sensation of pain is only one component of aversion as a general manifestation of the fluctuating central state. Pain would seem to play the same primary role relative to aversion as certain experiences of satisfaction do relative to pleasure. Similarly, the relations between pain and the cognitive functions are orchestrated by the dialectics of the vague and the cabled brain. Psychophysical experiments have shown how knowledge acts on the perception of pain. For example, a painful stimulus will appear weaker if it is preceded by a light signalling its imminence.

This may seem a little unnatural if we consider real-life situations, which are much more complex. There is no pure perception of pain devoid of historical contingency. Any pain is perceived relative to its context (corporal and extracorporal space) and to the sometimes distant past (temporal space). Pain offers us the possibility of following the progressive transformation of a sensation into an affection through the nervous pathways. Indeed, as soon as it enters the spinal cord, pain meets descending waves of information from the brain which attenuate it or clarify the message. In the cerebral structures, the painful message mixes with the neuronal groupings responsible for the general aversive processes. If there exist specific pathways for pain in the ventrobasal thalamus which relay it to the somesthetic cortex, they are now but a negligible fraction of the potentiality of the pain, which floats between limbo and the hemispheres.

'Who are these coming to the sacrifice?'

Pain is useful. It is the sign of something wrong somewhere in the body or of an injury which needs treating. Veterinary surgeons know this, and avoid putting a splint on certain fractures as the pain will immobilize the animal much more efficiently.

Pain is also an experience which is essential in defining the body. It is the point at which the corporal space meets the extracorporal. As Bergson says, the object of perception coincides with our body.

The metaphysical and moral meaning of pain is basic to Christianity. This will be the only reference to a Passion which is beyond biology. It is no minor paradox that pain should follow reassuring pathways in the nervous system and spinal cord, and at the same time translate man's powerlessness and tragic fate.

Let us side with pleasure rather than pain. Spinoza considered pain to be the most mediocre of passions. Of pain we say: the sooner this is over, the better. In contrast, we would like intense joy to last for ever, and this is the desire Keats whispers in his *Bright star* sonnet. But the opponent processes are there to remind us that during any party, even a Gatsby party, 'fruit rinds and discarded favours and crushed flowers' accumulate.

Sacrifice may give an ultimate meaning to pain. In its name, man has been burnt at the stake, used as cannon-fodder or crucified. Is this suffering the inevitable result of our cerebral development? If the presence of a vague brain bathed in constricting humours forces us to choose between the tree of pleasure and the tree of pain, why not choose the former along with Pascal, Luther and Montaigne? It is a choice which is always tempered by the opponent processes, a choice which needs to be negotiated, and which demands courage or inspiration.

Notes

1   On the impossibility of defining pleasure, see A. Lalande, 'Plaisir', *Vocabulaire technique et critique de la philosophie*, Paris, 13th edn, 1980.
2   R. Descartes, *Les Passions de l'âme*, Paris, 1649.
3   H. Cureau de La Chambre, *Les Caractères des passions: où il est traité de la nature et des effets des passions courageuses*, Paris, 1650.
4   J. Maisonneuve, *Les Sentiments*, Paris, 1948.
5   M. Scheler, *Le Sens de la souffrance*, Paris, undated.
6   A. Bain, *The Senses and the Intellect*, London, 1855.
7   M. Reuchlin, *Psychologie*, Paris, 1977.
8   J. Lacan, *Ecrits*, Paris, 1966.
9   B. Spinoza, *The Ethics*, transl. R.H.M. Elwes, New York, 1955.
10 'Joy is the passion which enables the spirit to reach a greater perfection.' *Laetitia* and *tristitia* in Spinoza have a more general meaning than joy and sadness in other philosophers.
11 E. Thorndike, *Animal Intelligence*, New York, 1911.
12 A lot has been published about pleasure in learning. See especially L.C. Crespi,

'Quantitative variation of incentive and performance in the white rat', *Am. J. Physiol.*, 55, 467–517, 1942.

13   N.E. Miller et al., 'Decreased hunger but increased food intake resulting from hypothalamic lesions', *Science*, 112, 256–9, 1950.

14   P. Teitelbaum, 'The use of operant method in the assessment and control of motivational states', in W.K. Honig (ed.), *Operant Behavior: Areas of Research and Application*, Englewood Cliffs, NJ, 1966.

15   M. Jeannerod, *Le Cerveau-machine*, Paris, 1983.

16   H. Bergson, *Matter and Memory*, transl. N.M. Paul and W. Scott Palmer, London, 1911.

17   'Alliesthesia' is a neologism formed from the Greek *alliosis*, 'change', and *esthesis*, 'sensory quality', and is used to express the subjective appreciation of the attractive or repulsive nature of food according to the internal state of the subject. See M. Cabanac, 'Physiological role of pleasure', *Science*, 173, 1103–7, 1971.

18   M. Cabanac and J. Leblanc, 'Physiological conflict in humans: fatigue vs. cold discomfort', *Am. J. Physiol.*, 244, 621–8, 1983.

19   J.D. Corbit and T. Ermits, 'Specific preference for hypothalamic cooling', *J. Comp. Physiol. Psychol.*, 86, 24–7, 1974.

20   J. Olds, 'Self stimulation of the brain', *Science*, 127, 315–24, 1958. On 'pleasure centres', see H.J. Campbell, *The Pleasure Areas*, New York, 1973.

21   J. Olds and M.E. Olds, 'Drives, rewards and the brain', in T.M. Newcombe (ed.), *New Directions in Psychology*, New York, 1965.

22   J.S. Deutsch and C.I. Howarth, 'Some tests of the theory of intracranial self stimulation', *Psychol. Rev.*, 70, 349–553, 1963.

23   J. Panksepp. 'Hypothalamic integration of behavior', in P.J. Morgane and J. Panksepp (eds), *Handbook of the Hypothalamus*, New York, 1981.

24   J.M.R. Delgado et al., 'Learning motivated by electrical stimulation of the brain', *Am. J. Physiol.*, 179, 587–93, 1954.

25   A. Sclafani, 'Appetite and hunger in experimental obesity syndromes', in D. Novin, W. Wyrwicka and G. Bray (eds), *Hunger, Basic Mechanisms and Clinical Implications*, New York, undated.

26   P. Schmitt et al., 'Periventricular structures, elaboration of aversive effects and processing of sensory information', in *Modulation of Sensorimotor Activity During Alteration on Behavioural States*, New York, 1984.

27   J.M.R. Delgado, 'New orientation in brain stimulation in man', in W. Wauquier and E.T. Rolls (eds), *Brain Stimulation Reward*, Amsterdam, 1976.

28   C.W. Sem-Jacobsen, 'Electrical stimulation and self stimulation in man with chronic implanted electrodes. Interpretation and pitfalls of results', in W. Vanquier and E.T. Rolls (eds), *Brain Stimulation Reward*, Amsterdam, 1976.

29   Panksepp, Hypothalamic integration of behavior.

30   J.P. Changeux, *Neuronal Man*, New York, 1985; D.H. Ingvar, 'L'idéogramme cérébral', *Encéphale*, 3, 5–53, 1977.

31   C.L. Hull, *Principles of Behavior*, New York, 1943.

32   M. Leiris, *Miroir de la tauromachie*, Paris, 1938.

33   N.E. Miller, 'Studies of fear as an acquirable drive. I: Fear as motivation and fear reduction as reinforcement in learning of new responses', *J. Exp. Psychol.*, 38, 89–101, 1948.

34   We cannot deal with the problem of psychosurgery in a brief note. We shall just

tell the story of Egas Moniz (1875–1955), Nobel prizewinner in 1949, whose career oscillates between the grotesque and the monstrous. As an elegant Portuguese neurosurgeon, Moniz heard the great physiologist Fulton expose the case of a female monkey called Becky whose emotive character had been improved by a partial ablation of the frontal lobes. Impressed by this observation, and on the sole basis of this information, Moniz went to see his surgeon friend, Almeida Lima, and they decided to operate on the frontal lobes of all the mentally sick people that they could persuade Portuguese mental hospitals to give them. Never was any mention made of a serious scientific study of the results, as if the affection alone justified the practice. In 1950, over twenty thousand people world-wide had profited from the 'therapy', including prisoners and children. One year after receiving the Nobel prize for medicine, Moniz also got a bullet in the spine from one of his grateful patients. Since then, methods have improved, particularly as a result of stereotaxis, and epileptics have been successfully treated, but this has nothing to do with psychosurgery, which is as unfounded scientifically as it always was, despite the proclamation of its rebirth by Gösta Rylander in *Proceedings of the Third International Congress of Psychosurgery – Surgical Approaches in Psychiatry*, Cambridge, 1972.

35   S. Freud, *Beyond the Pleasure Principle*, London, 1920.
36   H.F. Harlow and M.K. Harlow, 'The affectional systems', in A.M. Schrier, H.F. Harlow and F. Stollnitz (eds), *Behavior of Non-Human Primates: Modern Research Trends*, New York, 1965.
37   J. Bowlby, *Attachment and Loss*, London, 1970.
38   R. Halperin and D.W. Pfaff, 'Brain-stimulated reward and control of autonomic function: are they related?', in D.W. Pfaff (ed.), *The Physiological Mechanisms of Motivation*, New York, 1982.
39   R.L. Solomon, 'The opponent-process theory of acquired motivation: the costs of pleasure and the benefits of pain', *Am. Psychol.*, 35, 691–712, 1980.
40   C. Olievenstein, *Destin du toxicomane*, Paris, 1983.
41   C. Kornetsky and G. Bain, 'Effects of opiates on rewarding brain stimulation', in Smith and Lane (eds), *The Neurobiology of Opiate Reward Processes*, Amsterdam, 1983.
42   Y.F. Jacquet, 'β-endorphin and ACTH – opiate peptides with coordinated roles in the regulation of behavior?', *Trends Neurosci.*, 2, 140–2, 1979.
43   R. Melzack and P.D. Wall, 'Pain mechanisms: a new theory', *Science*, 150, 971–9, 1965.
44   P.D. Wall and W.H. Sweet, 'Temporary abolition of pain in man', *Science*, 155, 108–9, 1967.
45   D. Le Bars et al., 'Opiate analgesia and descending control system', in *Advances in Pain Research and Therapy*, New York, 1982.
46   D.J. Mayer, 'Endogenous analgesia systems: neuronal and behavioral mechanisms', in *Advances in Pain Research and Therapy*, New York, 1979.

10

Hunger and Thirst

The Creator, by forcing man to eat in order to survive, invites him to do so by giving him an appetite, and rewards him with the pleasure that comes of eating.

Brillat-Savarin, *The Physiology of Taste*, 1826

Hunger and thirst are the most basic of the passions: they ensure the survival of the body. Before studying hunger, let us recall the main metabolic phenomena which govern the functioning of the body.

It may seem incongruous to class hunger and thirst among the passions. Dying for love or hate may be construed as a noble fate, but dying of hunger or thirst if you are neither a victim of extreme poverty nor lost in the desert hardly provides the makings of stunning drama. Philosophers, probably because of their copious diets, have generally refrained from analysing a situation which nevertheless contains all the necessary ingredients. In the tragic vein, is there a better example than this fat red-faced gentleman who takes a one-way ticket to apoplexy by the feverish ingurgitation of gigantic quantities of steak and kidney pie, or that man who drinks his liver away supposedly under the pretext of quenching his thirst?

But there is a more general definition of the passions. They are the expression of a fluctuating central state and govern the relationships between us and the world: their common denominators are desire and the pleasure/aversion pair, and they are responsible for the management of life and the survival of the species. From this point of view, hunger is the most exemplary of the passions. Its object is ourselves, or rather our body: its growth and upkeep must be catered for by a regular supply of food. Seventy per cent of our body is water, but there is also meat, sugar and fat reserves, and all these suffer losses which must constantly be made up. Fats or lipids are the favourite object of the hunger passion. The regulations which keep the energy bill constant mainly concern fats. What is disparagingly called adipose fat is perhaps the most 'sculptable' part of our weight. Our constant weight depends on the constancy of the layers of fat. Adipose fat is also responsible for the pleasant forms of the female body. Fashion plays a role here, and the adipose fat of a woman, sated with peaches and cream or tortured with grated carrots, suffers from repeated disregard for homeostatic principles.

Hunger is the first passion, chronologically speaking. It drives the baby to the mother's breast. We shall never know if the first feeling a new-born baby expresses through its crying is its pain at arriving in our world or its impatience to eat its first meal, but there is no doubt that from the moment of birth there exist innate neurophysiological mechanisms that trigger hunger and stop it when the needs of the individual have been adequately covered.

The three dimensions of the fluctuating central state, the body, the world and time, are to be found in hunger. The corporal space of hunger is animated by energy-releasing substances: sugars, fats and proteins, the products of cellular metabolism and the hormones (insulin and glucagon) which regulate this metabolism. The brain, through its privileged receptors and endogenous secretions, offers a permanent representation of the biological drama being played out in the rest of the body. The extracorporal or sensorimotor space is the edible world, the food which has a different sensory representation from one species to another and differs also according to the internal state and the history of the subject. It is also the act of eating and the search for food, or feeding behaviour in general. The temporal space, which has become particularly important for the human species, fixes meal times, conditions our tastes and eating habits, and transforms hunger into the metronome of our social life.

Light my fire

To quote Conrad out of context, '. . . life is like an after-dinner hour with a cigar'; a combustion of substances which are inflammable in oxygen.[1] However, this is as indifferent a comparison for the writer as for the biochemist. The degradation of energy-releasing substances (catabolism) leads only indirectly to oxidation and more directly, by a still mysterious coupling, to the forming of adenosine triphosphate (ATP). This molecule has phosphorus-based chemical links which are rich in energy. When they rupture, they provide the cell with the energy it needs. Energy-releasing substances and oxygen are obtained from the external environment when we eat and breathe, two priorities we have in common with all animals and which condition the evolution of the species. The economics of feeding and breathing are very different. If we lack oxygen, we die immediately. Life ceases. If we lack food, however, the cells continue to be supplied with energy-releasing substances from internal reserves. Take a car engine. The air goes direct to the carburettor, whereas the petrol is pumped from a tank which it is wise to fill up from time to time. More poetically, Lavoisier compared animal life with a burning candle. However, hunger does not allow us to burn the candle at both ends. It is a saver's passion, only worried about how to manage what has not been spent. All animals possess an internal reserve of energy-releasing substances which the organism draws on permanently, and which feeding rebuilds periodically. There are short-term reserves in the digestive tract where food remains for a few hours before being digested and assimilated, and long-term reserves in the form of glycogen in the liver and muscles and above all in the form of fats in the specialized adipocyte cells. This adipose fat which accounts for between 10 and 15 per cent of our body-weight provides a man with two or three months' reserve supplies.

Cells can burn different substances: amino acids, fatty acids and sugars. However, their favourite fuel is glucose. The sugar content of the blood remains stable and fluctuates only very slightly from one day to the next. Some cells, like neurons, run only on glucose. With radioactive analogues of glucose, the consumption of this sugar in the brain can be measured locally and variations during different functions can be observed. There is a sharp drop during sleep, for example.[2]

Yang and yin

From the nutritional standpoint, two major modes of the fluctuating central state can be opposed: the state of fasting and that of satiety. In the state of satiety, energy-releasing substances are used directly for energy or stocked (lipogenesis). In the state of fasting, the situation is reversed in order to obtain an energy flow compatible with life through the burning of fats (lipolysis) and the synthesis of glucose from amino acids (neoglucogenesis).

Hormonally, these two states are characterized by the action of two pancreatic hormones. Insulin, which allows glucose to be used and fatty reserves to be formed, is the hormone of energy availability. Glucagon, which allows fats to be mobilized and glucose to be synthesized, is the hormone of energy requirements.

This duality would seem to be continued at the cellular level through the bringing into play by insulin and glucagon of two second messengers, cyclic guanosine monophosphate (cGMP) and cyclic adenosine monophosphate (cAMP) respectively which are each responsible for an opposite metabolic response.[3] An excess of available energy leads to the secretion of insulin which favours its use, and, reciprocally, a deficit leads to the secretion of glucagon which allows the build-up of an energy-releasing substratum. Hereafter we shall only deal with insulin, but the reciprocal evolution of glucagon should be borne in mind.

Energy bill and feeding behaviour

In order to maintain a constant weight in which the variable part corresponds to the energy reserves, the organism can control the input and output. The input control mainly concerns the frequency and size of the meals that make up the feeding sequence.

An ideal bookkeeper

Weight is a distinctive feature of the individual, like height or eye colour. Its constancy is a natural wonder. It signifies a perfect balance between the input and output of energy. One lump of sugar too many every day for thirty years would add 20 kilograms to your weight without an equivalent energy loss. What a marvel of balanced bookkeeping, even if we can observe a few exceptions in the undulating flesh on our summer beaches. It is a fact that man has lost the secret of perfect management in this field, because of his lack of adaptation to the external environment and the freedom which characterizes his way of life. The wild animal has kept the secret of a constant weight throughout its adult life.

Hunger administrates an inherited capital: 10–12 kilograms of fat deposited in the adipocytes. In adults, any fatty excess is converted into an increase in volume of these adipocytes. These cells lose the capacity to divide themselves up in early infancy. This explains why weight cannot be put on beyond a certain quantity relative to the number of available adipocytes and why only certain people with more fatty cells than others can become really fat.[4]

As we have already seen, rats presented with the wide choice of a self-service cafeteria endlessly guzzle the varied and tasty food until they become obese. It can be shown that, after a few days, heat loss through increased combustion of fat begins to compensate for the excess energy input and stabilize the weight of these consumer rats at a ceiling value. Western man, overnourished, also burns excess heat and this protects his weight balance. In contrast, undernourished animals thin down to a minimum weight beyond which they never go. Greater energy efficiency, an improved use of food and a reduction in heat loss compensate for the inadequate input. During a slimming diet, man sees his weight diminish spectacularly early on and then remain stable at a constant value which is the result of his reduced ration being used more efficiently by the body. This explains how under-nourished people can continue to work at a normal rate and how exaggerated the work-load of people suffering from mental anorexia can be.

The simplest way for an animal to balance its energy bill is to control the input, i.e. what it eats. We have always known that 'by eating we experience an indefinable and special instinctive well-being. Through what we eat we make up our losses and prolong our existence.'[5] As we shall try to show, eating results from the most typical of the passions. In this we follow Brillat-

Savarin, who in *The Physiology of Taste* shows how 'sensations, through repetition and reflection, have perfected the organ and widened the range of its powers; how the need to eat, at first only an instinct, has become an influential passion . . .'. In animals, meal times are determined by a scrupulous calculator which also fixes their size relative to the energy expended. Man has invented social time instead of biological time and this has led to complications and perversions of the regulation system. Hunger has become a secret passion which almost never announces meal times. It expresses itself in pathological disorders disguised as social convention, but it also explodes in the gratuitousness of art, i.e. gastronomy.

Alimentary, my dear Watson

Let us come back to the rat, that now familiar companion of our animal passions. Its habits are not the same as ours, neither does it share our taste in food. Since the town rat first invited the country rat to dinner, thousands of articles have been devoted to the alimentary behaviour of the illustrious rodent. Here it is not superfluous to recall the artificial nature of the laboratory animal, that experimental creature which exists only to help us understand what we are. The laboratory rat is the cousin many times removed of the grain-devouring field rat, and has become a kind of mirror image of planet-consuming man. But this standard is as far removed from man the metaphysical eater as from the wild animal in its natural environment. The laboratory rat is a calibrated and infinitely reproducible animal which inhabits a universe where the alternation of night and day is programmed by a clock. Food is provided in abundance, or distributed according to rules which determine its nature and quantity. Its food consumption is determined by two parameters: the number and length of the meals. The first depends on the stimuli which tell the animal that dinner is served; the second on satiety factors which fix the length and volume of meals and tell the animal that it has had enough.

Meals and the intervals between them form the alimentary sequence. The animal's timetable is organized around this. Strange as it may seem, the volume of a meal is not affected by the preceding interval. Long fasting does not necessarily induce heavy eating. However, the amount of food absorbed does determine the length of the following interval: the more the rat eats, the longer it will wait for the next meal. The animal eats periodically, but the cells consume permanently. Hunger expresses the relationship between the animal in search of food and its insatiable energy-devouring cells. The interval which follows a meal depends on food supply and cell demand. The larger the meal, the greater the stock of combustible substances in the digestive tube and the longer the cells can function without calling out for more.

Insulin is the master of cellular demand. It allows the main fuel, glucose, to enter the cell and be utilized. It also helps in the storage of energy-releasing substances in the form of fat in the adipocytes. The rat sleeps during the day and eats at night. Insulin strikes in the dark, forcing the night walker to follow the rhythm of its cells. The increased sensitivity of the insulin receptors at night amplifies its double action: the use and storage of fuel. The organism stocks and consumes simultaneously. The consequently high energy demand explains the considerable number of meals and the brevity of the intervals between them during the night. The opposite happens during the day. Cell sensitivity to insulin is weak. The energy demand is lower; the organism stores nothing but releases the fats accumulated during the night. In a self-cannibalizing act, the animal eats its nocturnal body during the day.

These biological observations apply to man, who is a diurnal animal, if we exchange day for night, as in a Hollywood film. The alimentary sequence in man is subject to the demands of social life which meddle with biological laws. In a situation where there are no temporal markers, in a pothole for example, the alimentary sequence which establishes itself spontaneously respects the relation between the volume of the meal and the length of the ensuing interval. Cultural habits often respect this law. Breakfast in France, for example, is relatively frugal despite the long interval of the night, and is followed by a short interval (three to four hours). The midday meal, generally copious, precedes a longer interval (five to seven hours) and the large evening meal prepares for the long interval of the night. When the meals and intervals are maladjusted, problems occur. An inadequate meal timetable contributes to certain forms of obesity. This dysregulation can affect an entire group of people, or even a nation which shares the same timetable. Visitors to France are sometimes surprised that the French are not all fat, after seeing the size of the meals there, but perhaps they are just miraculously adapted!

If we consider hunger only as the expression of the animal's energy requirements, we reduce the animal to its mere corporal space. Eating is the manifestation of the fluctuating central state, and the projection of its corporal, extracorporal and temporal dimensions. Any meal results from the coming together of a hungry subject and an edible object: it translates the concordance of internal signals and external stimuli.

What gives a meal man-appeal?

The interaction of internal factors linked to humoral variations and cellular metabolism, and external inciting factors, lead the individual to eat. The internal factors are dominated by the metabolism of sugar. The external factors are linked to the sensory qualities of food. The main senses called upon are those of taste and smell, for which we shall try to sketch a physiology.

Come and get it

There is no greater fusion of the individual with the world than when he sits down to eat. Opposite a divided Eros, Bacchus is calmly assured of union. A four-course meal in a three-star restaurant offers us incomparable ontological matter to get our teeth into, so to speak, and allows us to consider the three dimensions of the passionate individual.

What internal factors in the corporal space inform the individual of his dietary needs? Let us forget the old theory about a rumbling stomach signalling hunger, as that is just a case of confusing cause and effect.

We have seen that metabolic factors play a role in meal-taking. The glucose content in the blood was long thought to be the most important factor. A drop in glycaemia produces an uncomfortable feeling which resembles hunger. Here, cause and effect are again being confused. The diabetic, with his abnormally high glycaemia, is always hungry. In addition, glycaemia varies only minimally within strict limits and is extraordinarily well regulated by hormonal action parallel to that of hunger. It is nevertheless true that the determining factor in hunger is the cellular demand for energy-releasing substances, mainly glucose. Insulin produces increased consumption of glucose in the cell and, in the case of insufficient supply, creates a cellular deficit causing both hunger and hypoglycaemia. In the diabetic, insufficient insulin secretion prevents the glucose from entering the cells and being utilized, despite high glycaemia. The resulting cellular deprivation results in a permanent state of hunger. If false glucose, such as 2-D-oxy-glucose, is administered to animals or man, it causes an acute feeling of hunger. The chemical impostor, which cannot be utilized, takes the place of the glucose, preventing it from entering the cell and being metabolized. A cellular deficit results, and the organism retaliates by a massive mobilization of sugar reserves, creating acute diabetes, and by a passion-inspired state of hunger. The real internal signal of hunger is thus not the amount of glucose in the blood but its cellular availability.

How does the organism know when the cells lack glucose? Back to the brain, seat of the fluctuating central state, where we may suspect the existence of specialized neurons or glucoreceptors which are extremely sensitive to glucose. A toxic false glucose, aurothioglucose, replaces the real one and selectively destroys certain neurons in the hypothalamus. Electrical measurement of these cells shows that they respond selectively and progressively when glucose is administered. Glucose may be the tree that hides the forest, and the glucoreceptors may indicate more generally the energy available inside the cell in the form of the universal energy purveyor ATP.

However, whether the metabolite utilized by the cell be fat or sugar, it is always glucose which the neuron finally lacks, and this accounts for its important role in establishing hunger.

If we accept the equation in which cellular deficit equals hunger, we could conclude that everything in this passion boils down to a modification in the humours within the corporal space. But it should not be forgotten that the extracorporal space influences the corporal space through the objects of desire that occupy it. We know, for example, that the sight or smell of an appetizing dish brings about a secretion of insulin in the subject which accelerates the cellular utilization of glucose and increases cellular deficit and hunger. When we catch sight of delicious food, a spurt of insulin into the blood makes our mouth water.[6]

As with any desire, eating cannot be reduced to need alone, even if this need is cellular. External stimuli play just as important a role as internal signs in triggering eating behaviour. At the risk of sounding obvious, what is the point of feeling hungry if we have no appetite? Hunger expresses the need to eat in order to survive. Appetite, however, is a desire, and requires the edible object to be presented in reality or in the imagination. If we opposed workaday hunger to sensual appetite, however, we would have to abandon the concept of the central state. Experimental data will show us that the internal systemic and external sensory dimensions are closely linked.

Long John Saliva

The palate and the mouth judge the sensorial value of what is eaten, the palatability of the food. The mouth is the privileged site for the mingling of the senses and the humours. It is an ambiguous space which belongs to the outside and the inside, and where the extracorporal encounters the corporal. When my eyes settle on a dainty dish and my nostrils perceive its familiar aroma, my mouth fills with saliva and my pancreas inundates my body with insulin which increases the needs of my cells. As soon as the food enters my mouth it is already appreciated for its nutritive future. My mouth makes an assessment and my desire is satisfied long before my body is. The mouth is not only the conservatory of taste and preference, it is also the chosen site of anticipation, as we shall see.

The mouth and digestive tract can be cut out of the circuit by using a drip. Only 60–70 per cent of the energy value of the nutritive solutions thus administered is utilized. This percentage improves if the normal sequence of meals is imitated instead of a continuous system. An experiment which would exasperate a gourmet allows the animal to feed without eating: a catheter is left *in situ* in the right ear of a rat and connected to a nutritive injection device. By pressing a lever, the animal injects itself with a certain quantity of solution. It is capable of adapting the food supply to its energy demands by varying the frequency of the injections, and all this is done without any information from the mouth or digestive tract. If the solution is diluted or concentrated, it raises or lowers the number of injections. But such a balance only guarantees a minimal level, and the animal thus maintains its weight at a mere 70 per cent of its normal value. Taste is consequently no luxury, but the condition for regulation to function at a normal level.

The word 'taste' corresponds to the concept of the central state in that it is not only one of the five senses, but also the quality related to it, the taste of the food. The mingling of the subject and the world of sense is also expressed in the taste the one has for the other, but the definition of taste in this case is no longer a specifically oral desire: what is your taste in music, in women . . .? Taste is inseparable from pleasure, which is an emanation of the fluctuating central state. Aristotle remarked that the pleasant or unpleasant nature of a dish is not an inherent quality, but depends on whether we are hungry or not. We have already spoken of this change in the subjective appreciation of a sensory stimulus according to the state of the organism. This phenomenon is not the only organizer of our meals. We do not continue to eat a certain food until it becomes repugnant to us. If we did, we would probably never touch a similar dish again. Neither do we imagine a meal punctuated by nausea at the end of each course. Anticipation fortunately allows us to avoid disgust.

Pleasure has a bad name. It is often linked to excess. Increasing a source of pleasure would lead to infinite enjoyment and the ultimate ruin of the individual by leading him away from his natural penchant for virtue. The moralistic tradition, evoking this diabolical spiral, recommends us to steer clear of pleasure. Physiology goes counter to this: the seeking after pleasure leads to moderation. Wilhelm Wundt showed that the pleasure given by a sensory stimulus correlated with the intensity of it according to a biphasic curve (figure 50).[7] From a neutral level, pleasure increases with the intensity of the stimulus up to a peak and then decreases and becomes aversion at the very intense levels of the stimulus. Thus there exists an optimal intensity of average value which gives the subject the maximum pleasure. Here we should remember what has already been said about the optimal level of activation (figure 40).

We can use Wundt's curve for each of the four basic sensations of taste: sweet, sour, salty and bitter. The peak is reached at low intensities for salty and bitter tastes, which rapidly become unpleasant. For sweet and sour tastes the curves are distinctly biphasic. They are variable from one individual and substance to another, according to age, upbringing and culture, which make the individual prefer bitter to sweet, sweet to salty, salty to sour, or vice versa (*omnia gusta in naturam*). Taste is thus not a property of the stimulus but an integral part of the taster. This can be demonstrated in animals.

An animal's pleasure can be appreciated only indirectly and a certain circularity cannot be avoided. The animal generally has to choose between pure water and aqueous solutions of a substance at increased concentrations. Preference is expressed by the amount of pure water that the animal drinks. Preference presupposes that the animal consumes the substance because it likes it, whereas we could equally well say that it likes the substance because it consumes it. For sweeter and sweeter solutions, it is shown that preference passes through a maximum, diminishes afterwards and changes into aversion according to Wundt's general model. When a

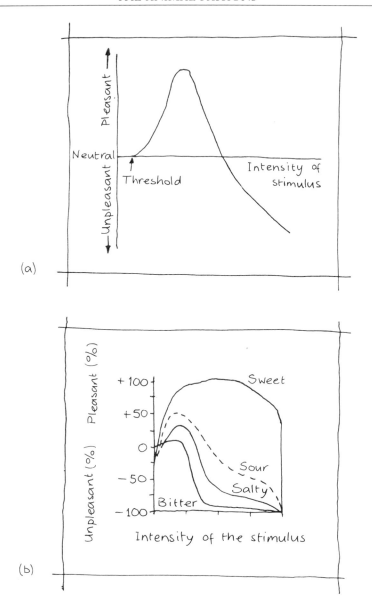

FIGURE 50   (a) Wundt's curve showing the pleasant and then unpleasant nature of
a stimulus according to its intensity; (b) the curves represent the pleasant or
unpleasant value of different taste stimuli (bitter, sweet, sour or salty) relative to the
concentration of the solutions. (After C. Pfaffmann, 'Taste a model of incentive
motivation', in D.W. Pfaff (ed.), *The Physiological Mechanisms of Motivations*,
Springer, New York, 1982.)

fistula is made in the oesophagus of the animal in order to deprive it of the food it has just swallowed, it becomes a glutton and is no longer capable of organizing its meals in a discontinuous sequence. The preference curve goes constantly upwards with no aversion for very sweet solutions. This is not surprising. Eating is no longer the expression of the fluctuating central state for the animal with a fistula, because the body, except for the mouth, has been withdrawn from the feeding process. The animal has become nothing but a mouth, and the brain which is consequently freed from the limitations of the body no longer controls its pleasure. As with Tantalus, desire is never satisfied and the mouth has become a Danaid's jar.

This experiment shows that post-ingestive factors play a role in taste. Upon arrival in the digestive tract, an over-rich solution slows its own ingestion and changes former pleasure into displeasure. The pleasure of taste is an expression of the fluctuating central state and demands continuity between the corporal and extracorporal spaces. If we inject a very sweet solution into the stomach or glucose into the blood while we are testing preference, the curve is displaced to the right and disgust appears for weaker solutions since the organism is already 'sweetened'.

The body and the garden

Electrodes placed on the taste nerve of the tongue measure action potentials. The nerve fibres have a relative specificity and respond preferentially to one of the four basic stimuli: sweet, sour, salty and bitter. The curve of the electrical responses is parallel to that of the behavioural responses: the frequency of the discharges increases with the intensity of the stimulus up to a maximum and then decreases. Saccharose, which is preferred to lactose, produces a higher electrical response at the same concentrations. It can be assumed that there exist receptors for the different kinds of sugar present in nature on the sensory cells of the tongue. The abundance of receptors for such and such a sugar conditions the intensity of the response to that sugar. Saccharose, which is plentiful in fruit, leaves, flowers and roots, is also the most richly represented in specialized receptors on the surface of the tongue. The order of preference reproduces the order of presence in nature. One sugar, maltose, seems to be an exception, since it provokes a strong behavioural response while being rare and only slightly sweet. What is the reason for this preference which has little to do with taste and does not respect the nature of the garden? The biological significance of this sugar may provide the answer. A molecule of maltose is hydrolysed in the body into two molecules of glucose, a preferential metabolite. Its biological value, superior to that of other sugars, may explain the choice of the organism.

The corporal and extracorporal spaces mingle on the periphery, in the mouth itself. The palatability of a foodstuff which determines the amount ingested is a function of the product tp in which t represents the taste of the substance and p its biological significance. The term t varies with the concentration of the substance and the sensitivity of the taste receptors;

the term p changes according to the internal state of the animal. For example, in a subject deficient in sodium or suffering from an adrenal gland disorder inducing the loss of salt, p for sodium chloride will be very high and the palatability of salt will increase. An extremely salty solution which would disgust a normal individual will in this case be gulped down avidly.

The physiology of taste

Brillat-Savarin says that the number of different flavours is infinite. To process this immense range man has only a few inches of tongue. If we believe Brillat, a man's tongue and the various membranes around it are so fine in texture that they are perfectly fitted for the sublimity of the tasks they have to accomplish. Reality is more prosaic. What is mysterious is the simplicity of the tongue compared with the complexity of its role. The tongue, that universal organ, is a better active symbol of a being's presence in the world than the penis, which half the human race lacks. There is no need to remind anyone of its role in language or sexual relations. Hunger, language and sex are united in the tongue, which incarnates the concept of the oral stage in psychoanalytical parlance.[8]

The surface of the tongue is covered with papillae in the shape of mushrooms or valleys which are covered with taste buds. A human tongue has no more than two thousand of these. Each bud contains sensory cells with nerve fibres leading away from them. None of these cells is specific to one of the basic sensations: sweet, sour, salty or bitter. One nerve fibre receives impulses from several sensory cells and one sensory cell innervates several nerve fibres. Therefore there are overlapping receptor fields which cover the surface of the tongue. The discharge of a fibre depends on the nature and intensity of the stimulus. Without knowing anything of the modern notion of the relation between a molecule and its receptor, Brillat-Savarin states that 'the sensation of taste is a chemical operation which requires moistness', and that 'the only sapid things are either dissolved or soluble'. He also says that 'the sapid molecules must be dissolved in a fluid in order to allow them to be absorbed by the nervous tufts and papillae which cover the inside of the tasting apparatus'. After this contact with the sensory membranes, the sapid molecules are recognized by specific receptors. It is as yet impossible to say how this recognition is coded in the electrical message carried by the fibres and how the four basic sensations become the subtle perception of a one-in-a-thousand taste which is immediately identifiable. Brillat-Savarin speaks of the sensation and compares it to 'the judgement which the soul passes on the impressions transmitted by the organ'. Today we would not speak of the soul, but of the cognitive functions. Through its neuron networks, the brain disposes of a cognitive map covering the whole range of flavours.

There is no need to prefer the company of gourmets to that of scientists, as the one is perfectly compatible with the other when treating the question of the physiology of taste. The impression food makes on our organism cannot be explained merely by the functioning of our 'tasting apparatus'. A knowing eater will tell you that taste is the least self-centred of the senses and that it equally calls on the other four. In his preface to *The Life and Passion of Dodin-Bouffant, a Gourmet*, James de Coquet summarizes this association: 'Dodin-Bouffant's passion is that of a man governed by his senses. Not the vulgar, primitive senses, but those which one keeps under control, rather like Ben Hur's quadriga, except that here there are five, not four. They all play a role in taste. We first devour things with our eyes, and this helps us to bear the ensuing pleasure. Smell then plays the herald to taste, which also adds the touch of the tongue. And what about hearing? The ears perceive the music of the culinary instruments. They appreciate the sharpening of a knife or the pouring of a gravy.'[9]

Smell is the indispensable partner of taste, and we can subscribe wholeheartedly to Brillat-Savarin's opinion that 'smell and taste form one sense only: the mouth is its laboratory and the nose its chimney'. Everybody has experienced that 'when the nasal membrane is irritated by a bad cold, taste is entirely obliterated; what we eat has no flavour; the tongue is nevertheless in its normal state.' Anaesthesia of the olfactive mucosa blunts taste. This shows that what we commonly call taste is in fact largely olfaction. The aroma of ingested food, passing into the nasopharynx is a stimulant which is a thousand times more active for the olfactive system than for the taste receptors. For example, a sensitive nose can help you recognize the taste of an alcohol in a concentration twenty-five thousand times less than what would be necessary without the sense of smell. Other basic sensations share in taste because of the presence all over the buccal mucosa of thermoreceptors, mechanoreceptors and nociceptive terminals. The latter are the target of spices.

Taste is both a sensation and an action. What a marvellous muscle the tongue is! It is boneless like the penis, but much more mobile, capable of rotating, sweeping, folding etc.

We have seen that taste in animals can only be indirectly observed through their choice of different foods or through licking movements or other instrumental responses to alimentary stimuli. In man, we can obtain a direct measurement of pleasure by means of psychophysics. Brillat-Savarin should be considered a pioneer in this field. He imagined experimental measurements concerning the desire for food. 'We have pursued this study with the obstinacy which brings success, and our perseverance allows us to present . . . the discovery of gastronomic tests which will do honour to the nineteenth century; . . . the method is the following: each time a morsel well-known for its tastiness is served, the guests will be closely observed and those whose features do not show delight will be considered unfit . . .' It is not so much the behaviouristic observation of expression and gestures which is original, but the fact that language and social class are also taken into consideration. Roland Barthes, in his preface to a new edition of *The Physiology of Taste*, notes that in his gastronomic tests, Brillat-Savarin, however hare-brained the idea may seem, takes two very serious and very modern factors into account: social class and language. The dishes he serves to his experimental subjects are different from one class to another. Thus steak and kidney pie is served to the poor, a filet of beef to the well-off, and rose-flavoured meringues to the rich etc., which suggests that taste is sculpted by culture and class. Next, in order to read the pleasure of his subjects (this is the aim of the experiment), Brillat-Savarin surprisingly suggests examining their language, a social medium *par excellence* which changes with the class of the taster. The steak and kidney pie may draw a 'Goodness me' from the poor man, while the meringues may draw a 'Your chef is an admirable man, sir,' from the rich one.[10]

The social aspect of hunger is also present in the distinction between the pleasure of eating and the pleasure of meal time. 'The pleasure of eating is the sensation of a need being satisfied. The pleasure of meal time is the sensation born of diverse circumstances, places, things and people that go with the meal.' A meal is a social ritual if ever there was one, even in a self-service cafeteria. The choice of food available, the way it is prepared, is an expression of our culture, our way of life. Our tastes are the reflection of our education and the habits that have been handed down to us. Concerning hunger, then, an extra dimension is to be added to the fluctuating central state: the social space.

What makes us stop eating?

Why do we stop eating in spite of the pleasure a meal gives us? Why is eating so often associated with sleep?

A surfeit of pleasure

The fact that we find some foods pleasant and others unpleasant does not tell us why this should be so. A general principle is that neither the taste nor the smell of nutritive substances is unpleasant. From birth, an infant distinguishes what it likes from what it dislikes. Innate expressions show its natural attraction to certain foods or, conversely, its rejection of unwelcome substances. The choice is different from one species to another, but it can be assumed that, in general, what is good for the species is good for the individual.

Jacob Steiner observed new-born babies whose first alimentary experience was the sweet, sour or bitter solution which was applied experimentally to their tongues. A sweet solution produces a satisfied expression, a smile and sucking action. A sour solution makes the baby tighten its lips, screw up its nose and blink. A bitter solution produces a frankly disgusted expression and the baby sticks out its tongue. A one-day-old baby shows its growing satisfaction with sweeter and sweeter solutions by both its expression and consumption. It has a clear preference for sugar and maltose, and the measurement of the pressure of its tongue on the teat according to the solution in the bottle follows Wundt's curve.[11]

Taste preferences and their behavioural expression are thus present from birth in the cabling and organization of the central nervous system. Acceptance or refusal of food depends on reflexes that are still present in animals deprived of the upper parts of their brains, and can also be observed in anencephalic foetuses.[12] Before language appears, approach and avoidance behaviour are the only translations of pleasure and aversion. The central state organizes itself on the hereditary cabling layout that learning complicates, fine-tunes or disturbs. Heredity is in the kitchen but society decides on the menu! Tastes, preferences and aversions are created by repetition and association. Natural aversions can change into acquired preferences. Sourness, bitterness and saltiness are attractive characteristics of food for some people and unpleasant for others.

The phenomenon of delayed learning (conditioned aversion and preference) has already been mentioned in the chapter on desire. Certain effects which appear several hours after the absorption of a food or drink can induce almost irreversible aversion or attraction. It is obvious that the brain is not the only agent in the process of association. The central state also plays a part with all its bodily components. The beneficial nature of the food, whether it be due to its caloric value or its vital substance content, makes it preferable to any other upon its being presented for a second time. An animal lacking in vitamin B1 or in certain amino acids will quickly learn to recognize and prefer the taste of food which contains them.

Preference for a food expresses itself in the way it incites the central mechanisms of desire. We know that a chain reaction can be set up in which the alimentary stimulus leads to a feeding response which reinforces the desire to consume even more. Our attitude to salted peanuts is a good illustration of the self-activating nature of the desire. The first peanut is popped into the mouth with indifference, while the second is taken with more attention . . . our consumption accelerates and sometimes ends with our feverishly gobbling a whole handful.

Preference does not involve only the brain but also the entire corporal space, including hormonal secretions. A rat presented with several foods consumes a different quantity of each according to its taste. The amount of insulin secreted during the cephalic phase differs from one food to another according to the degree of preference. The sight of a dish, its aroma and the flavour of the first mouthfuls trigger a reflex secretion of insulin with an intensity which shows our taste for the dish. All our gastronomic yesterdays are expressed in this spurt of insulin.

The insulin released increases hypoglycaemia and cellular deficit, increasing hunger, and so eating does indeed whet the appetite. This conditioned hunger expresses the temporal dimension in the fluctuating central state.

This temporal dimension is basic to the sensation of surfeit. What makes us stop eating despite the pleasure eating gives us? The simple explanation that we eat until we have satisfied the needs of our organism and then stop, will obviously not hold. Several hours elapse before the digestion process finally satisfies these needs. If we spent all this time eating we would experience acute indigestion. The organism has to anticipate future absorption of foodstuffs and foresee their delayed metabolic effects. This anticipation takes place in the mouth. Each food seems to possess a surfeit index or rating. This surfeit power can be conditioned just like hunger. The same food is presented to a rat in two different caloric versions of different richness, identified by scent markers. The animal learns to satisfy its hunger more rapidly with the richer food. The scent marker associated with the richer food subsequently reduces the consumption of any food it is added to. It has become a surfeit-conditioning stimulus. Learned anticipation does not work only in discriminating between foods. For any food given *ad libitum*, the rat seems to eat and simultaneously anticipate the metabolic effect to come, producing an implicit 'body forecast'. Man, with his fixed meal times, does the same. When he tucks into a 1500 calorie meal, he is not making up a corresponding deficit, but storing enough food to supply the systemic compartment in the following hours.[13] He is filling up his gastro-intestinal tank in order to be able to cover the distance which separates him from his next meal.

Therefore the mouth is not only the seat of taste, it is also a forecasting bureau, a kind of budget balancer succeeding in the task of reconciling income and expenditure. A sense of surfeit does not come from an immediate satisfaction of needs but from foreseen satisfaction. Let us compare what happens after sexual relations. Mounting sexual excitement is never the expression of a systemic need, and ends abruptly in the wiping-out of all the senses without there having been either the making-up or even the estimate of a deficit. In contrast, eating leads to pleasure which is not only here and now, but also future oriented. Barthes mentions that 'lust and gastronomy do not have much in common. There is a basic difference between the two pleasures, and that is orgasm, or stimulation and release. The pleasure of eating does not transport us to extremes of ravishment or ecstasy, and the enjoyment is not climactic. There is no rising pleasure, no culminating point, only duration . . .' The pleasure of eating, adds Brillat, 'gains in duration what it loses in intensity . . . and is remarkable for the way it disposes us towards others or comforts us in their absence'.

While dealing with the physiology of alimentary behaviour, we could hardly ignore its relations with sexual behaviour, but we must admit that there are hardly any experimental data in this field. The essential information can be found in literature from Casanova to de Sade. Scientists have, however, recently examined how sleep and eating behaviour are related.

Chief nourisher in life's feast

Recent experiments on the rat confirm what Brillat-Savarin thought, namely that 'he who needs to eat cannot sleep . . . whereas he who has eaten beyond a certain limit immediately falls into a deep sleep'. There is a correlation between the size of the meal and the length of time that the rat sleeps afterwards. This would seem to depend on the metabolic utilization of the foodstuffs by the cells. Sleep, the expression of surfeit, would seem to depend on the energy supplied to the cells by the meal. As Virginia Woolf says, 'One cannot . . . sleep well, if one has not dined well'. In contrast, a lack of available energy in the cell would lead to wakefulness and hunger. Insulin encourages sleep. Diabetics are often insomniacs, and rediscover 'great nature's second course' when treated with insulin. Intravenous or intracerebral injections of insulin lengthen the time spent sleeping. Insulin, by helping glucose to penetrate the cell, increases the amount of energy available there, and hence the resulting sleeping time.[14]

It is not surprising that sleep and alimentary behaviour, which together take up more than half the life of any normal person, should be associated in maintaining a well-balanced metabolism. They also obey the same regulation factors. As in the case of all the expressions of the fluctuating central state, these factors concern the internal milieu and the central nervous system in parallel. Duplicating the systemic action of pancreatic insulin, a peptide manufactured by neurons (cerebral insulin) would seem to act at the same time on the specific receptors situated inside the brain. It should be remembered that these apparently superfluous actions which take place simultaneously in the brain and the rest of the body are characteristic of the action of peptides in the fluctuating central state (see chapter 5).

Insulin could also have a more specific influence on sleep than that which depends on its general metabolic effect. It appears to help an amino acid, tryptophan (the precursor of serotonin), to enter the brain. This neurotransmitter appears to play an important role in the onset of sleepiness. Parallel to this, serotonin also apparently intervenes in the nervous mechanisms of satiety.

While metabolic factors help to bring on sleep, sleep itself helps to regulate the metabolism. We shall speak later of sleep, 'sore labour's bath', which allows the organism to recover the losses that take place during wakefulness. Sleep also allows the growth hormone to be secreted. This hormone plays a role in metabolizing the amino acids supplied by food. We shall also see that growth hormone releasing factor (GHRF), the hypothalamic factor which regulates the hypophyseal secretion of the growth hormone, is perhaps instrumental in triggering feeding behaviour.[15]

Thirst

The other bodily passion concerns water, the volume of which must remain constant. Hunger and thirst are often considered together, but in fact follow different mechanisms. There are two kinds of thirst, with different causes. We shall analyse their humoral and nervous mechanisms and locate them relative to the central state.

Food and drink

Eating and drinking are inseparable. They maintain or restore body weight. Drink looks after the 70 per cent of water that contributes to this weight. The need for water has its specific passion, thirst, just as the need for energy-releasing substances has hunger.

For simple mechanical reasons, eating without drinking can be unpleasant. Boiled rice unaccompanied by some sort of liquid is not the easiest thing to ingurgitate in any considerable quantity. If you destroy the lateral hypothalamus of a rat, it recovers in time a modified kind of feeding behaviour. It drinks only while eating. Drinking is no longer an autonomous passion for this animal, but merely a mechanical consequence of the act of mastication.

Drinking without eating is, however, extremely frequent behaviour in man or animals. Drinking is the first manifestation of the oral stage in Freudian terms, it is the behaviour which occurs to you in response to a non-specific activation of the fluctuating central state. When you repeatedly give a hungry animal too small a quantity of food every two minutes, it develops drinking behaviour which increases at each interval. Drinking here is a response to the frustration of a pleasure too soon interrupted. It is what ethologists call displacement activity. This irrelevant behaviour (the animal is hungry, not thirsty) is the expression of the opponent state which develops when an animal is suddenly thwarted of an expected reward (see chapter 9). According to Robert Dantzer, these displacement activities offer the central activation an outlet which permits the individual in a conflictual situation to control tenseness.[16] Drinking is the most common of these activities. In certain experimental situations, the animal can be led to the kind of behaviour that we see in the innumerable men who are compulsive drinkers.

The drinks men have invented increase the difficulty of distinguishing between eating and drinking. There is as much food as drink in some beers and wines, for example, and their energy value certainly contributes to middle-age spread etc. The Dublin double chin and the Burgundy belly are eloquent witnesses here. What we have already said about taste and smell concerning hunger also applies to thirst. The palatability of a drink depends on its qualities and meaning for the organism at the moment when it is presented. The mouth plays the same role for fluids as for food, anticipating future needs and their satisfaction. As with hunger, time organizes desire in terms of pleasure and aversion, learning and conditioning. In the desire for water, we can distinguish two different kinds of thirst, two versions of the same fluctuating central state, corresponding to the intracellular and extracellular liquid compartments of the organism.

Two different kinds of thirst

Baron de Crac, whose horse was shot in two by a cannonball, observed that the front half of his mount continued to drink while the water absorbed immediately flowed out behind. This rather primitive homeostasis thus ensured a perfect balance between input and outflow (figure 51). Like the baron's horse, our organism constantly loses water through the skin, lungs and kidneys. The water contained in food and drink makes up these losses. While the hormone vasopressin regulates the outflow by controlling urinary elimination, drinking regulates the input. Those two pub standards 'Have another drink' and 'All right, but I must go and have a pee first' go together like a horse and carriage: the regulation of the one influences the regulation of the other. Thirst, the passionate state which corresponds to the need to drink, is not due simply to the mouth feeling dry, as Cannon thought, but is the product of multiple factors including input and outflow which interact in the central state.

FIGURE 51   The Baron de Crac (François Durkheim).

Water is unequally distributed between the inside and outside of cells. The intracellular and extracellular liquid compartments are separated by the cellular membrane. When the osmotic pressure of the extracellular environment rises, i.e. when the concentration of dissolved substances increases, either by the addition of solutes (salty meal) or through the loss of water (evaporation or urination), the water in the cells passes through the membrane in order to maintain the balance between the two compartments. Cellular dehydration results. The higher the osmotic pressure of the extracellular environment rises, the worse the intracellular dehydration becomes. This dehydration manifests itself by a feeling of thirst (intracellular thirst) of osmotic origin. When the extracellular environment diminishes in volume, after a haemorrhage for example, osmotic pressure, i.e. the relative proportion of water and dissolved substances, does not change. Any reduction in extracellular volume also manifests itself by a feeling of thirst (extracellular thirst).

A thirsty man, even with training in physiology, will find it very hard to tell just from what he feels whether the thirst is intracellular or extracellular. The disturbance in the internal milieu and the regulation brought into play are nevertheless totally different. Therefore we cannot reduce thirst to merely sensory data. It concerns the entire intracorporal space.

A rise in the osmotic pressure of the plasma after a heavy salt intake or a long period without water can be seen in drinking behaviour and the secretion of the antidiuretic hormone vasopressin, which keeps water in the kidney. Having a drink, but not a pee, are the two responses of the organism to intracellular dehydration. These responses bring into play a desire and a hormone. They are the expression of a fluctuating central state and follow the rules already described for hunger. Anticipation, for example, puts an end to thirst as soon as water enters the mouth and digestive tract, long before cellular dehydration is corrected. Similarly, a few mouthfuls of water are enough to block the secretion of vasopressin, long before this water enters the cells.[17]

The role of the brain is to match the behavioural and hormonal responses. It knows how much water there is in the cells through osmoreceptors in the hypothalamus. The existence of nerve cells which are selectively sensitive to changes in osmotic pressure in the blood was suggested as early as 1937 by Verney. For the first time, it was shown that the brain is sensitive to variations in the physical parameters of the internal milieu. If a serum saltier than blood was injected into the cerebral circulation of a dog it caused a drop in diuresis (by vasopressin secretion) and drinking behaviour. By tying up the various branches of the carotid artery, Verney showed that only a narrow region of the brain, forward of the hypothalamus, was sensitive to rises in the osmolality of the blood. He drew the conclusion that it was here that the nerve cells capable of measuring the osmotic pressure of the plasma were to be found. In 1970, using surgically implanted microelectrodes, we were able to measure variations in the electrical activity of nerve cells in the hypothalamus of the monkey. These variations were proportional to the osmolality of the blood (figure 52).[18]

The brain is not the only part of the body which is sensitive to fluctuations in osmolality. There are osmoreceptors in the mouth, stomach and intestine, and above all in the walls of the vein which carries blood from the intestine to the liver. The whole organism is in fact a network of information contributing to the unity of the fluctuating central state.

Extracellular thirst is another example of this unity. The brain triggers it after summing up and reproducing the experience of the body in which hormonal secretions mingle with visceral mechanisms etc. During the Hundred Years War, a famous battle pitted thirty Frenchmen against thirty Englishmen for the succession of Brittany. During this battle, a French captain, Jean de Beaumanoir, wounded in the arms and face, called for water while he was fighting. One of his companions, who were all tough customers, shouted to him, 'Drink your blood, Beaumanoir, that will quench your thirst!' Haemorrhages, even when they are internal, cause intense thirst, which is a consequence of hypovolaemia, an abnormally low circulating blood volume. Angiotensin II, a hormone released in Beaumanoir's blood in response to his haemorrhage, was directly responsible for his thirst.

Let us sum up the action of this homeostatic play. Loss of blood leads to a drop in the volume of circulating liquid. Hypovolaemia stimulates the kidney which secretes renin, an enzyme which transforms a protein of hepatic origin, angiotensinogen, into angiotensin. This hormone has a constricting effect on blood vessels which it adapts to the reduced volume of blood flowing through them and so restores blood pressure to a normal level. It also stimulates the secretion of aldosterone by the adrenal gland, and this induces retention of water and salt and helps to restore normal blood volume. But angiotensin also acts on the brain. It triggers thirst and drinking behaviour by stimulating receptors in the brain. Behavioural and visceral responses thus contribute to restoring the same balance. The brain is not just a passive observer of peripheral disorders. It reproduces the systemic problem inside its protective barrier. Under the influence of hypovolaemia, the brain, informed by cardiac and vascular receptors, secretes its own angiotensin. We have already seen that this hormone induces drinking behaviour, high blood pressure and vasopressin secretion when applied to certain parts of the brain. Vasopressin helps angiotensin to restore normal blood pressure. Thirst, in this complex matter, is only one factor amongst others which shake up the central state when it ceases to fluctuate and so threatens to founder.

In the ordinary circumstances of everyday life, the sensitivity of the organism to variations in osmotic pressure and blood volume allow it to react before there is any real danger of imbalance. Under normal circumstances, intracellular dehydration and hypovolaemia work together to produce imperceptible internal signals which join with external signals and temporal factors to affect the desire to drink. The organism seems to ask us to drink before we are thirsty. But what a pleasure thirst gives us when we have water to quench it! The only painful passion is one which cannot be satisfied. But if we feed passion's flame too much, it may burn itself out. The economics of pleasure hinges on this contradiction.

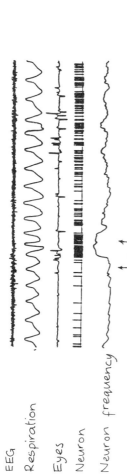

EEG

Respiration

Eyes

Neuron

Neuron frequency

Salt

50 μV

100 μV

5 Sp/s
0

10 s

Drinking

FIGURE 52   Recording of the electrical activity of a neuron in the hypothalamus of a monkey. This activity speeds up when the osmotic pressure of the blood is raised by an injection of salty solution into the carotid. The cell is probably an osmoreceptor. In contrast, the presence of drinking water in the mouth of the animal inhibits the activity of this neuron, although the osmotic pressure of the blood has not had the time to vary. It is thus an anticipatory mechanism contributing to satiety. (After Vincent et al., 'Activity of osmosensitive single cells in the hypothalamus'.)

The centres and the humours

Back to square one, the desire and pleasure centre, because the sites we described there are the same as those involved in hunger and thirst. With a little repetition, we shall now speak only of feeding and drinking behaviour.

If we consider the first experimental results, the facts are simple. If we destroy the ventral and medial region of the hypothalamus of a rat, it becomes a compulsive eater. The animal becomes obese. If we stimulate the same region electrically, it stops eating. We can draw the conclusion that there is a satiety centre there, opposed to a hunger centre situated in the lateral hypothalamus. If we stimulate this region electrically we can induce feeding in certain cases. If we destroy it bilaterally, however, the rat stops eating and drinking for several days.

A satisfactory diagram can be recalled here (figure 33). The excitor stimulus (a drop in cellular glucose) activates the appetite centre. Feeding provides an inhibitor stimulus which activates the satiety centre, which in its turn inhibits the appetite centre, despite the persisting excitor stimulus, and stops consumption. It is only after the metabolic imbalance has been regulated that the excitor stimulus disappears. At this point, let us call on the fly for help, as it is a model that we have already used. The highly developed tasting apparatus of the insect, which is sensitive to sweet substances, activates a nervous ganglion which controls ingestion. The sensory effect of sugar can be considered as a positive reinforcer of feeding behaviour. However, ingestion finally stops. Indeed, as the digestive pouch fills up, nerve impulses are sent out from it which are proportional to its distension. These inhibitor messages slow down and finally halt the activity of the ganglion and, consequently, ingestion. If the nerve which transports these messages is severed, inhibition stops and the insect eats itself to death.

The higher vertebrates run no such risk. The reinforcer stimuli are multiple and parallel, as we have seen, and the inhibitor circuits are superimposed and repeat each other's roles.

The very idea of a hunger centre or satiety centre is open to doubt. The destruction of the ventromedial region of the hypothalamus increases the pancreatic release of insulin. Its stimulation, however, inhibits this secretion. This region of the brain thus normally slows down the utilization of glucose and lipogenesis. Its effect on hunger is only indirect, and is secondary to its metabolic effects. When the vagal nerves linking the brain to the pancreas are severed, the destruction of the ventromedial hypothalamus no longer produces obesity. This region has other roles which are not metabolic. Various sensory and systemic data enter it and take on an affective colouring after passing through the limbic circuits. Aversion, avoidance and aggressiveness, as well as hunger, are expressed there. Once again, faced with the unity of the central state, anatomy takes a back seat.

The same sort of thing can be said of the lateral hypothalamus. Its heterogeneity has already been pointed out. The stimulation of the lateral region induces a secretion of insulin which can be responsible for hunger. Humoral and sensory information floods into this region and their convergence generates specific desires oriented towards peripheral stimuli. Thirst and hunger cohabit in the lateral region even if specialized areas receive different specific information (volaemia, osmolality, glycaemia).

The hypothalamic machine is only one link in vaster circuits (see chapter 7). The amygdala is a kind of limbic double of the hypothalamus. If the lateral part is destroyed, it produces overeating and obesity. If the medial part is destroyed, it stops eating activity. Through the limbic circuits, the regions involved in hunger and thirst are connected to the cortex, which links the cognitive to the affective and the emotional to the vegetative.

This uncertainty which reigns over the centres and nervous pathways is added to by the confusion over the chemical messengers used. In this field also, we are far from the initial optimism. In 1960, Grossman injected a few microlitres of acetylcholine into the lateral hypothalamus of a rat and immediately observed drinking behaviour. Noradrenaline injected into the same place induced eating behaviour. Each type of behaviour had its mediator. Chemical centralism was replacing anatomical centralism. Then came dopamine. The selective poisoning of the dopaminergic fibres in the lateral hypothalamus by 6-hydroxy-dopamine induced the same absence of eating and drinking behaviour as the surgical destruction of the region. It should not be forgotten that dopamine does not only concern feeding behaviour but also desire and pleasure as a whole (see chapter 9).

Noradrenaline would seem more particularly to concern the sensory side. The destruction of the ventral noradrenergic fasciculus between the locus coeruleus and its destination, the ventromedial structures of the hypothalamus, induces the same symptoms (overeating followed by obesity) as lesions of the ventromedial hypothalamus. The particularly noticeable sensory factor in this syndrome is that the animals stuff themselves with food but will let themselves die of hunger if the food tastes bad.

Serotonin seems to have some influence on the links between feeding behaviour and sleep. It may be the amine of satiety, but we know neither where nor how it intervenes. Does it use a neuropeptide as an intermediary, for instance?

Several neuropeptides play a role in the hunger and thirst mechanisms. Amongst these, endomorphines, which were evoked relative to desire and pleasure, intervene in reinforcement mechanisms and so are the privileged accomplices of pleasure and communication. It is difficult to attribute a specific role to them in hunger, even if their release, induced by repeated daily tail-pinching in rats, stimulates hunger and causes obesity. Is there an explanation to be found here for the obesity which often accompanies stress in certain people, or for the ever-growing waves of overweight people inundating the pavements of large cities? But it is a far cry from the laboratory rat to the victims of consumer society, and we must beware of facile comparisons.

Cholecystokinin has been put forward as the hormone of satiety. This hormone is secreted by the intestine during digestion, but does not cross the haemato-encephalic barrier. It must therefore be recognized that cholecystokinin is also released in the brain and acts in parallel with the systemic hormone. The brain is once again seen to be the image of the body, in this case because the same substance is released in the nervous centres and at the periphery, and for the same purpose. Another recently isolated hypothalamic hormone, GHRF, which controls the hypophyseal secretion of the growth hormone (involved in metabolic regulations), triggers feeding behaviour when it is injected into the hypothalamus. This is another example of the functional cooperativeness of one substance in both the body and the brain (see chapter 4).

To be continued

Look at those two lovers face to face drinking each other's health, bodies bending forward over the table, glasses held up in front of their eyes which are bathed in the golden liquid. Imagine the biology over and under the table. Eros and Bacchus are frolicking between the hypothalamus and the limbic brain. What synapses should be thrown to the amines and peptides for this moment's bliss? Forget the tiresome neurons, let us enjoy for an instant the pleasures of the soul . . .

Notes

1 J. Conrad, *Lord Jim*, London, 1900.
2 R.A. Hawkings et al., 'Measurement of the rate of glucose utilization by rat brain *in vivo*', *J. Neurochem.*, 23, 917–23, 1974.
3 The opposition between the two second messengers (cGMP and cAMP) suggested by Nelson Goldberg has not been verified. However, the hypothesis of dual systems is verifiable at other metabolic levels and clarifies some of the complexity of metabolic regulations.
4 In medicine, the tendency to become fat can be identified by measuring the cellularity of the adipose tissue which is given by the number of fatty cells per cubic millimetre and their average volume. The figure obtained is a fixed characteristic of the individual.
5 A. Brillat-Savarin, *Physiologie du goût*, Paris, 1826.
6 J. Louis-Sylvestre and J. Le Magnen, 'Palatability and preabsorptive insulin release', *Neurosci. Biobehav. Rev.*, 4, 43–6, 1980.
7 W. Wundt, *Grundzüge der physiologischen Psychologie*, Leipzig, 1874.
8 In Freudian theory the oral stage is the first stage of libidinal development and ego development. The mouth is the main source of pleasure and satisfaction and so oral experience is the prototype of fixation of desire on a certain object. Psychoanalytical theory suggests that desire and satisfaction are permanently marked by this first experience (J. Laplanche and J.B. Pontalis, *Vocabulaire de la psychanalyse*, Paris, 1967).
9 M. Rouff, *Vie et passion de Dodin-Bouffant*, Paris, 1984.

10   A. Brillat-Savarin, *Physiologie du goût, avec une lecture de Roland Barthes*, Paris, 1975.
11   J.E. Steiner, 'The gusto-facial response: observation on normal and anencephalic newborn infants', in J.F. Bosmas (ed.), *Fourth Symposium on Oral Sensation and Perception*, Washington, DC, 1973.
12   Ibid.
13   J. Le Magnen, 'Bases neurobiologiques du comportement alimentaire', in J. Delacour (ed.), *Neurobiologie des comportements*, Paris, 1984.
14   J. Danguir and S. Nicolaïdis, 'Feeding, metabolism and sleep: peripheral and central mechanisms of their interaction', in D.J. MacGinty (ed.), *Brain Mechanisms of Sleep*, New York, 1985.
15   F.J. Vaccarino et al., 'Stimulation of food intake in rats by centrally administered hypothalamic growth hormone releasing factor', *Nature, Lond.*, 314, 167–8, 1985.
16   R. Dantzer, 'Psychobiologie des émotions', in J. Delacour (ed.), *Neurobiologie des comportements*, Paris, 1984.
17   E. Arnauld and J. Dupont, 'Vasopressin release and firing of supraoptic neurosecretory neurones during drinking in the dehydrated monkey', *Pflügers Arch. Eur. J. Physiol.*, 394, 195–201, 1982.
18   J.D. Vincent et al., 'Activity of osmosensitive single cells in the hypothalamus of the behaving monkey during drinking', *Brain Res.*, 44, 371–84, 1972.

11

Love, Sex and Power

I ask you, what credit can you give to a feeling which depends on half a dozen bones, the longest of which measures under an inch? This is no blasphemy. Would Juliet have loved Romeo with four front teeth missing? No, she wouldn't. Despite the gaping black hole, he would have had exactly the same soul and the same moral qualities! So, why do they keep on at me about the importance of the soul and moral qualities?

Albert Cohen, *Belle du Seigneur*

By one of those paradoxes that only the universal creator could invent, two human beings, a man and a woman, blend into one another, becoming a suprapersonal unit by the fact that their relationship magnifies each to the point of greatest autonomy, to total and eternal self-centredness.

Lou Andreas-Salome, *Eros*

The other person, other people and being in love

Hunger and thirst, as we have described them, are passions of our own body. Sex and power concern our passionate relationships with someone else's body. Before suggesting a definition of what being in love is, we would like to point out certain dangers of the task.

The other person

Faced with the other person who is the object of his desire, man's only resort is love or a test of strength. There is no place for the other as a separate being in the fluctuating central state. Narcissus forgot that, and drowned.

Man needs another person just as he needs water or proteins, and this

need is expressed in sexual desire. What is love for? Reproduction really
interests only demographers or sociobiologists, and the child-fruit is present
during sexual intercourse only as a mythical third person, a far-off
projection of desire. There remains the other person that pleasure and desire
attach us to (see chapters 8 and 9).

Between heaven and earth, between the calling of the sublime and the
running of his nose, man has no choice. He loves with all his being: brain,
hormones and moonlight included. The essence of love is to enable the
soarings of the soul to cohabit with the flutterings of the flesh. There are
those who pretend to ignore the one or the other, but this comfortable
dualism is extremely reductionist. Being in love is just a particular form of
the fluctuating central state. It expresses the presence of the other person in
the extracorporal space, that other person language links us to. All the
complexities of love derive from the fact that language takes root in it. As
Kristeva says, 'the love test is a putting to the test of language'.[1]

Desire is specified by its object. In the case of love, it is specified by the
sexual partner chosen by the central state. The central state integrates the
other person amongst its component parts. Far from being the mere 'contact
of two fleshes',[2] the meeting-point of two solitary corporal spaces, love
represents a state of fusion in which the whole being is realized.

Sex, in so far as it is both opposite and identical, embodies this unity. We
shall try to show how the radical difference between feminine and masculine
is based on a fundamental ambivalence and how any sexual union is the
result of the formidable battle between opposites.

In the end, the other person cannot escape sex, which is the principle of
unity amidst otherness. This leads us to the fact that all social life is
governed by sex. Without going so far as to say that sex is the only root of
all power over others, we shall try to show how the central state expresses
the encountering of other individual central states and how an inter-
individual organization and the establishment of a hierarchy result from
this.

Other people

Before entering on biology, we should like to point out two pitfalls to be
avoided. The first consists in a reductionist interpretation of experimental
data or human observations with a view to constructing a sexual
machine with alternative pleasurable or reproductive ends in order to
ensure maximum profitability. These technicians of love call themselves
sexologists. They are the workaday accountants of female orgasm and
describe an orgasmic function as if it were like blood pressure or other
constants of homeostasis. We are presented with 'biologies of love'. These
are quite happy in most cases to put sex under house arrest in the brain or
the glands. We are told, for instance, of a centre in the hypothalamus
which is responsible for sexual behaviour. Its destruction, carried out
by a neurosurgeon with a vigilante's knife, is supposed to correct a

criminal's deviant sexual behaviour.[3] Chemical substances are sometimes made responsible for sexual desire. An American biologist mentioned phenylethylamine as a neuromediator in this respect and then added that it was to be found in chocolate. Who said black magic was a thing of the past?

The second pitfall consists in a biased choice of animals used as models for man. Moral prejudice is never totally absent from these demonstrations. Some of the examples taken from animal life are used in such a way that they would not be out of place in a gossip column instead of serious scientific literature. The snail will soon be used as a sign outside transvestite clubs and the sex-life of the gibbon will be used to sing the praises of Christian marriage! Studying the sex-life of animals in order to understand the sex-life of man can only be justified in an evolutionistic perspective. A man has four limbs but does not walk on all fours; he can even travel about without using his legs. By observing his ancestors, we may detect what remains in modern man's love behaviour, even if man has learnt to make love without his genitals, thanks to his brain, and even if love of God sometimes replaces love of another person . . .

What is 'being in love'?

Being in love can last for an hour or for ever. It is an iceberg of chemistry and fancy. Sexual behaviour is only the visible part of this iceberg. Who claims that love is just a question of pulling a few faces and then engaging in copulatory gymnastics? However, these are the only observable phenomena, and so we shall mainly deal with sexual behaviour rather than love.

'When shall we three meet again?' Here are our old friends, the corporal, extracorporal and temporal dimensions of the central state. Being in love demands the actual or imagined presence of the loved one in the extracorporal space. The paradox of love is that the object of desire also has a central state, and so the extracorporal space of the one is occupied by the corporal space of the other. The other's attitude is not irrelevant. Love demands reciprocity, and our desire is influenced by the other person's. Two dogs of opposite sex may politely cohabit all the year round; for short periods when the female is in heat, the male ceases to be indifferent and becomes a lover. The central state of the female induces this change in the male: 'Your love is what I love . . .'.

The corporal space

When two people are in love, bodily transformations take place. These can sometimes be spectacular, but most often concern inner disturbances, mainly of hormonal secretions and the workings of the central nervous system. The genital glands obviously play a basic role, as can be seen in the effects of castration. Sex hormones act directly on the brain because of the presence of receptors in the neurons. Other hormones, such as prolactin and luliberin, also play a role in the arousing of sexual desire. But testicles or ovaries overflowing with secretions are not enough. There are desire systems inside the brain which must also function properly. The sexual organs are necessary for orgasm to be experienced and for the purposes of reproduction, but play little or no role in recognizing or identifying the person you were 'meant for', which in man remains the highest function of love.

Arrows of desire, or every body needs some body

The body sometimes loses its ordinary outer appearance. Fur becomes shiny, eyes light up, horns start growing and buttocks change colour. But it is inside that desire, through its hormones, has the greatest effect. Sexual desire in the female is more heterogeneous, being a mixture of active and passive components. If we use Beach's terminology, we can distinguish between attractivity, which is the power of seduction over a male, proceptivity, which is the attraction felt towards a male, and receptivity, which is the taking-up of a posture permitting mating.[4] There is not a one-to-one relationship between hormones and these three components.

Attractivity consists of a number of signs used by the female to arouse desire in the male. There are specialized works dealing with their extraordinary diversity in the animal kingdom. We shall come back to this question relative to the extracorporal space.

Proceptivity is the active part of desire, and can be spectacularly visible in some species. The darting runs and trembling ears of the female rat, for example, signal its desire to the male. The obscene gestures and pelvic movements of the female monkey are explicit solicitations for the male. The degree of proceptivity in the female monkey can be measured by observing how often and how eagerly it overcomes obstacles placed between itself and the male.

Receptivity is a posture facilitating penetration by the penis, usually involving curvature of the spine, or 'lordosis'. It is a veritable reflex triggered by lumbar pressure if the female is in heat, or 'oestrus'.

Oestrus is a particular hormonal state which coincides with ovulation. The ovaries, under the action of hypophyseal gonadotrophin hormones and ovarian steroids, undergo a cyclical maturation which results in the release of ova into the genital pathways. Very roughly, the first half of the cycle is governed by oestradiol which allows the growth of the follicle (the cellular structure inside which the ovum develops) and the extrusion of the ovum. The second half is governed by the progesterone secreted by the follicle which has become the corpus luteum in order to prepare for the coming pregnancy (figure 53). If fertilization does not take place, a new cycle begins. In most species, sexual desire (rut) exists only during oestrus, when the secretion of oestradiol is at its height. This is when the female is desirable

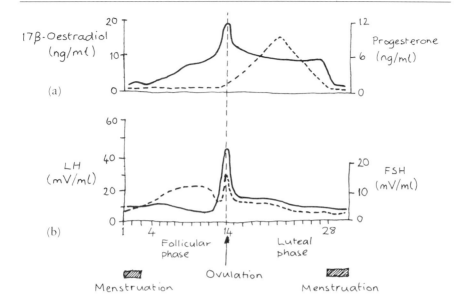

FIGURE 53   Menstrual cycle: (a) it can be seen that there is a rise in oestradiol in the first half of the cycle and a rise in progesterone in the second half; (b) the abrupt rise in oestradiol which precedes the middle of the cycle induces a peak in the luteinizing hormone (LH) (the hypophyseal hormone) which in turn causes the extrusion of an ovum by the ovary.

and accepts the male, the moment when the finality of sexual relations – reproduction – asserts itself.

In the primate, oestrus is not so tightly controlled by the brain. Generally, the female monkey is never in heat. This does not mean that there is no variation in desire during the cycle. Statistically, sexual relations are more frequent as ovulation nears, in the middle of the cycle, and become less frequent afterwards. These are the results of a study carried out by Persky, concerning not only female monkeys, but also female students at American universities.[5] They show that sexual drives become more intense during the hormonal peak period preceding ovulation. The desire of female monkeys in captivity shows more permanence throughout the cycle than is the case with females in the wild, where fecundity is obviously much more important for the survival of the species. The loss of rut in the primate coincides with the birth of Eros. The latent period between the act and its fruit, the birth of the young, allows a cultural dimension to be introduced into the relations between the sexes, and otherness replaces reproduction as the explicit aim of sexuality.

The ablation of the genital glands which secrete the sex hormones soon results in the loss of all sexual activity in most species. In the female, this loss concerns proceptivity, attractivity and receptivity. A spayed female cat would scratch any overgallant male, but of course none approaches since all attractivity has been lost. If oestradiol is injected, desire and seduction are restored after a few dozen hours. The second sex hormone, progesterone, has a more complex and varied action from one species to another. If it is injected between thirty-six and forty-eight hours after oestradiol, it potentializes the effects on receptivity. Injected later, progesterone has an inhibiting effect on desire and acts as an agent of sexual surfeit.

Hormones have less contrasted effects in primates. A spayed female monkey continues to engage in copulatory activity for a certain time. In women, desire does not seem to be affected by the ablation of the ovaries, and this shows once again that, in humans, sexual activity has lost its direct links with the reproductive function.

Spaying in the female monkey does not affect the three components of desire in equal measure. Neither proceptivity nor receptivity seem to be altered. However, there is a spectacular drop in attractivity. The male monkey wants nothing to do with a spayed female, and its advances are unsuccessful. The female monkey recovers its charm with an injection of oestradiol, which acts on its vaginal secretions and changes the smell given off. Attractivity here is not linked to the effect of oestradiol on the brain, but merely to a smell.

In the female monkey, and probably in woman, the female hormones progesterone and oestradiol do not regulate proceptivity and receptivity. This is done by the male hormones testosterone and androstenedione, which are also secreted by the ovaries and adrenal glands. Their action is exerted directly upon the brain. There is a testosterone peak in the period before ovulation, when desire is the strongest. Certain contraception pills bring about a drop in the male hormone content of the urine, which coincides with a weakening of desire. It may seem paradoxical, or at least ambiguous, that desire in woman depends on the cerebral action of her male hormones.

What about desire in the male? It is tempting to say that it resides in the memory. Indeed, sexual activity declines quite slowly after castration. A dog still fornicates energetically almost a year afterwards. A monkey, albeit with less vigour, is able to mount for a long time after castration. If castration is carried out before puberty, or on an inexperienced animal, the effects are all the greater. If the animal has had sexual experience before castration, the memory of this will influence its subsequent sexual activity. Eunuchs have a fair reputation for lubricity. If Brattleboro rats are deprived of vasopressin, they lose their memory and cease all sexual activity immediately after castration. If they are injected with vasopressin, they recover their memory and continue their sexual activity after castration.[6]

It is nevertheless true that all males, including men, experience a progressive loss of sexual activity after castration. Ejaculation is the first thing to disappear, followed by erection and consequently any chance of penetration. If testosterone is injected, sexual activity is restored, beginning with the last capacity to be lost and so on. Testosterone acts directly on the brain, as has been shown by placing crystals of this hormone in the anterior

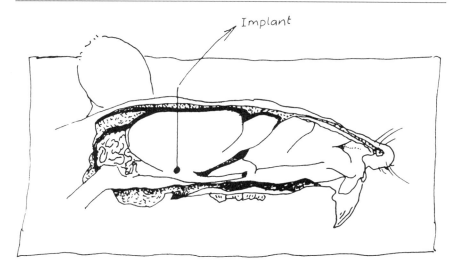

FIGURE 54 Sagittal section of rat brain showing the presence of testosterone implant in the hypothalamus.

hypothalamus of a castrated rat, which then recovers its sexual activity (figure 54).

Neurons under the influence

The hormones which circulate freely in the body work only on precise sites in the brain. If the testosterone implant were a few millimetres from the normal zone of action of this hormone, it would have no effect whatsoever. This is because there exist selectively sensitive neurons in certain regions of the brain. These neurons are revealed by the technique mentioned in chapter 4. The steroid hormone, marked by a radioactive product, fixes itself selectively on its receptor sites (figure 9). These are mainly situated at the base of the brain, in and around the hypothalamus: the ventral and medial regions on the one hand, and the anterior and lateral regions on the other. There are also fixing sites in the limbic brain (amygdala and septum), in the brainstem and even in the spinal cord (figure 55).

There is no real difference from male to female in these regions. It is difficult, as we shall see later, to distinguish the regions where testosterone and oestradiol fix themselves. The progesterone-sensitive zones coincide with those sensitive to oestradiol; the same neurons can have receptors for both these hormones.[7]

The steroid receptors in the brain are not different from those in the uterus or prostate, for example. The steroid, after passing through the cell membrane, finds a cytosolic receptor and forms a complex which transports the steroid to the genome. It fixes itself to the nucleic acids and modifies

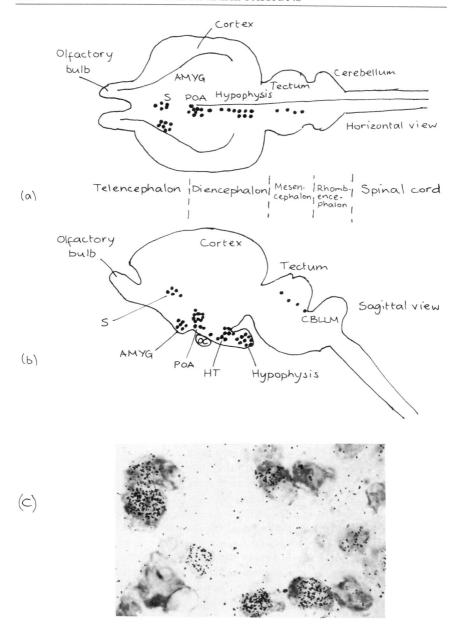

FIGURE 55 (a), (b) Representation of the distribution of oestrogen-sensitive neurons in the brain; (c) macrophotography used on a radio-autograph of the medial preoptic region of a guinea-pig brain an hour after a radioactive oestradiol injection (magnification 1520×). (Document provided by M. Warenbourg, INSERM, U.156.)

their activity. In the nucleus, the steroid induces enzyme synthesis. Its action is generally complex, multiple and not yet well understood. When the brain is developing, oestradiol, for example, directs cellular division, neuron differentiation, axon growth, the establishment of intercellular contact and the formation of networks.[8] Once the brain has completed its development, the various steroids affect the workings of neuronal networks and help or block the synthesis and release of hormones and neurotransmitters.

These actions affect the regions of the brain which regulate the functioning of the gonads: the secretion of hormones on the one hand, and the production of ova and spermatozoa (gametes) on the other. The various neuronal networks which play a role in sexual behaviour are also under the influence of steroids, as we have seen.

Typically, the action of a steroid lasts several days because of the slow and cumbersome mechanism of enzyme synthesis. Today, steroid hormones are credited with faster interventions in the brain. In a matter of minutes, they can work on neuron membranes, modifying their excitability (figure 21).

Whether sexual steroids have a short- or long-term action, we shall insist on their importance, as they are permanently present in the brain, first to direct its construction and then to modulate its expression.

In addition to their elective affinity for the brain, sex hormones act on the afferent and efferent sides of the reflex structure. In the male rat, there are motoneurons in the spinal cord gathered in a nucleus situated in the lumbar region. They innervate the muscles which allow erection of the penis.[9] This nucleus and these muscles do not exist in the female and disappear in a male which is castrated at birth. However, if a female foetus is treated with testosterone before birth, the muscles develop and so does the corresponding spinal motor nucleus.[10] This example shows that the male hormone is capable not only of inducing the appearance of specific nerve structures in the spinal cord, but also of influencing the development of the peripheral organ, in this case the penis.

The male hormones which act on the motor output of the penile reflex also influence the input. They increase the sensitivity of the glans to tactile stimuli. In the female rat, oestradiol widens the receptor fields of the sensory nerves which innervate the perineal region.[11] The ear of the toad is receptive to the charming song of the female only under the influence of androgens.[12]

Let us now consider the multiple levels of action of steroids and the problems that this poses. Tinbergen thought that steroids could only act on the higher nervous centres and that the action of a hormone on a muscle seemed incompatible with a specific action on particular behaviour, as no muscle was involved in only one behaviour pattern.[13] We can immediately remark, with all respect to this great ethologist, that the muscles of the penis rarely serve for anything other than sexual behaviour. Birds are a good example of the hierarchy of peripheral and central effects of steroids. In the chaffinch, the muscles used for the lovesong which attracts the female to the male are directly impregnated with testosterone which tunes the vocal instrument of the animal to its sexual desire. The testosterone also causes an upheaval in certain regions of the brain where the neuronal networks which control singing are to be found.[14] It is worth pointing out, as being contrary to the general rule, that if an adult castrated canary is injected with testosterone, this can induce neuron division leading to a new organization of the centres which control singing.

There would seem to be a lot of overlapping in the hormonal feedback at the different hierarchical levels which regulate the different components of sexual behaviour.

Another difficulty is that it is impossible to attribute a precise role to such and such a steroid in such and such a nervous structure.

These roles change from one species to another. Progesterone is indispensable to the sexual activity of rodents, for example, but seems to play a negligible role in primates. The number of steroid receptors and their specificity are not constants either. One of the properties of oestradiol is to induce the production of progesterone receptors in the hypothalamus. The action of progesterone is thus reinforced by the increase in the number of specific receptors.[15] The sequential action of these two hormones in inducing a type of sexual behaviour in the rat can perhaps be explained in this way.

A final factor resides in the chemical versatility of steroids. Through the presence of an enzyme or aromatase in certain regions of the brain, testosterone, the male hormone, is changed into oestradiol, the female hormone. Specific receptors for male hormones probably exist, but it is difficult to say whether, when testosterone acts on a target cell, it does so in its own form or after being changed into oestradiol. Another transformation of testosterone is its reduction to 5-α-dihydrotestosterone, a form in which it acts above all on the genital organs. But progesterone in reduced form can also recognize testosterone receptors.[16] Male hormones, female hormones . . . the difference between the sexes seems so clear, and yet even at the hormone level, difference is born of ambivalence.

Other amorous hormones

The corporal space of desire is not animated by steroids alone. Prolactin, a hormone secreted by the hypophysis, is not only responsible for the production of milk by the mammary glands, but also has other roles, particularly in the male.[17] Too high a level of prolactin has been held responsible for some cases of male impotence.[18] This may be an indirect consequence of the inhibiting action of this hormone on the secretion of testosterone. In women, an overabundant secretion of prolactin causes numerous cases of sterility. It would seem to block the hypothalamo-hypophyseal mechanisms of ovulation. It would also seem to regulate sexual behaviour, inhibiting the nervous centres which control female receptivity by blocking the release of luliberin there.[19]

Luliberin has already been mentioned several times (see chapter 4). When this peptide hormone is injected into the hypothalamus of a rat it induces sexual behaviour (see chapter 5). All we have said about the role of various steroids in inducing sexual behaviour shows that luliberin does not act alone, and cannot be considered as the exclusive hormone of sexual desire. But it does seem to be the key element. A nervous pathway using luliberin as a neurotransmitter apparently links the hypothalamus to the mesencephalon.[20] This allows communication between two strategic levels which are essential for the sexual act. We have already described the complexity of these nervous structures, the catecholamine playground. Here, the action of luliberin is linked to that of dopamine.[21] These two substances seem to facilitate and amplify each other's action.[22] As a hypothesis, we could say that luliberin may give a sexual orientation to non-specific desire systems. As desire is specified by its object, the catecholaminergic desire systems are specified by luliberin, with the conditions being looked after by the local presence of sex hormones.

One swallow does not make a summer

The drop in the testosterone level is not responsible for impotence and loss of desire in old people. Male hormone injections do not allow old men to recapture their sexual vigour. It is desire which ages more than the testicles. There is a degenerescence of desire systems, including the dopaminergic system, in old people.[23]

Your head's desires

A simple observation confirms the primacy of the brain in sexual activity. There are genetic strains of guinea-pigs which differ by their level of sexual activity. Let us call them the Casanova strain and the Joseph strain. When castrated, both strains become equally impotent. If both strains are subsequently injected with the same massive dose of testosterone, Casanova recovers a much higher level of sexual activity than Joseph, which confirms that the initial difference did not come from glandular differences but from nervous factors. Desire is in the head, not the heart or the genitals.

In the brain, the neuronal structures are common to different expressions of desire (see chapter 8). The different components of the central state specify the desire. Hormones play a crucial role. During growth, they trace networks in the vague brain which permit each sex to accomplish sexual acts after puberty. They determine the levels of activation, excitability and response of the nervous structures. They determine attractivity and are responsible for a desiring individual also becoming an object of desire.

Desire caught by the tail[24]

In all we have said up to now, we have often mentioned desire, the brain and hormones, but hardly ever those singular accessories, the penis and its female sheath. While speaking of love, were we coyly avoiding references to its instruments? We do not refuse to see Romeo's bulging fly, we only wish to show that the seat of his desire for Juliet is nearer to his cap than his pants, and that the ladder, the balcony and the nightingale are just as important to his desire as any lower form of upward mobility.

Far from pretending to ignore the importance of erection and ejaculation in man, or of the contractions and secretions in woman during coitus, we have deliberately chosen to leave this field to specialists. An experiment by Stefanick (1983) shows that male rats, after their penis has been anaesthetized, continue actively to mount females although they are incapable of erection.[25] Thus desire and sexual excitement in animals can clearly be dissociated from the peripheral mechanisms involved in copulation.

In fact, we do not know much about the peripheral and central nerve mechanisms of erection and ejaculation. These are reflexes induced by tactile stimulation and compression of the penis. Erection involves the parasympathetic centres situated in the sacral spinal cord, while ejaculation is mainly orthosympathetic. If the spinal cord of a dog is severed in the dorsal region, rhythmical movements of the pelvis and ejaculation can still be obtained in response to stimulation of the penis. It is important to note that these reflexes disappear in a castrated animal but are restored by the injection of testosterone or the implantation of testosterone crystals in the spinal cord. Therefore these reflexes are neuroendocrine in nature, and require the presence of testosterone, which can act as a modulator because of hormone receptors on the neurons of the spinal cord. Like any reflex organized at the medullar level, copulation is integrated in a controlling hierarchy involving the higher levels of the nervous system. After being relayed in the brainstem, the sensory afferents of sexual origin arrive in the hypothalamus. Here, the triggering of the copulatory sequence is linked to all the components of the central state. We shall come back to the regions of the hypothalamus which are specialized in the control of sexual behaviour in the male. Similarly, at this point we shall mention only briefly the nervous structures of the brain involved in male sexual behaviour, not in order to belittle their importance, but because they are the same as those already involved in all the animal passions. The amygdala, when stimulated, induces erection or its inhibition. The ablation of the temporal lobe induces the syndrome of Klüver and Bucy (see chapter 7). The septum would seem to facilitate erection. Finally, the role of the neocortex is crucial in psychogenetic sexual impotence or the fiasco dear to Stendhal.[26]

Once again, bearing in mind the concept of the central state, it is better to avoid dissociating the nervous structures which have a facilitating or inhibiting influence on the neuron systems which are responsible for the copulatory sequence. Concerning the pleasure which goes with copulation and the satiety which follows it (see chapter 9), we shall only add that there is no particular centre of sexual pleasure and that the neurovegetative storm which carries the lover away is nothing other than a paroxystic flaring of the common nervous structures (perhaps the septum) which may even lead to a momentary loss of consciousness.

As far as female sexual behaviour is concerned, it is even more difficult to extrapolate from the female rat to woman than it is from the male rat to man. It is impossible to reduce the postural inventions of woman to the stereotyped lordosis of the female rat. In both cases there is an obvious reflex component relative to the importance of tactile stimuli and uterovaginal pressure in the triggering of copulatory action. The extreme variety of erogenous zones in woman and the diversity of postures used in sexual intercourse, bear witness to the secondarization in humans of the process of love-making. Therefore we need only briefly evoke the central nervous structures in the female rat which organize lordosis. There is a reflex medullar level, a mesencephalic level and a hypothalamic level where the zone involved is different from that concerned in the male, as we shall see.

What about orgasm? Both men and women experience orgasm, but they differ in quality and length. Today the man in the street tends to make orgasm the mythical property of women, thereby making any housewife the equal of Saint Teresa of Avila. Whereas in man, orgasm accompanies the spasms of ejaculation, orgasm in woman comes a few seconds before the perineal response. Whatever the biological or philosophical significance attributed to it, orgasm bears witness to the participation of cerebral nervous structures in the unfolding of the copulatory sequence. In its reductionist version, orgasm is presented as a kind of reflex epilepsy.[27] Beyond a threshold reached via sensory afferent impulses and facilitating influences of cerebral origin, there would seem to occur synchronous self-sustaining discharges of neurons in the septum, amygdala and thalamic nuclei.[28]

We also know that rhythmical stimuli, using intermittent light for example, can bring on epileptic fits. Could the parallel rhythms of penis, pelvis and voice which accompany normal sexual intercourse merely be intermittent stimuli destined to trigger orgasmic epilepsy? The rare electrophysiological measurements taken during the orgasm of certain subjects (moreover, affected by nervous disorders) can only take a back seat to more subjective data. Until we are able to make intracerebral electrical measurements on normal people, men and women will probably continue to have orgasms without knowing whether they are epileptic or not.

Pure love

We have not yet drawn any distinction between sex and love. This attitude could appear narrowly reductionistic if it were not for the proclamation of the unity of the central state. Christian love, for all its sublimity, believes in the transubstantiation of bread and wine within man's body, at least in its Roman Catholic version. As Kristeva says of Saint Bernard, 'the more the mystic transcends his poor flesh, the more he treats it as an animal residue, the more the poor flesh imposes itself in the affect and love dictated and implanted in us by the grace of another' (figure 56).

From the neurobiologist's point of view, it would be too easy to attribute the role of angel to the neocortex because it is nearer the sky, and then relegate the beast to the ditch of the hypothalamus and spinal cord. Desire involves man entirely, from his eyeballs to the balls of his . . . feet, and there is no nervous structure which is not solicited. The corporal space, the space of desire, in so far as it is a component of the central state, participates in all forms of love.

Paraphrasing Freud, we can say that the essence of what we mean when we use the word 'love' is the same thing as what is sung of by the poets, i.e. sexual love which tends towards sexual union. However, there are many other kinds of love, such as self-love, love for one's parents, love for one's children, friendship, philanthropy, love of an object, of an abstract idea or ideal etc., which are all varieties of the same group of tendencies. In some cases, there is an invitation to sexual union; in others, this is excluded. Using the word 'love' for all these different things is a perfectly justified linguistic synthesis.

Similarly, desire, which we could also have called love, is at the heart of all our passions.

The extracorporal space

Love is an exchange of information between two bodies. It requires reciprocity, with each extracorporal space being constituted of signals emitted by the other's body. The information is taken in by the nose, ears and eyes. The face of the beloved, perceived by the eyes, is a veritable signature in the love-space, and deserves special attention. Environmental factors such as climate, temperature, light and food are crucial for some species but seem unimportant to humans, who can love in all seasons. The same cannot be said of social factors, as lovers, whether they are animals or human beings, are never alone in the world.

Led by the nose

The attraction a female exerts on a male is related to the presence of odoriferous substances in its urine and vaginal secretions. In humans, the smell of breath apparently plays a role in sexual attraction, and we should remember in this connection the importance of the face in love relationships.[29]

The destruction of the olfactory bulbs in certain species leads to a disappearance of sexual behaviour which may be complete (in the hamster) or partial (in the rat). In primates, however, neither the sense of smell, nor any other sense, is indispensable to sexual activity.

Smell is not perceived only by the nose; licking also allows subtle or acrid exhalations to reinforce desire. Taste, then, plays a complementary role to smell in the love feast.

Smell is also often the sign of oestrus, which allows the male to pick out the fecund female in a group. If the genital region of a ewe which is not in heat is smeared with secretions taken from another ewe in oestrus, a ram can be tricked into thinking it is the right time to mate, to the acute displeasure of the unwilling partner!

We have already pointed out that ovarian hormones affect the attractiveness of the female monkey by modifying its vaginal secretions. A touch of oestradiol on its sex will make the beauty much more attractive than flooding its hypothalamus with hormones.

Fragrance is not exclusive to the female and it plays a noticeable role in male attractiveness. In the pig, a sow with no sense of smell can no longer distinguish between a male and a female and so cannot show its preference. The glands of the boar secrete various compounds and at least one of them is capable of immobilizing the sow in the same way as the smell of the boar itself.

The preputial secretions of a man, the smell of which is reminiscent of sandalwood, would seem to attract women and repulse men. Therefore some smells attract, and may even be aphrodisiac, while others repel or signal satiety. Consequently, if you are thinking of using perfume for the purposes of seduction, experiment carefully with it beforehand.

Certain substances, no different from those identified in the boar, have been isolated in concentrated form in the urine of man and in the secretions from his armpits. Testosterone increases male seduction, probably by increasing the quantity of scented secretions.

In the study of the role of odour in determining desire, we should mention the perfume of childhood. Mice raised with violet-scented parents show a preference for males who are marked with the same perfume when they grow up and become adults.[30]

Language participates in the attraction–repulsion game by referring to smells. We say 'he's a stinker' of someone we thoroughly dislike. Such a person does not attract us. It is in the domain of sexual behaviour that smell, that forgotten sense, fully recovers its communicative function.

Sounds like love

Despite the importance of the love song in folklore, we must admit that auditory communication seems less important than smell and sight in the sexual activity of most mammals.[31] Obviously the case is quite different in birds and certain invertebrates. As for fish, since we do not quite know

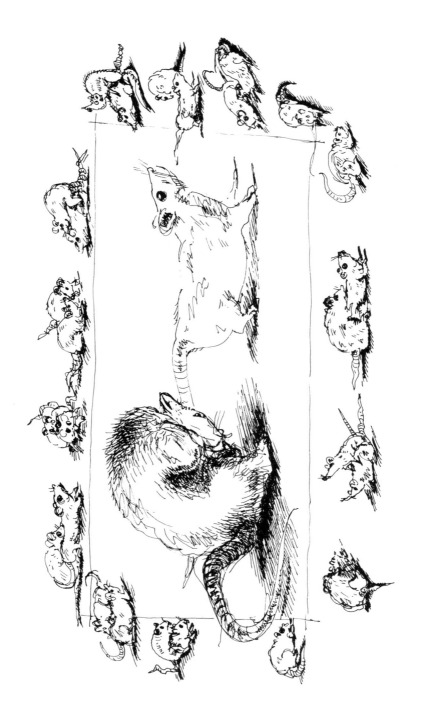

FIGURE 56   Mr and Mrs Rat (François Durkheim).

whether to class sirens with marine life or amongst humans, we shall leave them out of our discussion.

The importance of auditory information varies from one species to another, and we cannot judge its importance; therefore we shall simply note its presence amongst the wave of signals which trigger and sustain desire. In certain species, ultrasounds are used to attract a partner or repel a rival.[32]

Monkey business

The rump of the male mandrill in periods of sexual activity is a rainbow of colours which are a love-call to the female. The turgescent and colourful skin in the genital region of the female chimpanzee is a permanent invitation to the male. Certain postures of the female favour the display of the crucial region and, consequently, the visual signals it sends out. The behaviour of females, absolute immobility in the sow and cow or, in contrast, the darting runs of the female rat, are all invitations for the male. Signals are sent out not only to potential partners, but also to rivals, sometimes announcing combat.

The role of sight in sexual activation in humans is more a question of sociology than biology, and so we shall examine only briefly the different aspects of the question. Kinsey insisted on the disparity between men and women concerning the role of visual stimuli in arousing desire.[33] He noted that representations of naked women are more frequent than those of naked men and that pornographic pictures are produced for a male public, even when these pictures show other men. More recent studies have confirmed Kinsey's findings.[34] There is no equivalent in woman of man's efforts to get a glimpse of the female sexual organs. In primitive societies hiding the female genital organs is a more widespread practice than hiding the male's. The function of this is to exalt the vision of them and reserve this privilege for the chosen one.[35] Symons notes that when a woman looks at a man, a reasonable estimation of future profit, whether it be economic or physical, is more to the fore than an immediate arousal of desire, unlike what happens in men.[36]

It must not be forgotten that, in humans, one of the principal functions of love resides in the discovery of the other person. Consequently, the face is singularly important as a major element of identification. The function of the kiss may simply be to bring two faces close together. The face-to-face love-making of man and woman, which is unique in the animal kingdom, can also be seen in this light. G.E. King remarks that the universality of ventroventral copulation can be understood as a personalization of sex, and that this heterosexual position, which offers the greatest probability of female orgasm (according to women), also offers the greatest number of visual interactions to the participants.[37]

However, many couples turn out the light before making love, and this argues against the importance of visual stimuli, until we remember the pictures stored up in the head, including the idealized face of the beloved . . .

Day in, night out

Daylight imposes a rhythm on the love-making of certain animals. This has been shown since 1924, when Rowan noticed that birds which normally fly south for the winter, and which were kept in captivity in artificial light, had testicles and ovaries in perfect working order when they were examined in mid-winter. This was in stark contrast to the atrophied organs of other captives left in natural light.[38]

The importance of the daily ratio of light to darkness in determining the seasonal rhythm of sexual activity has since been confirmed in the study of numerous species, including mammals. Ewes become sexually active from September to January in the northern hemisphere, when days are shorter. If the ewe is exposed to short periods of light by artificial means at any time of the year, a procreative phase is triggered. In nature, as the length of the days is immutably determined, so is the season of love-making. The light factor is what chronobiologists call a *zeitgeber*, a time-giver. It has an obviously adaptive value. Young born at a certain time of year will have more chance of surviving than those born at others, because of scarcer grass or colder weather. Natural selection thus favours individuals conceived at a certain time of year. If this photoperiodic sexual response is genetically determined, these individuals will procreate in their turn at the most favourable time of year.

Other environmental factors have a more limited influence on sexuality.[39] Temperature, for example, only affects the libido of a ram if it is very high, but this may simply indicate a weakness in the cooling system of the testicles, which, as everyone knows, must be kept below body temperature in order to function properly.

Nutritional factors also affect reproduction. Much contradictory work has been done in this field, which is of the greatest importance, especially in agriculture.

What about man? The study of the influence of environmental factors on human sexuality has fuelled a flood of studies and statistics in which biology has little say. In temperate regions, conception is most frequent at the end of spring and in summer. Malnutrition hardly seems to affect sexual desire in man.[40]

Of mice and men

Love involves the search for the presence of another, but there is also the presence of others to be taken into account. Mice are interesting in this connection.

When three or four female mice are shut up in a small cage, their oestrus comes a week later than usual and pseudo-pregnancies can be observed, with the presence of a corpus luteum unaccompanied by gestation. This phenomenon is called the Lee Boot effect. When a larger population (fifteen to thirty females) is brought together, the oestral cycle of each individual becomes irregular or disappears. If a male is put into the cage, all the females start synchronous cycles. This is the Whitten effect. All the females are thus in heat at the same time to welcome the lucky visitor. Another strange thing can be observed if the male is taken away from the female after fecundation, and another male is put into the cage. The female is furious, but the fertilized egg cannot fix itself in the uterus, and our female finds itself once again in oestrus. This is the Bruce effect. The immediate cause of these phenomena is to be found in the urine of the male, which contains highly volatile substances (pheromones) which cause physiological reactions in other individuals of the same species.

Other studies, particularly on rabbits, show the importance of population factors on sexual activity. The adaptive element in these inter-individual regulations is obvious. It would nevertheless be irreverent, and totally unscientific, to extrapolate from our mice to female communities such as convents or girls' boarding schools. It is extremely difficult to get a male inside these places at the right moment and measure the onset of oestrus with all the necessary accuracy.

The fact that sociobiology studies sexual matters is not surprising, given the adaptive value of sex in the evolution of the species.[41] In the data we are presented with, it should be noted that there is more sociology than biology. The torrents of literature, serious investigations and field studies are not devoid of interest in so far as they try to draw up the laws governing human sexuality. Nevertheless it would be dishonest to use biological arguments obtained in the animal kingdom to corroborate the 'truths' which are put forward. Here are a few examples of misleading assertions.

The female orgasm is supposed to be the privilege of humans. This is in fact incorrect, since animals in captivity experience climax.[42] Should we conclude that prison is the price to be paid for sexual enjoyment? The loss of oestrus and the fact of being receptive outside the period of fecundity is thought to be exclusive to woman. This is again incorrect, since certain female monkeys accept the male all the year round. What about faithfulness in marriage? All possible combinations are to be found in primates, from the monogamous gibbon to the orgy-loving macaque. The sexual behaviour of woman is sometimes presented as a service. For example, woman scrupulously manages a stock of ova and lets man profit from this to the best of her own interests. For some people, the only difference between a woman's love and a greengrocer's apples is in the nature of the goods. No biological data allow such hypotheses to be confirmed. Whereas woman is monogamous, man is supposed to be polygamous by nature.[43] Claude Lévi-Strauss suggests that the universal and natural tendency of man towards polygamy means that we are always short of women. Symons concludes that the demand is greater than the supply. The profitability of commerce in which the seductiveness of the product and the desire of the consumer are the basic components would seem to augur well for the demographic future of our descendants.

There is a little more biology in masculine jealousy. In many animal species which live in groups, like monkeys, seals or deer, adult males are sometimes extremely aggressive with young males and keep them at a good distance from the females. A sea-elephant, capable of procreating at the age of four, will sometimes have to wait until it is fifteen before being able to approach the creature of its dreams. The hormonal determinism of this aggressiveness between males is not always clear and its adaptive value is a matter for speculation. In woman, jealousy would appear to be a primarily cultural phenomenon.[44] Ford,[45] Kinsey and others affirm that husbands are more concerned about the faithfulness of their wives than wives about that of their husbands.[46] This difference can be explained by evolutionistic biology. A man may have doubts about being the father of his wife's children, whereas a husband's infidelity never endangers a woman's fertility.[47]

The reader who is avid for explanations can only find biology disappointing as regards love. Once more we must evoke our neocortex, our proliferating culture and our disrupted natural environment. Our brain may weigh 700 grams more than that of a chimpanzee, but we should not forget that our testicles weigh about the same.

The temporal dimension

'For ever wilt thou love, and she be fair.' Whatever Keats may say, clocks in our brain give a rhythm to our love-life. There is a time for learning to love, the waiting which heightens desire, habit which withers love, orgasm in which all notion of time vanishes . . . Biology may not offer explanatory mechanisms but does offer analogies for the role of time in love.

Clockwise

We have already pointed out the existence of biological cycles which regulate sexual activity. In the females of certain mammals (rodents and primates), a cyclical ovulation coincides with maximum sexual receptivity. The species in which the biological clock is to be found in the deep regions of the brain (rodents) should nevertheless be distinguished from those more highly developed species in which the periodicity of ovulation seems to have escaped from the control of the central nervous system.

Alongside this highly specialized system of cyclical ovulation, other periodic factors may intervene in sexual activity. Circadian rhythms in all animals cause particular phenomena to take place at set times every day, and regulate on a twenty-four-hour basis certain biological activities, such as hormone secretion. Cortisol secretion, drinking behaviour and eating behaviour are cases in point. A master clock situated in the suprachiasmatic nucleus of the hypothalamus is in charge of all these rhythms. Is there a circadian rhythm for sexual activity? In the rat, the effect of oestradiol depends on when it is injected.[48] A hormone can act only if its target is receptive, and this receptivity often varies according to a circadian rhythm. The four-day oestral rhythm observed in rodents seems to be produced by the circadian oscillator itself or at least to be coupled with it.[49]

In the course of twenty-four hours, shorter rhythms can be observed, particularly during sleep, in the form of periodical activations corresponding to phases of rapid eye movement (REM), called paradoxical sleep. Paradoxical sleep is a dreaming period and in men the penis is erect. These erections, which are periodical during sleep, can be recorded by a plethysmograph (figure 57). We often wake in the morning during a phase of paradoxical sleep, as these phases are particularly frequent at the end of the night. How many furtive desires are satisfied at the break of dawn thanks to a brief erection which is the mere consequence of nocturnal rhythms?

Other rhythms, such as the oestral rhythm, are much longer and go far beyond the twenty-four hours of the day. There are annual rhythms in animals with a varying synchronizing role played by external factors. There are also more mysterious rhythms, the seasons of the heart, which abandon our loves to the hazards of time.

Getting to know you

The lessons of love last throughout childhood and adolescence in all human societies, and include sentimental education and technical initiation. We shall avoid fastidious discussion of how much is innate and how much is learned in sexual behaviour. The taboo on sexual relations with the mother has been observed in chimpanzees and Japanese macaques.[50] However, this does not prove that the prohibition upon incest in man is of biological origin.

Male rats raised in isolation can neither recognize nor behave normally towards a female. However, male rats which are deprived of their sense of smell but raised with females show satisfactory sexual behaviour as adults, which proves that they have received a suitable education from their young companions. Female rats learn to mark their territory with their vaginal secretions before and during oestrus, according to whether fellow creatures are present or not, for fear of competition or undesirable advances from males. The sexual games of childhood, which are common in the animal world, are perhaps the rehearsals which pave the way for adequate love behaviour in adulthood.

Absence, habit and sensitization

'Consider, my love, just how far you lacked foresight.' The passionate love of the Portuguese nun is the archetype of desire caused by the absence of the loved one: *rerum absentium concupiscentia.*[51] At the other extreme, endless

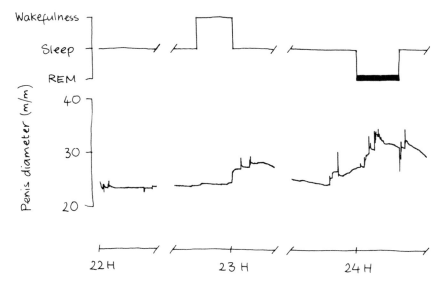

FIGURE 57   Plethysmographic measurement of penis diameter variation during sleep. Erections occur periodically at night during phases of paradoxical sleep.

repetition, excessive presence and dull routine generally end up by putting out the fire of desire. Wilson has shown that the stimuli associated with mating with the same female rat lose their power of attraction over the male when frequently repeated.[52] However, the male exhausted by this repetition can begin its copulatory activity again with another female, especially if no other male has preceded it.

The Portuguese nun and the worn-out rat are two vexing examples of what time can do to love. What choice is there between a passion consuming itself in a vacuum and an ecstasy stifled by routine? What would have become of Tristram and Isolde if they had not died? Would the endless repetition of knightly embraces in some Cornish castle have led to the routine love-making and twilight tenderness we associate with faithful no-fuss couples?

We have no wish to use biological explanations to demystify behaviour which is the privilege of man, but let us briefly flirt with the pleasures of a little dangerous analogical reasoning to show the parallels between certain love situations and what happens in the communication systems of the organism.

When a messenger, whether it be a hormone or a neurotransmitter, is released in excess or uninterruptedly, the receptors lose their capacity to respond, producing a desensitization. Consequently, when the cells of the hypophysis are permanently inundated by a hypothalamic hormone, they cease to respond. This may explain why hormones are released discontinuously, in a pulsatile way, in order to allow the receptors to

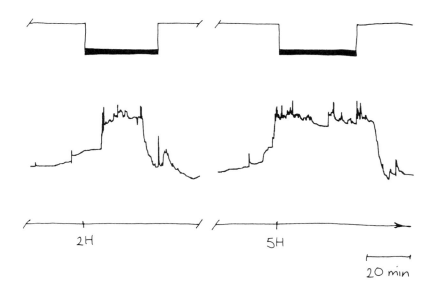

recover their sensitivity to the hormone during the interruptions. However, if no messenger is released, this leads to hypersensitization, a heightened sensitivity and a proliferation of receptors.[53] In these circumstances a very small quantity of messenger is enough to cause an explosive response.

We are not trying to say that sensitization processes govern love, but so many hormones serve as go-betweens in sexual matters that it would be surprising if events of this nature did not take place in the brain and glands at the very moment when the chemistry of love starts to work.

Come together

We have already mentioned the links between orgasm and death, and the fact that orgasm kills all sense of time. The cerebral storm of orgasm results in a temporary interruption of the biological perception of time. When a man and a woman try to synchronize their orgasms, is this an attempt to complete the fusion of both fluctuating central states in a unified temporal dimension?

Masculine, feminine

How is the function of otherness based on the difference between male and female established? Does the brain retain a kind of bipotentiality or is it definitely marked by the sex hormones secreted in the foetus? To what extent are the brains of a man and a woman different? Are the extracorporal space and education of an individual the only determining factors in sexual tastes or does hormonal determinism make the choices? Without claiming the status of absolute truth for what we are about to say, we can nevertheless try to answer these questions.

The birth of sex

The sex chromosomes determine whether the gonads become testes or ovaries. The secretion of testosterone by the testes transforms the neuter outline into an individual of the male sex. The secretion of oestradiol by the ovary or the absence of a gonad lets the outline evolve towards a female individual.

Up to the age of two months, a human foetus has no gender. Early on, the genital apparatus possesses both male and female characteristics. Between 1947 and 1952, Alfred Jost established the dogma concerning sex differentiation in mammals.[54] The sex glands, or gonads, are the architects of this differentiation. If a foetus is castrated in the uterus, the result is the birth of a female. In mammals, therefore, female sexual differentiation is of a neutral type.

The gonads of the embryo develop in accordance with its chromosomal sex (XX for the female, XY for the male), producing ovaries or testicles. Very early on, while the differentiation is just beginning, the gonads secrete their hormone: oestradiol for ovaries and testosterone for testicles. The latter hormone causes the regression of the potentially female genito-urinary tract and the development of male genitalia and secondary sexual characteristics. In the presence of ovaries or in the absence of gonads, the potentially male genitalia regress and the individual takes on the characteristics of a female.

Once it has begun, hormone secretion remains abundant during foetal life and continues for some time after birth. Testosterone is especially active in the development of the internal male genito-urinary tract and, in the form of dihydrotestosterone, in that of the external genitalia. Oestradiol, however, does not seem to be essential to sex differentiation, since the female genitalia can develop without it. During childhood, the secretion of sex hormones is reduced to a trickle after the abundant flow of the foetal period, but the flow picks up again during puberty, when everything that was prepared for before birth is brought to completion.

Behaviour is just as much a sexual characteristic as a mane, a beard or genitals. It is the result of the differentiating action of embryonal hormones. For the brain to function subsequently in a masculine way, it must be subjected before birth to the action of testosterone. Otherwise, the adult individual will be unable to behave adequately in female company. Immediately after birth, testosterone completes its action by defeminizing the individual. If this were not the case the castrated adult male would behave like a female when injected with oestradiol.[55]

The differentiation of female sexual behaviour does not require hormonal action. Testosterone, we should remember, is changed into oestradiol in order to act on the brain, and brings about defeminization in males. Why does oestradiol not have the same effect in females? In females, it seems to be neutralized by a blood protein, alphafetoprotein.[56] Another hypothesis is that the progesterone secreted at the same time as oestradiol would seem to protect the brain from its action.[57]

Before drawing any conclusions about the absolute power of embryonal hormones in the differentiation of sexual behaviour, we must insist once again on the fact that we are speaking of rodents, not humans. But even in rats, the determinism of sexual behaviour is far from being irreversibly fixed during the perinatal period. Female rats can indulge in male copulatory behaviour as adults, and castrated males can act like females if they are given prolonged oestradiol treatment. These observations would seem to suggest that both male and female potentialities continue to exist somewhere in the adult brain.

Hermes and Aphrodite's child

From Hermaphrodite to Musil's goldfish, the myth of bisexuality has traversed time and cultural frontiers. It echoes the fundamental ambivalence of the individual. Biology has rediscovered this mythical figure in the hypothalamus of animals.

According to Krafft-Ebing, male and female cohabit in the same brain and allow individuals of either sex to show behavioural bisexuality. Psychoanalysis and biology, at different levels, try to check the hypothesis. We shall limit ourselves to biological data.

We have already mentioned that male and female sexual behaviour are governed by different coexisting regions of the hypothalamus (figure 58).

When testosterone crystals are placed in the pre-optic region of the hypothalamus of a castrated male adult, the animal will behave normally in the presence of a receptive female. If oestradiol is applied to the ventromedial region of the hypothalamus, however, it causes female behaviour in the castrated male rat.[58]

The same duality can be observed in the female. An oestradiol or testosterone implant in the pre-optic region of a castrated female induces male behaviour, while the same hormones inoculated into its ventromedial hypothalamus trigger female behaviour.[59]

It should nevertheless be understood that this latent bisexuality normally never expresses itself. The brain, because of the foetal and postnatal conditioning it receives, favours either the male or the female centre. The other centre merely retains a potential capacity to direct behaviour in its turn if ever the central state of the animal so demands.

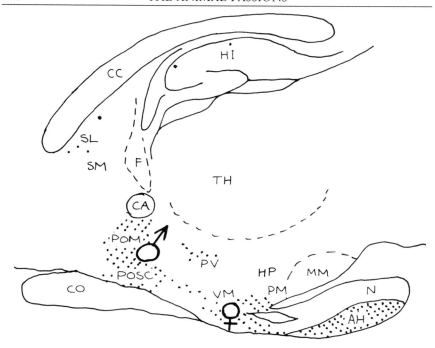

FIGURE 58   Sagittal section of the diencephalic region of the rat brain showing the male and female sexual centres.

   This apparent changeability in the male or female expression of sexual behaviour should not make us forget the basic differences which separate the two sexes.

Vive la différence!

The theme of the double here joins that of the hermaphrodite. The double is simultaneously similar and opposite. The difference between male and female is the test which allows the statement of a deep unity of being.

It is difficult for man to remain insensitive to the bodily differences between the two sexes, and so it is hardly surprising to read of Doctor Johnson saying to a theatrical friend that the 'white bosoms of your actresses excite my amorous propensities'. What is more surprising is the slightness of the difference between the brain of man and that of woman. A small hypothalamic nucleus in the male, a few neurons containing vasopressin, roughly 100 grams of cerebral matter and perhaps an unequal development of the hemispheres do not add up to much compared with such dissimilar bodies, behaviour and social status. It is as if otherness were the domain of the body and behaviour, while the brain would seem to express the deeper identity of masculine and feminine beings.

Nevertheless, for more than a century, physiologists and anatomists have been desperately trying to pinpoint differences in the brain of man and woman. The aim is clear. If there are two different functions, there must be two different machines, even if these must ultimately be married.

Crichton-Browne (1880), after examining the brains of thirty corpses, concluded that the weight difference between the hemispheres is less marked in woman than in man.[60] More recent studies have confirmed that there exists a greater degree of asymmetry between the hemispheres in man than in woman.[61] The vascularization of the hemispheres is also more asymmetrical. This is true not only of humans. Primates, cats and rodents show the same type of characteristics, except that in rodents the asymmetry is more noticeable in females.

We have already mentioned the functional difference between the two hemispheres. No recent data have confirmed Buffery and Gray's model, according to which the male brain is organized more symmetrically than the female brain.[62] The opposite seems to be the case.[63] Indeed, the domination of each cortex in their respective fields would seem to be more pronounced in man.[64]

Differences in the cognitive capacities of the two sexes have been demonstrated. Women seem to be better at verbal skills, while men are better at spatial perception.[65] Appropriate tests have established these differences in schoolchildren, showing in particular that the maturation of the right hemisphere may be inhibited in girls.[66] It should be borne in mind, however, that these differences appear only after statistical studies and concern minimal variations. It would be ridiculous to claim a scientific basis for the opposition of two stereotypes, on the one hand the man-manipulating sweet-talking word-weaving woman, and on the other the abstract-thinking music-loving space-probing man.

Anatomical differences in the subcortical structures of the brain have been described recently. They are as yet relatively few in number and fragmentary. Raismann and Field were the first to show a difference between male and female in the synaptic organization of the pre-optic region in the rat. This difference could be inverted by an appropriate manipulation of neonatal testosterone levels. Also in the rat, Gorski (1978) has described a nucleus in the pre-optic region which is larger in the male.[67] We have already pointed out the existence of a motor nucleus for the penis in the spinal cord of the male rat. Van Leeuwen has observed that neurons containing vasopressin are particularly numerous in the septum of the male rat.[68]

There is one last difference we should like to point out between the male and female hypothalamus, concerning their functional signification. In the rat, the 'masculine centre' is located in the pre-optic region. This region is part of the group of anterior and lateral structures which would seem to control the parasympathetic functions and be involved in approach and self-stimulation behaviour. It would seem to represent the pleasure side of the pleasure—aversion pair.[69] In this connection, it should be noticed that the sexual behaviour of the male is strongly parasympathetic. Erection is the most visible evidence of this.

In contrast, the 'feminine centre', located in the ventromedial hypothalamus, belongs to a group of medial and posterior structures which would seem to be involved in the orthosympathetic functions as well as flight and aversion behaviour. Pfaff remarks that the sexual behaviour of the female rat, in its preparatory phase at least, includes a strongly orthosympathetic sequence of flight and defence reactions which finally help the penis to penetrate.[70] Outside the receptive period, the sensory stimuli from the male are frankly aversive in character and unavoidably cause hostility in the female. The joint action of oestradiol and progesterone would seem to abolish the painful and aversive nature of these sensory messages. Once again, it is difficult to extrapolate from rats to humans, but a rape victim will not deny the unpleasant, painful and intolerable character of sexual stimuli perceived when no desire is associated with them.

We are not trying to say that sexual pleasure is man's privilege while aversion is woman's lot. Women are not the victims of their hormones and a plot hatched by men to make them take for pleasure what is in fact a painful chore. We only wish to show that in any male and female pair, the same conflict of opposites is to be found as within the individual. The essential function of love, as we have said, is the discovery of oneself in this confrontation with somebody of the opposite sex. How can we explain, then, that some people choose to make love with other individuals of the same sex?

'I would not be a queen'

Our biologist's training would have us look for the causes of homosexuality in 'abnormal' hormonal secretions. We would then draw examples from the animal kingdom which would tend to show the common bestiality of things sexual. On the other hand, forgetting our training, we could claim that homosexuality is exclusive to man, and that it is the mere product of his unconscious, a Blakean 'poison tree' of his own cultivation. In the first case, there would be an anomaly to treat, and in the second, we would acknowledge through its erring ways the all-powerful mind. Both attitudes seem to us equally unacceptable. Homosexuality, which is a variety of passionate love, is only one of the modalities of the fluctuating central state. Therefore the corporal space, hormonal secretions and neuronal activity are no more important than the objects in the extracorporal space, including daddy, mummy and the social milieu. Furthermore, as the fluctuating central state represents a being in the making from the moment the male and female gametes meet, each event contributes to the building of this central state, whether it is inscribed in the neurons or in the cultural environment.

Homosexuality is the expression of a sexual orientation towards a partner of the same sex, resulting generally in 'heterotypical' sexual behaviour, in contrast with 'homotypical' sexual behaviour involving a partner of the opposite sex. The animal kingdom offers numerous examples of heterotypical sexual behaviour, which takes place spontaneously, especially in females. Beach has found thirteen species which indulge in heterotypical practices, including lionesses, female dogs and cats, and even those apparently lethargic cows which people our fields. In males, however, spontaneous heterotypical behaviour is rare, with the exception of macaques in captivity and a special strain of rats.

Above all, atypical sexual orientation, or the choice of a partner of the same sex, should be distinguished from sexual differentiation disorders. The latter result in sexual dimorphism which influences not only bodily appearance but also certain behaviour patterns. Indeed, apart from copulatory activity, there exists in animals and in men a behavioural dimorphism which manifests itself in violent games, physical and verbal aggressiveness, parental imitation games, choice of friends, a tomboy or effeminate character etc., which distinguish the young male from the young female.

Sexual differentiation, as we have seen, depends on the sex steroids. Experiments on rodents have shown that the bipotentiality of the foetus can be oriented towards either sex according to the programme of hormonal secretions.[71] Any anomaly leads here to atypical sex differentiation. For example, Dörner has shown that female rats subjected to stress or harmful stimuli during gestation give birth to insufficiently masculinized or imperfectly defeminized males. If these males are castrated upon reaching adulthood, and given an oestradiol injection, they will indulge in heterotypical behaviour more frequently than males from a different litter.[72] Dörner, on the basis of these observations, undertook a retrospective study of men in an attempt to find the effect that stress during their mother's pregnancy may have had on their sexual orientation. The results of this work cannot be accepted without reservations, however seriously it was carried out. In a population of one thousand males born between 1934 and 1948, homosexuality is more common in those conceived during the war.[73] Furthermore, in a population of one hundred male homosexuals, the number of those whose mother underwent a traumatic experience during the pregnancy (rape, death in the family) is higher than in the control population.[74] In rats, as in men, heterotypical behaviour or homosexuality would seem to be the expression of an abnormal behavioural differentiation due to insufficient secretion of testosterone in the foetuses of mothers under stress. These observations reinforce the opinion of those who refuse to separate sexual differentiation from sexual orientation. Human homosexuality, according to them, is a disorder linked to inadequate behavioural differentiation and is thus a case of intrinsic determinism.

Numerous observations lead to opposed conclusions. In humans, abnormal sexual differentiation does not necessarily lead to atypical sexual orientation. Conversely, atypical sexual orientation does not always imply differentiation anomalies. The notion of gender identity is also important in humans. Gender identity is the sex that the subject identifies with. This has nothing to do with homosexuality. A homosexual does not try to hide the sex he belongs to, quite the contrary. According to the theory defended by Money and most Anglo-Saxon authors, gender identity is formed in the early years of childhood, parallel to language acquisition.[75] It depends almost exclusively on the educational influence of the parents. The sex adopted by the child is the one imposed by the environment. This theory is mainly based upon the observation of children whose mothers received hormone treatment during pregnancy and on the study of cases of congenital adrenal hyperplasia.

Thirty years ago it was fashionable to treat pregnant women in danger of having a miscarriage with progestogens. Their androgenic action was comparable with that of testosterone, and so the result for female infants was a more or less accentuated masculinization of their external genital organs, which led to some of them being taken for boys. The later the mistake was finally discovered, the more difficult it was for these false hermaphrodites to accept their new sexual identity. It finally transpired from these observations that the sexual identity of the future adult depended almost exclusively on the parents' conviction about the sex of their child in the first two or three years after birth.[76]

Congenital adrenal hyperplasia offers an almost experimental situation since the subjects suffering from it secrete an excess of adrenal androgens at the expense of other adrenocortical hormones. A female foetus is thus submitted to an overstrong impregnation with androgens, causing its masculinization. At birth, the little girl has male genital organs. Cortisone treatment, however, normalizes androgen secretion and early surgery gives the infant an appearance in conformity with her sexual identity. She will be brought up as a girl and her sexuality and adult fertility will not be endangered. These cases are particularly interesting, since they allow us to determine the responsibility of foetal androgens in sexual identity, differentiation and orientation. These children are brought up as girls and accept themselves as such. A certain deviation in differentiation of behavioural dimorphism can nevertheless be observed. The personality, games and parental imitation are more like those of a boy. However, their sexual orientation is not atypical. Most of these girls are heterosexual, a few are bisexual and none of them are homosexual, either in behaviour or erotic fancy. In these cases, we can at the very most speak of a certain inversion of behavioural differentiation, but there is no deviation in gender identity and sexual orientation.

This confirms our opinion that it is useless to look to the foetal gonads or adrenal glands for the exclusive source of adult homosexuality, even if it is possible totally to exclude the role of abnormal androgen secretion during foetal life in the later appearance of homosexuality or lesbianism. We cannot isolate hormones in this context from the global fluctuating central state.

Lacking in personal experience and specialist knowledge of homosexuality, we can speak of it only as we would of an unknown planet. Indeed, there seem to be as many varieties of homosexuality as there are stars in the sky. What is certain is that no endocrine anomaly is at play here. All attempts to 'treat' homosexuality with hormones have failed. Homosexuality in identical twins is no proof of a genetic origin.[77] There is no proof of sex chromosome anomalies in homosexuals. Neither is it possible to show that chromosome anomalies inevitably lead to deviant sexual behaviour. We shall say nothing of the psychoanalytical interpretations of homosexuality. The role of the parents is that of an element in the extracorporal space which interferes with the sexual bipotentiality of the corporal space. This attitude leaves psychoanalytical theory plenty of elbow room. To our knowledge, there is no better theory with which to account for the interactions between a child's bisexuality and affective environment.

Finally, we should like to say a word about the common opinion that homosexuality is an excess of ambivalence. The homosexual male is seen as too feminine and the woman as too masculine. The opposite would often seem to be the case. The homosexual male, for example, can be excessively masculine. Indeed, an injection of testosterone only reinforces the homosexual tendency. Male homosexuality often takes the form of an exaltation of virility. Erection is all important to both active and passive partners. The phallus becomes an object of worship. Leather and other attributes of male aggressiveness abound. The homosexual population is not exclusively composed of those glorious cohorts of 'queens'. How does the homosexual see himself through the eyes of others? Can Proust's two-faced Charlus, in whom the incarnation of war-like virility gives way to the powdered face of effeminate senility, help us here? Homosexuality would seem to result from a deficit in the function of otherness. When it comes to recognizing one's 'better half', which is the main function of love, the homosexual would seem to choose the same as himself, like Narcissus, eliminating the risk which invests love with all its meaning: the confrontation with difference.

We should like to quote Lou Andreas-Salomé at this point, in order to summarize this essential function of love.

> when we are in love, that is to say, when our creative agitation requires its external complementary half in order to undertake bodily tasks outside itself, this does not attenuate the antithesis of the sexes. On the contrary, it accentuates the antithesis to the point of total opposition. Everything which is concentrated, woven and mingled within us under the influence of the erotic stimulus seems to be so to one end only, a very partial one, and the individual seems to become overladen with meaning as a representative of his sex. It is only as a complement, as a representative of otherness, that he is placed on a pedestal worthy of the beloved 'one and only' . . .
>   . . . If it is true that all love is based on the ability inwardly to experience the nature of another person by sharing in it, and if we can say . . . that the experience of the two lovers in this respect is identical, then love possesses a

double human face. It absorbs the sex of the other in its affective expression, a little as it does physically in conception. This makes love capable of acquiring, alongside the accentuated sexual character of the relationship, traits in which it reflects its own sexual opposite.[78]

Power

Every subject's duty is the king's;

Shakespeare, *Henry V*

When the other person is not an object of desire, he is a stranger and a competitor. Relations of domination and submission provide a solution to conflictual situations between individuals and allow everyone the possibility of satisfying their desires according to their rank. We shall not treat the general and theoretical problems raised by the notions of domination and rank in animal groups. We shall only try to show the importance of the notion of domination in the fluctuating central state with a few examples. Rank and social hierarchy are integrated in the extracorporal space and influence the individual's corporal space, namely the hormonal secretions. Reciprocally, the latter help to establish the hierarchy.

Biology tells us that domination is a universal tendency in animal groups which have a social organization.[79] It only remains to list the factors that are associated with the power that some individuals exert over others, but do not necessarily explain it. Amongst these factors, those concerning sex are probably the most important.

Monkey nuts

A strongly hierarchical social structure characterizes most species of primates. This is a determining factor in individual behaviour.

The composition and structure of a group of monkeys would seem to influence the individual's behaviour by acting first of all on its hormonal secretions. Many studies insist on the fact that the aggressiveness and sexual activity of leaders are almost always associated with a high testosterone level in the blood.[80] It is difficult to say whether the social rank determines the level of testosterone, or vice versa.

In the social group we find once again the reciprocal exchange between the corporal and extracorporal components which characterizes the individual central state. Once again, time intervenes as a third party, regulating the relations between the other two. The hierarchical position of four monkeys A, B, C and D depends on the outcome of past conflicts. When A has beaten B, B has beaten C, and C has beaten D, it is apparently easy to understand who dominates and who is dominated, and what rank A, B, C and D occupy in the hierarchy. Neither weight nor strength, nor testosterone level, nor even the size of the testicles is directly responsible for rank, which is determined by what we might call a true collective central state which integrates all these factors in the light of the history of the group.

We would not wish to be accused of speaking exclusively of males in relation to power. There exists a comparable hierarchy amongst females and even between male and female monkeys.

Sex and social rank

A study of a group of talapoin monkeys by the Cambridge group will allow us to make a few remarks.[81] In these experiments, the monkeys were put together in groups of four males and four females. The females were spayed and made desirable at differing intervals by means of oestradiol implants.

When the females receive oestradiol, male desire flares up and is shown by repeated inspections of the female genitalia. The chiefs indulge in frequent and detailed inspections, while those of lower ranks are brief and furtive. Copulation and ejaculation are the privilege of the higher-ranking monkeys. As for the females, their invitations are addressed to the leaders. The latter are the almost exclusive beneficiaries of the seduction ploys of the love-struck females. Under these circumstances, masturbation is the only resource of the lower-ranking males.

If a low-ranking male is left alone with receptive females, however, it displays intense sexual activity and is as efficient in this field as its higher-ranking colleagues. If the group is re-formed, each member returns to its former rank in the hierarchy.

Hormones and social rank

If a dominant male is castrated, this deprives it of sexual activity but not of its rank. A testosterone injection restores the sexual vigour of the castrated leader. On the other hand, a low-ranking male has nothing to lose or gain from castration and hormone injection. A large injection of testosterone does increase the female's interest, but only results in intensifying the low-ranking male's onanistic tendencies and multiplying the number of beatings it receives.

The females also have their hierarchy, which is very different from that of the males. If oestradiol is injected into a spayed dominant female it restores its power of attraction and increases male attention. The only honour an injection of oestradiol confers on a low-ranking female is the doubtful one of receiving more copious beatings from its hierarchical superiors.

Conversely, the social hierarchy seems to have an influence on the internal state of the animal. The level of testosterone in the blood is not an absolute reflection of rank. However, it seems that prolactin, the hormone which inhibits fertility, and cortisol, the hormone released under stress, are at lower levels in males and females of high rank. Thus it would seem that fertility and serenity are the attributes of power in monkey society.[82]

By using anthropomorphic language to speak of monkeydom and the relationship between sex and power there, we did not wish to denounce the monkey surviving in man's make-up, but . . .

It is not just literary admiration which made us quote Lou Andreas-Salomé and Albert Cohen at the beginning of this chapter.

> Baboonery everywhere, baboonery and animal admiration of strength . . . passionate crowds of slave baboons, trembling crowds in orgasm when the square-jawed dictator appears, he who is licensed to distribute death . . . strength-loving baboons, those young American girls who invaded the Prince of Wales's compartment to caress the cushions which pillowed his posterior and who offered him a pair of pyjamas hand-stitched by each . . . What they call original sin is nothing more than the confused and shameful conscience we have of our baboonish nature and its awful affects.[83]

We could add the gangs of young suburban baboons who follow the petty chief with the big penis, or the baboonish cocktails or society parties where decorations and fat wallets are substituted for the penis as the objects of adoration for bejewelled females. Power and hierarchy undeniably intervene constantly in the regulation of relationships in the society of monkeys and men. We do not dispute the adaptive value of domination or reject its importance in the survival of the species. We only wish to underline what distinguishes power from love.

The former allows a man to die rich or forces him to live out his life in poverty and slavery. The latter leads to the discovery of oneself through the recognition of the other and allows those famous words to be pronounced, that bubble lost in the whirlpool of the humours: 'Listen to me . . . I love you'.

Notes

1 J. Kristeva, *Histoires d'amour*, Paris, 1983.
2 S.R.N. Chamfort, *Maximes et Pensées*, VI, 359, 1803.
3 F. Roeder et al., 'The stereotaxic treatment of pedophilic, homosexuality and other sexual deviations', in *Proceedings of the Second International Conference of Psychosurgery*, Copenhagen, 1972.
4 F.A. Beach, 'Sexual attractivity, proceptivity and receptivity in female mammals', *Horm. Behav.*, 7, 105–38, 1976.
5 H. Persky et al., 'Plasma testosterone level and sexual behavior of couples', *Arch. Sex. Behav.*, 7, 157–73.
6 B. Bohus, 'The influence of pituitary neuropeptides on sexual behavior', in *Hormones et Sexualité*, L'Expansion scientifique française, 'Problèmes actuels d'endocrinologie et de nutrition', No. 21, Paris, 1977.
7 B.S. MacEwan, 'Neural gonadal steroid actions', *Science*, 211, 1303–11, 1981.
8 C.D. Toran-Allerand, 'Gonadal hormones and brain development: cellular aspects of sexual differentiation', *Am. Zool.*, 18, 553–65, 1978.

9   S.M. Breedlove and A.P. Arnold, 'Hormone accumulation in a sexually dimorphic motor nucleus of the rat spinal cord', *Science*, 210, 564–6, 1980.

10 S.M. Breedlove, 'Hormonal control of the anatomical specificity of motoneuron-to-muscle innervation in rats', *Science*, 227, 1357–9, 1985.

11 B.R. Komisaruk et al., 'Genital sensory field: enlargement by oestrogen treatment in female rats', *Science*, 178, 1295–8, 1972.

12 D.B. Kelley, 'Auditory and vocal nuclei of the frog brain concentrate sex hormones', *Science*, 207, 553–5, 1980.

13 N. Tinbergen, *The Study of Instinct*, New York, 1951.

14 A.P. Arnold, 'Quantitative analysis of sex differences in hormone accumulation in the zebra finch brain: methodological and theoretical issues', *J. Comp. Neurol.*, 189, 421–36, 1980.

15 MacEwen, 'Neural gonadal steroid actions'.

16 Ibid.

17 R.M. MacLeod, M.O. Thorner and U. Scapagnini (eds), *Prolactin, Basic and Clinical Correlates*, Berlin, 1985.

18 M.O. Thorner, 'Prolactin: clinical physiology and the significance and management of hyperprolactinemia', in L. Martini and G.M. Besser (eds), *Clinical Neuroendocrinology*, New York, 1977.

19 C.A. Dudley et al., 'Inhibition of lordosis behavior in the female rat by intraventricular infusion of prolactin and by chronic hyperprolactenemia', *Endocrinology*, 110, 677–9, 1982.

20 P. Riskind and R.L. Moss, 'Midbrain central gray: LH-RH infusion enhances lordotic behavior in oestrogen primed ovariectomized rats', *Brain Res. Bull.*, 4, 203–5, 1979.

21 M. Al Satli et al., 'Involvement of dopaminergic mechanisms in the control of ovulation and sexual receptivity in cyclic female rats', *Biol. Behav.*, 6, 305–15, 1981.

22 M.M. Foreman and R.L. Moss, 'Effects of subcutaneous injection and intrahypothalamic infusion of releasing hormones upon lordotic response to repetitive coital stimulation', *Horm. Behav.*, 8, 219–34, 1977.

23 D. Samuel et al., *Aging of the Brain*, New York, 1983.

24 A play by Pablo Picasso, written about 1920.

25 M.L. Stefanick et al., 'Penile reflexes in intact rats following anesthetization of the penis and ejaculation', *Physiol. Behav.*, 31, 63–5, 1983.

26 Stendhal, *On Love*, London, 1957. Stendhal turns the fiasco into a fine art.

27 J.P. Changeux, *Neuronal Man*, New York, 1985.

28 R.G. Heath, 'Pleasure and brain activity in man. Deep and surface electro-encephalograms during orgasm', *J. Nerv. Ment. Dis.*, 154, 3–18, 1972.

29 R.L. Doty et al., 'Communication of gender from human breath odors: relationship to perceived intensity and pleasantness', *Horm. Behav.*, 13–22, 1982.

30 E. Alleva et al., 'Effets d'une expérience olfactive précoce sur les préférences sexuelles de deux souches de souris consanguines', *Biol. Behav.*, 6, 73–8, 1981.

31 J. Herbert, 'Behavioral patterns', in C.R. Austin and R.V. Short (eds), *Reproduction in Mammals*, London, 1972.

32 O.R. Floody et al., 'Testosterone stimulates ultrasound production by male hamsters', *Horm. Behav.*, 12, 164–71, 1979.

33 A.C. Kinsey et al., *Sexual Behavior in the Human Female*, Philadelphia, PA, 1953.

34 D.G. Steel and C.E. Walker, 'Male and female differences in reaction to erotic

stimuli as related to sexual adjustment', *Arch. Sex. Behav.*, 3, 459–70, 1974.
35   W.H. Davenport, 'Sex in cross cultural perspective', in F.A. Beach (ed.), *Human Sexuality in Four Perspectives*, Baltimore, MD, 1972.
36   D. Symons, 'Precis of the evolution of human sexuality', *Behav. Brain Sci.*, 3, 171–214, 1980.
37   G.E. King, 'Pair bonding and proximal mechanisms', *Behav. Brain Sci.*, 3, 191–2, 1980.
38   W. Rowan, 'Relation of light to bird migration and developmental changes', *Nature, Lond.*, 115, 494–5, 1925. Rowan had not understood the role of light in sexual function. This was demonstrated by Jacques Benoit in J. Benoit, 'Activation sexuelle obtenue chez le canard par l'éclairement artificiel pendant la période du repos génital', *C.R. Acad. Sci.*, 199, 1671–3, 1934.
39   Herbert, 'Behavioral patterns'.
40   Ibid.
41   E.O. Wilson, *Sociobiology: The New Synthesis*, Cambridge, MA, 1975.
42   F.D. Burton, 'Sexual climax in female *Macaca mulatta*', in *Proceedings of the Third International Congress of Primatology*, Basle, 1971.
43   Symons, 'Evolution of human sexuality'.
44   Ibid.
45   C.S. Ford, *A Comparative Study of Human Reproduction*, New Haven, CT, 1945.
46   Kinsey et al., *Sexual Behavior in the Human Female*.
47   Symons, 'Evolution of human sexuality'.
48   S. Hansen et al., 'A daily rhythm in the behavioral sensitivity of the female rat to oestradiol', *J. Endocrinol.*, 77, 381–8, 1978.
49   C.E. MacCormack and R. Sridaran, 'Timing of ovulation in rats during exposure to continuous light: evidence for a circadian rhythm of luteinizing hormone secretion', *J. Endocrinol.*, 76, 135–44, 1978.
50   Herbert, 'Behavioral patterns'.
51   'Desire is a longing for absent things', Saint Augustine, *Letters*, London, 1872.
52   J.R. Wilson et al., 'Modification in the sexual behavior of male rats produced by changing the stimulus female', *J. Comp. Physiol. Psychol.*, 56, 636–44, 1963.
53   J.C. Schwartz et al., 'Modulation of receptor mechanisms in the CNS: hyper and hyposensitivity to catecholamines', *Neuropharmacology*, 17, 665–85, 1978.
54   A. Jost, 'Development of sexual characteristics', *Science*, 6, 67–71, 1970.
55   N.J. MacLusky and F. Naftolin, 'Sexual differentiation of the central nervous system', *Science*, 211, 1294–1302, 1981.
56   MacEwen, 'Neural gonadal steroid actions'.
57   Ibid.
58   P.G. Davis and R.J. Barfield, 'Activation of masculine sexual behavior by intracranial oestradiol benzoate implants in male rats', *Neuroendocrinology*, 28, 217–27, 1979.
59   G. Dörner et al., 'Homosexuality in female rats following testosterone implantation in the anterior hypothalamus', *J. Reprod. Fertil.*, 17, 173–5, 1968.
60   J. Crichton-Browne, 'On the weight of the brain and its component parts in the insane', *Brain*, 2, 42–67, 1880.
61   Studies by Jurgutis (1957), quoted in the Russian edition of Blinkov and Glezer

(*The Human Brain in Figures and Tables*, New York, 1968), have shown that the average length of the left hemisphere of the cerebellum of an adult man is 61.32 ± 0.30 mm compared with 62.08 ± 0.28 mm for the right hemisphere. In woman, there is practically no asymmetry: 58.22 ± 0.23 mm on the left compared with 58.25 ± 0.22 mm on the right. A woman's brain is smaller and less asymmetrical than a man's.

62 A. Buffery and J. Gray, 'Sex difference in the development of spatial and linguistic skills', in C. Ounsted and D. Taylor (eds), *Gender Differences, their Ontogeny and their Significance*, Edinburgh, 1972.

63 J. McGlone, 'Sex differences in human brain asymmetry: a critical survey', *Behav. Brain Sci.*, 3, 215–63, 1980.

64 Ibid.

65 Ibid.

66 R. Harter Kraft, 'Lateral specialization and verbal/spatial ability in preschool children: age, sex and familial handedness differences', *Neuropsychologia*, 22, 319–35, 1984.

67 R.A. Gorski et al., 'Evidence for the existence of a sexually dimorphic nucleus in the preoptic area of the rat', *J. Comp. Neurol.*, 193, 529–39, 1980.

68 F.W. van Leeuwen et al., 'Vasopressin cells in the bed nucleus of the stria terminalis of the rat. Sex differences and the influence of androgens', *Brain Res.*, 325, 391–4, 1985.

69 D.W. Pfaff, 'Neurobiological mechanisms of sexual motivation', in D.W. Pfaff (ed.), *The Physiological Mechanisms of Motivation*, New York, 1982.

70 Ibid.

71 MacLusky and Naftolin, 'Sexual differentiation'.

72 G. Dörner et al., 'Prevention of demasculinization and feminization of the brain in prenatally stressed male rats by perinatal androgen treatment', *Exp. Clin. Endocrinol.*, 81, 88–90, 1983.

73 G. Dörner et al., 'Stressful events in prenatal life of bi and homosexual men', *Exp. Clin. Endocrinol.*, 81, 83–7, 1983.

74 Ibid.

75 J. Money and A.A. Ehrhardt, *Man and Woman, Boy and Girl: The Differentiation and Dimorphism of Gender Identity from Conception to Maturity*, Baltimore, MD, 1972.

76 Herbert, 'Behavioral patterns'. The description of cases of pseudo-hermaphrodites observed in Central America seems to contradict Money's opinion. These genetically male individuals are born with female external genital organs because of an enzyme deficiency (5-α-reductase). These children are brought up as girls, but at puberty, perhaps because of a higher testosterone secretion, the girls change into boys. These adolescents accept themselves as boys and use their new male organs quite normally, which counters the idea that gender identity is linked to social factors (J. Imperato-McGinley et al., 'Androgens and the evolution of male-gender identity among male pseudo-hermaphrodites with 5-α-reductase deficiency', *New Engl. J. Med.*, 300, 1233–7, 1979).

77 Herbert, 'Behavioral patterns'.

78 Lou Andreas-Salomé, *Eros*, Paris, 1984.

79 On dominance, see I.S. Bernstein, 'Dominance: the baby and the bathwater', *Behav. Brain Sci.*, 4, 419–57, 1981.

80 I.S. Bernstein et al., 'Behavioral and environmental events influencing primate testosterone levels', *J. Human. Evol.*, 3, 517–25, 1974.

81 E.B. Keverne, 'Sexual and aggressive behavior in social groups of talapoin monkeys', in *Sex Hormones and Behavior*, Amsterdam, 1979.
82 L.A. Bowman et al., 'Suppression of oestrogen-induced LH surges by social subordination in talapoin monkeys', *Nature, Lond.*, 275, 56–8, 1978.
83 A. Cohen, *Belle de Seigneur*, Paris, 1968.

12

The Smile at the Foot of the Ladder

> Now that my ladder's gone
> I must lie down where all the ladders start,
> In the foul rag-and-bone shop of the heart.
>> W.B. Yeats, *The Circus Animals' Desertion*

Shall I climb up, wait, or walk away? Here are three of the possible courses of action for someone at the foot of a ladder, that symbolic representation of the world which can take on the shape of a promise of freedom or a terrifying obstacle. Here we are confronted with the ultimate passion. After the passion of the body expressed in hunger and thirst, after the passion which feeds on love and power, here is the passion of the being in the world. A hostile or benevolent world with which the fluctuating central state is faced.

At the foot of the ladder you can smile, cry or shake with fear, but these are just words to describe what we call an emotion. An emotion is nothing more than the changing face of the central state. A glance, a blush, a beating of the heart, a dilation of the blood vessels are just the physical manifestations of the body running through the boring catalogue of human emotions. About as interesting as a description of the stones on a New Hampshire farm, according to William James.[1]

Just as the description of a horse's gallop, no matter how perfect, cannot tell us what a horse is, so the portrait of an emotion cannot inform us of the nature of the being who feels that emotion. If we consider that emotion is a manifestation of the being in the world, we must accept that emotion does not exist as a bodily phenomenon, since a body cannot be moved for lack of the ability to confer a meaning on its own manifestations. To paraphrase Sartre, emotion expresses in its own way the whole human consciousness, or, on the existential plane, human reality. Emotion can only be approached, therefore, through psychological phenomenology. It falls outside the field of biology with its systematizations based on the exclusive observation of body movements. Psychology will immediately look beyond vascular or respiratory phenomena to the meaning of joy or sadness. But as this meaning is not an external reality stuck like a label onto joy or sadness, as it exists only in so far as it appears and is assumed by humans, psychology will question consciousness itself, since joy is only joy in so far as it appears to itself as such.[2]

Such a position, however well founded it might be from an anthropological point of view, is obviously unacceptable for a biologist. A recent attempt to reconcile introspection and behavioural biology does not seem very convincing.[3] Panksepp is convinced that the study of emotions in men and animals is impoverished by our inability to combine both sources of knowledge. He believes that recent progress in neurobiology means that anthropomorphism can become a useful strategy for understanding basic psychological processes in animals.

This optimistic stance leads to the description of four basic emotions, expectation, rage, fear and panic, each of which is supported by an executive neuronal circuit in the hypothalamus. We do not wish to deny the existence of such circuits or their importance in the regulation of the passions, but to refute the excessive nature of such a systematization, which merely leads to the construction of yet another unmarried machine, as sterile as all its predecessors.

But if we limit ourselves to considering the emotions of sadness, fear, joy, disgust, surprise etc., as a specific bodily message, they are reduced to the status of partial elements of the fluctuating central state engaged as a whole in its passion. In our opinion, there is no need to revise the traditional opposition between the James–Lange 'peripheral theory', which considers the emotions as secondary to the physiological manifestations of the body, and the 'central' theory, which considers them as the products of cerebral activity.

Does this mean, as Mandler suggests, that the best way of studying emotion is to ignore it?[4] We do not think so. The biological significance of emotion, however, must remain subordinate to the biological significance of the adaptive passion of which it is part. We shall mainly study the expression of emotions on the subject's face, where they are a communicative element of the extracorporal space in the fluctuating central state.

The fluctuating central state and the world

Each basic emotion has a background of nervous and hormonal changes peculiar to it.

J.P. Henry and P.M. Stephens, *Stress, Health and the Social Environment*

The world is not taken here in the sense of an external reality cluttered with stimuli which can trigger individual responses. We do not wish to ignore such a reality, which provides the basis for the associative world of reflexes and learning processes, any more than we do the cognitive world, which is reality organized by knowledge. What we call the passionate world is a projection of desire through space. It is the domain of subjectivity.

By subjectivity we mean the fluctuating central state in so far as it is simultaneously the creator and the creature of the desiring being. It will be remembered that desire is the source of primordial feelings and that these evolve along a continuum from positive to negative, which allows us to consider joy and sadness, surprise and boredom, enjoyment and disgust, calm and anxiety, pride and shame etc. as modes of subjectivity.

The passionate world is first of all that of the mother, the starting-point of all later subjectivity. Then come the territory and its occupants, the family and fellow creatures, various types of social organization and finally a universe of objects which are sources of aggression, frustration or reward.

Subjectivity manifests itself in the three dimensions of the central state. Within the corporal space, it accompanies the movements of the organs, the secretions of the glands and the interplay of neuronal circuits which all allow the organism to adapt to the contingencies of the world. In the extracorporal space, subjectivity is to be seen in facial expressions and gestures which form the basis of systems of communication between individuals and establish intersubjectivity. We shall come back to this dimension of the central state. The temporal dimension represents the adaptive fluctuations of the central state throughout life. Some modes can be learnt, such as fear or resignation, while others are inscribed in the very functioning of the organs and lead to illness. This gigantic field, which covers the whole of psychic and somatic pathology, will not be treated here, as a brief treatment could hardly do justice to it.

The world of the mother

The young know their mother before meeting her. Immediately after birth, the baby rat crawls blindly but directly, and with the determination of one who knows, towards the teats of its mother. Pulling a young rat away from its mother gives much the same sensation as pulling fruit off a tree; you need to give a good tug to detach it. We know the biological factors behind this attachment. If the olfactory mucosa of a baby rat is destroyed at birth by the intranasal injection of zinc sulphate, it is incapable of finding the teat and rapidly dies of hunger, unless the mother eats it, in which case death is even quicker. If the teats of the mother are washed with detergent, the young can no longer find them. If these same teats are then smeared with amniotic fluid collected at the birth, the young can suckle again normally. For the young to suckle normally from birth, the mother in fact licks the amniotic fluid which covers its new-born and then licks its own teats. The young, attracted by the smell, crawl up and start feeding. The pheromone responsible for this has been isolated. It is methyl bisulphite, which is also found in the saliva of the mother and the young. This explains the mutual licking which strengthens attachment.[5]

The natural smell can be masked by the synthetic smell of citrol. When this essence is injected into the uterine horn of the mother some time before the birth of the young, they choose the citrol-smelling teats. If a choice of several mothers is given, they will adopt those with citrol-seasoned teats.[6] The story does not stop there. As adults, these rats will show a marked preference for females with a citrol-perfumed vagina. Animals with an experience of citrol at birth take twice as long to ejaculate with ordinary females as with citrol-perfumed ones. We simply wish to recall the importance of this perfume of infancy in the sexual attachment of the adult, without taking the liberty of concluding that every male seeks the image (in this case olfactory) of the mother in the female partners chosen in adulthood.[7]

The young make the mother, just as the mother makes the young. If a virgin female rat or deserted mother is repeatedly presented with new-born young for several days running, it will at first refuse to accept them, but will finally adopt maternal behaviour, soon followed by lactation.[8] In normal conditions, i.e. after giving birth, maternal behaviour springs spontaneously within the maternal central state from the meeting of the corporal dimension represented by oxytocin and progesterone with the extracorporal dimension embodied by the young.[9] Maternal behaviour is always the result of an interaction between mother and young in which mutual licking plays an important part, as we have seen. The mother is attracted to its young by the smell given off by the secretions of their preputial glands. This smell is stronger in young males, which may explain both the greater attraction that the mother feels for them and their future behavioural dimorphism.

This attachment between mother and infant is to be found in all species of mammal. In primates and man it begins in the minutes which follow birth and lasts months, even years, throughout an extraordinarily complex system of exchanges.[10] Smell gives way to sight and touch, according to a series of interactions programmed in advance in the brains of mother and young.

Klauss,[11] and more recently De Chateau,[12] have observed mother and infant during post-partum, and then periodically during the first months of the infant's life. During the first minutes (mother and child are alone), the mother lies on her side and places the child opposite her. Their eyes are on the same plane. Here is the first face-to-face encounter, the first exchange of looks and smiles. Next come the kisses, the caresses of the mother's hands on the baby's body, the creation of a world made for two out of sight, sound and touch. The more intense the contact is during the first forty-five minutes, the stronger the attachment to the breast will be during the first feed.[13] The earlier and the more prolonged the first encounter is, the more frequent and attentive the mother's care will be in the following months. Reciprocally, a baby who benefits from this kind of treatment will cry less and smile more. Klauss observes that the difference is even more striking if the baby is a boy.

Early contact is also a determining factor in the way a mother holds her baby. Eighty per cent hold the baby on the left-hand side of the breast, whereas a mother deprived of her infant during the first twenty-four hours will most frequently carry it abnormally on the right-hand side. This 'right-side' baby will subsequently need twice as much medical care as a 'left-side' baby. De Chateau concludes that there exists a 'biogrammar' in the brains of the mother and child which fixes attachment behaviour between them in the same way as syntax rules determine language use. The sequence of innate acts would seem to be influenced by what actually happens between the two partners in the first post-partum hours.

Desire inaugurates the relationship of the subject to the world with this mother–infant attachment, the first test which determines the rest. Awakening desire is specified by its first object, the mother. The mother's desire enters into resonance with it and creates the basis for intersubjective communication. Bowlby, in his work on attachment and loss, has magisterially defined this primordial expression of desire.[14]

The link between mother and child is next extended to brothers and sisters, and then to other members of the social group. For Harlow,[15] as well as for Hamburg,[16] these links and those with lovers and spouses, not to mention the equally strong if more distant attachment to an ideology, institution, political party or country, are only ramifications of one basic behaviour type. Traces of this are to be found in the corporal contacts which materialize all these links, from handshakes to kisses, caresses and beyond. However, any breaking of attachment represents the worst aggression an individual has to bear, and has the greatest consequences on his health. If we fix a scale of seriousness with which to measure the negative impact of such events, the worst is the death of the spouse (100), followed by divorce (79), separation (65) and the death of a relation (63), all of which represent a kind of tearing away, a special kind of loss.[17]

We may now better understand that the passion we are concerned with here is above all the management of those links which unite us to others. But the world is also the territory where those links are expressed.

The world of the father

Attachment is the mother's realm, and territory is the father's. It is his role to widen the family circle and mark out the ground onto which the child will progressively sally forth. The father is not alone here, however. There are other male or female individuals who navigate amidst certain privileged zones, bristling with threatening objects, abysses and walls. The society of others with its hierarchy of chiefs and underlings is to be found in this territory, which is also characterized by physical phenomena such as heat, cold and noise. Faced with this threatening or comforting world, the central state fluctuates, adapting itself to the circumstances.

The adaptive passion

The adrenal glands are at the heart of the adaptive mechanisms. Each of them is in fact a double gland with a duality which reflects two possible modes of being in the world. In the centre is the adrenal medulla, the gland of aggression, combat and flight. On the periphery is the adrenal cortex, the gland of submission and resignation. One gland is for winning and the other is for losing, two opposed solutions in the existential negotiation which most often leads to compromise. This endocrinological Manicheism should not hide the complexity of the facts. The adrenal gland is only a relay for feedback systems involving the hypophysis and the different levels in the hierarchy of the central nervous system. Hormones other than adrenal ones are involved in adaptation. Inside the brain, the play of neurohormones reproduces the complexity of the peripheral phenomena.

The adrenal medulla is an integral part of the orthosympathetic nervous system and represents a differentiation of it in gland form. Each time an individual acts, the sympathetic system intervenes by giving logistic support. This system releases the catecholamines, adrenaline and noradrenaline, the former being above all secreted by the adrenal medulla, the latter by the sympathetic nerve terminals. The system is solicited each time an emergency demands an immediate reaction from the organism. Faced with a threat, whether it is an enemy or a dangerous situation, an individual can choose to fight it out or run away. In both cases, the response is action. The decision to stand and fight means that immediate victory is considered possible. The decision to run away means only that this possibility is being deferred.

Noradrenaline makes superficial blood vessels contract and diverts blood to the muscles. Adrenaline makes the heart beat faster and stronger, and mobilizes the reserve sugar in the liver. Thanks to the action of these two hormones, fuel and oxygen pour into the liver and towards the cells to help satisfy the increase in energy demand. They are thus complementary in organizing the energy response of the organism, but appear to have a different significance as far as passion is concerned. They are released in different proportions according to the situation that the individual is confronted with. This can be seen in the work of Frankenhaeuser and Gardell.[18] Certain workers in a sawmill are subjected to the tyranny of their machine which forces them to carry out alternating movements that are not only rapid but also very dangerous. The adrenaline level in the blood of these men is higher than that of the maintenance workers in the same mill. Noradrenaline is released massively each time a worker gets cramp or feels annoyed. This seems to corroborate the old and very controversial hypothesis put forward by Funkestein that adrenaline would seem to be associated with fear and noradrenaline with annoyance. The psychological analysis can be carried further by observing that basketball players secrete noradrenaline when they are on the court playing, and adrenaline when they are on the bench watching. In short, adrenaline would seem to be released whenever a situation is marked by uncertainty or lack of control, whereas noradrenaline release apparently accompanies determined action. This association of adrenaline with fear and flight corresponds fairly closely to what we shall say later about the adrenal cortex. The cortisol secreted by the adrenal cortex helps noradrenaline to be transformed into adrenaline. There remains an essential difference, however. Adrenaline may represent a loss of control, but it nevertheless continues to favour action such as flight, for example. This is not the case with cortisol.

When an individual accepts defeat, his incapacity to react is accompanied by the release of cortisol by the adrenal cortex. An increase in cortisol secretion is to be noticed in situations of stress. Stress is linked to an infinite number of physical or psychological factors and is characterized by the inability to act which leads to depression. Must cortisol consequently be associated with the world of nervous breakdowns? Not necessarily, because depression and resignation are not always the expression of an existential loss, but may merely be the best means of surviving after a failure.[19] Cortisol allows a long-term adaptation by reconstituting the hepatic sugar reserves, helping the action of catecholamines and slowing down the immune defences of the organism. However, gastric ulcers may be the price to pay.

Each time a new situation appears (when a monkey changes cages or a civil servant changes desks), each time frustration is felt (when a monkey is deprived of food while others around it are eating), each time uncertainty is great or certainty unpleasant, an abundant secretion of cortisol shows that there is a state of stress (figure 59). Weiss has shown that if it is possible to act, stress does not develop. When two rats simultaneously receive an electric shock and one of them can stop the stimulation by moving a wheel, only the passive rat develops a high level of cortisol in the blood as well as gastric ulcers. Two rats placed on an electrified grid rapidly develop stress with a high level of cortisol. Strange as it may seem, if the two animals are allowed to fight each other, their cortisol level drops dramatically.[20] The possibility of action, even violent and indirect action as far as the stress agent is concerned, inhibits the cortisolic response. Social factors are also a determining factor in cortisol level. Dominated individuals who by definition are uncertain about the future, generally have a higher level of cortisol than dominant individuals. This is true of all species where power means security. What about man?

What we have said about the opposition between the respective adaptive functions of the adrenal medulla and the adrenal cortex is applicable not only to the two glands but also to their regulation systems, involving the different levels of the neuroendocrine hierarchy. At the top of the pyramid, the frontal cortex, confronted with a threatening situation, would seem to choose a strategy according to the problem and the personality of the subject.[21] Depending on whether the situation is under control or not, the prefrontal cortex would seem to bring into play either the sympathetic adrenal medulla axis through the amygdala and posterior hypothalamus, or

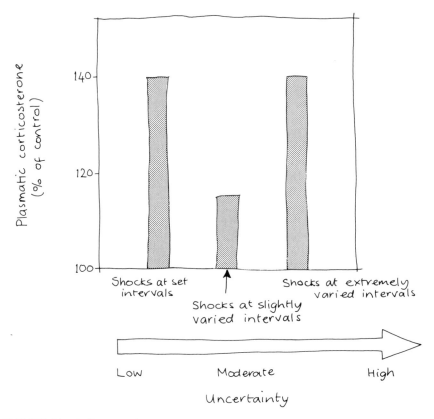

FIGURE 59   Influence of uncertainty on cortisol secretion in the rat. Three groups
of rats are submitted to a series of ten electric shocks given at regular three-
minute intervals (minimal uncertainty), at extremely irregular intervals (maximal
uncertainty) and at slightly varied intervals (moderate uncertainty). Cortisol
secretion is maximal in cases of minimal or extreme uncertainty, and minimal in
cases of moderate uncertainty. (Quoted by R. Dantzer, 'Physiologie des émotions', in
J. Delacour (ed.), *Neurobiologie des Comportements*, Paris, Hermann, 1984.)

the adrenal cortex axis through the hippocampus, hypothalamus and
adenohypophysis. The first system follows a scenario in which the situation
is under perfect control. The amygdala intervenes in deciding on the value of
the stimulus which must be fled from or taken charge of in a concert of
sympathetic activation.[22] The hippocampus is the star of the second
scenario, as it is the specialist on territorial questions and social convention.
The hippocampus is the memory of the subject in the world and
consequently has the maps and instruction sheets. It exerts permanent
control over the secretion of corticotrophin-releasing hormone (CRH) by
the hypothalamus. This hormone in its turn controls the secretion

of adrenocorticotropic hormone (ACTH) which finally regulates the release of cortisol by the adrenal cortex. Let us briefly recall that retroactive control is exerted at each nervous and endocrine stage on this axis. In the hippocampus there are receptors for the glucocorticoids located in the neurons. The balance of the system would be endangered by any disturbance of these controls. According to Carroll, in cases of primary depression the hippocampus appears not to carry out its normal action of slowing down adrenocortical response because of some breakdown in feedback.[23] Even if this explanation is contradicted by many data, we can retain the general idea of an illness being produced by an adaptive mechanism which goes beyond its own limits because of failures in the control systems. Retroactive control failure can be caused by the disappearance of receptors. If these are solicited by an excessive quantity of cortisol during prolonged and repeated stressful stimulations, their number drops.[24] In the long term the very survival of hippocampal neurons could be endangered by the absence of corticosteroid receptors. We would then witness the passage from adaptive passion to ageing and cell death.

After reading these explanations, one could be forgiven for thinking that the passionate world is governed by two neuroendocrine axes only, and that their subtle balance decides on who is a winner and who is a loser. We know in fact that it is impossible to reduce a passionate being to the confrontation of two hormones. All hormone secretions probably contribute to some extent to the adaptive functions. The traditional view that the activation of the neuro-hypophyso-adrenocortical axis automatically means that the other endocrine systems are at rest is almost never confirmed. The thyroid axis, the gonadal axis, growth hormone, prolactin and insulin, for example, are diversely solicited in different situations. Endomorphines, which play an important part in the brain, are also released on the periphery by the adenohypophysis in the form of β-endorphins and by the adrenal medulla in the form of encephalins.

The adrenal cortex and adrenal medulla are therefore not the only actors in the passionate dramas which unfold in parallel on the periphery and within the brain. Adrenaline and noradrenaline of adrenal origin do not cross the haemato-encephalic barrier, but are released both on the periphery and in the central nervous system, where they imply the activation of the desire systems. ACTH, which stimulates the secretion of cortisol is also, as we have seen (figure 16), manufactured in the brain from a precursor common to several endomorphines. Its intracerebral actions, perhaps by influencing memory and learning, become part of those systemic and hormonal actions which are capable of influencing brain function.

The complexity of neuronal and hormonal endomorphine intervention in adaptive passions is also easy to imagine. It is enough to peruse the non-exhaustive list of opioid neuropeptides formed from only three precursors (appendix 5). One of the several roles of endorphins could be to constitute a system of protection against the nastiness of the world. After a painful stimulation, for example, the release of endorphins in the brain would seem to prevent pain lasting longer than is necessary for it to fulfil its role of alarm system. According to Bolles, fear would seem to be the emotional translation of an endorphin-induced state which inhibits pain in order to make flight easier.[25] Similarly, endorphins would seem to prevent aversive behaviour from setting in too easily, making the individual more resistant to the unpleasantness of the world.[26] As always in matters of adaptation, certain excesses can lead to a pathological situation . . .

To each of the passionate versions of the fluctuating central state there would seem to correspond a profile of hormonal secretions and cerebral activities which theoretically should allow us to distinguish between them. These neuroendocrine factors would seem to evolve on a continuum between a pleasant positive pole and an unpleasant negative pole. The level of cortisol in the blood, for example, would seem to oscillate between very high values corresponding to deep despair and low values accompanying the euphoria characteristic of an exalting and well-controlled situation.[27]

There is no question of replacing a machine made of anatomical cogs and wheels with an equally unmarried magic potion which is supposed to explain the passionate fluctuations of a being by its chemical composition. A hormone does not make a passion. It is enough to observe the effects of an injection of adrenaline on a volunteer. The same quantity injected into different volunteers will result in euphoria or anger according to the situation that the subject finds himself in.[28] Therefore it is the whole central state of the subject, including the extracorporal space, which confers a special value upon the hormone level. In this context, the face of emotion takes on its true significance.

The face of the fluctuating central state

The facial expression of emotions constitutes an innate repertoire of signs by which communication is established by different individuals. There is a close correspondence between the biological signs of emotions and the facial expression of them. Rather than asking which depends on which, we should consider them as inseparable elements of the fluctuating central state. They show its essentially unitary nature.

On the face of it

To explain the facial expression of emotions, Darwin wrote that one must understand why different muscles are activated in different emotions, for example why the inner extremities of the eyebrows are raised and the corners of the mouth lowered when a person is suffering from grief or anxiety.[29] Darwin was right to think that a certain number of muscular contractions are enough to paint the precise emotional state of a subject. He based his remark on the contemporary work of Duchenne de Boulogne who wrote a book on facial expression and whose preface ends thus: 'I shall show how to paint the expressive lines of the human face correctly by using electrophysiological analysis and photography. These lines can be considered as a kind of alphabet used for the spelling out of physiognomy in movement'[30] (figure 60).

Without being able to give their biological significance, Darwin established that the emotions constitute a universal attribute of man independently of race or culture, that they are innate and that their trace can be found in the evolution of the species. Darwin's theory was strongly criticized when researchers in the social sciences began to give credit to the hypothesis that what can be read on a man's face is written there by culture. At a time when theories about learning in human behaviour were triumphant, the Darwinian theory of the universality and innate nature of facial expression seemed slightly indecent. Despite the 'cruel smile' of Asians evoked in order to uphold the culturalist thesis, nobody doubts today that the expression of emotions is universal. The same muscular contractions express anger, surprise or disgust in different peoples. We read emotions in the same way, whatever the face or culture concerned. Papuans who had never before seen Americans contracted the same muscles as them when they were asked to show what expression they would use if they lost a child.[31] Their faces were photographed, and when these photographs were subsequently shown to American students, the emotion seen in them was immediately identified as grief. These results do not totally eliminate the influence of culture on the expression of the emotions. It is obvious that education, rites and conventions can attenuate, disguise or, on the contrary, exaggerate the expression of an emotion.

For Hecuba!

Is it not monstrous that this player here,
But in a fiction, in a dream of passion,
Could force his soul so to his own conceit
That from her working all his visage wanned,
Tears in his eyes, distraction in his aspect,
A broken voice, and his whole function suiting
With forms to his conceit? And all for nothing.

Shakespeare, *Hamlet*

Professional actors with perfect control over their face muscles are given precise instructions and asked to represent six classic emotional expressions: anger, fear, grief, joy, disgust and surprise. Cardiac rhythm, temperature and cutaneous resistance are measured during the representation. Remarkable differences are to be observed according to the emotional expression represented. Cardiac rhythm rises when the subject represents anger, fear or grief, and slows down when the face expresses joy, disgust or surprise. Furthermore, it is possible to distinguish between grief and other negative emotions according to skin temperature which reflects blood flow

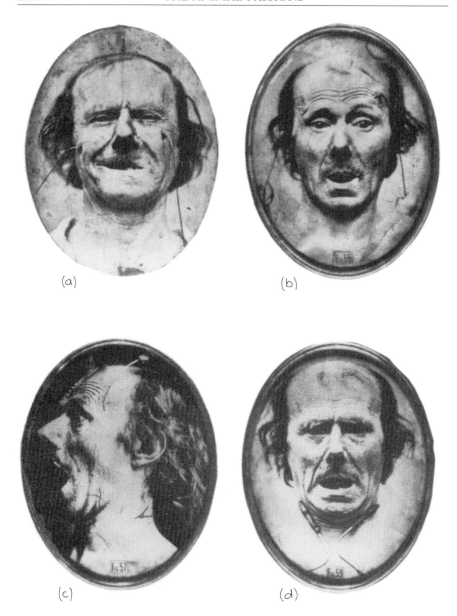

near the surface of the skin (figure 61). These results of the work of Paul Ekman contradict the cognitive theories which claim that a non-specific neurovegetative activation accompanies emotions of all kinds.

In these experiments, we notice that the subjects are moved because they appear to be moved. According to Ekman, the activity of the facial muscles would seem to trigger specific neurovegetative reactions directly, either by feedback of peripheral origin or by a connection between the motor programmes of the cerebral cortex and the hypothalamus.[32] These recent observations can be compared with a forgotten theory developed by the Frenchman Waynbaum (1907). According to this doctor, the contractions of the facial muscles, through the modifications in blood flow in the head which they cause and the resulting variations in irrigation of the regions of the brain, would seem to be responsible for the different sensations we feel under the influence of the emotions.[33] What we should conclude from Ekman's work is that a whole palette of humoral and neurovegetative modifications corresponds to the muscular repertoire of the emotions. Once again, the extracorporal dimension appears to be inseparable from the corporal dimension. Could there be a better example of the unity of the fluctuating central state?

Passion shared

In its first face-to-face encounter, the infant looks fixedly at its mother. Despite common belief, a baby is not blind. Its visual acuity is about 14 per

FIGURE 60   The expression of the emotions according to Duchenne de Boulogne. This nineteenth-century anatomist tried to obtain the expression of specific emotions by causing different face muscles to contract with the help of electrodes applied to the skin. We give here his commentary on the photographs of the results obtained from different stimulations (Duchenne de Boulogne, *Mécanisme de la physiologie humaine*):

(a) a comparative study of the different expressive lines of the greater and lesser zygomatic muscles . . . On the left, the lesser zygomatic muscle is contracted and the expression corresponds to moderate sadness or tenderness. On the right, the greater zygomatic muscle is moderately contracted, resulting in an expression of false laughter.

(b) a study of the combined moderate contraction of the frontal muscles and those responsible for the dropping of the lower jaw. The voluntary dropping of the lower jaw and the proportional electrical contraction of the frontal muscles express surprise. We feel that the subject has just been given some unexpected news, that he has seen something surprising.

(c) a study of the combined maximal contraction of the frontal muscles and those responsible for the dropping of the lower jaw. The maximal voluntary dropping of the lower jaw and the strong electrical contraction of the frontal muscles express astonishment and stupefaction.

(d) inexpressive contraction of these neck muscles which stretch the skin, rather like a curtain behind which the sternomastoid relief is hidden.

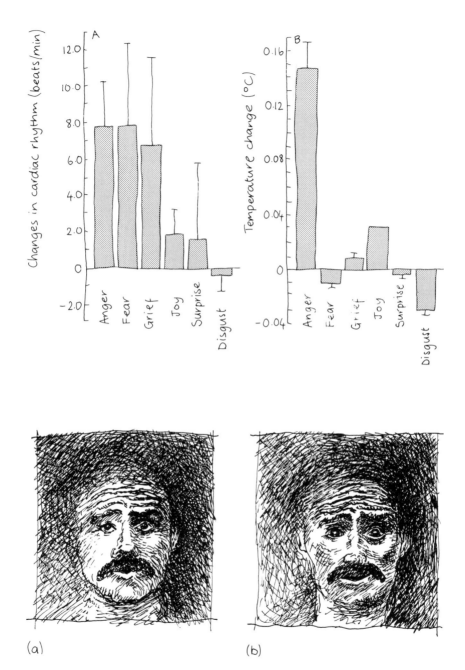

FIGURE 61 An actor is asked to carry out these instructions: (a) raise your eyebrows and pull them together; (b) now raise your eyelids; (c) stretch your lips out horizontally towards your ears. The results of the vegetative measurements are given in the upper part of the figure. On the left, the changes in cardiac rhythm and skin

High —— Skin
          temperature

High
= Anger

Low = Fear
        Grief

Cardiac
rhythm

Slow   Joy
       Disgust
       Surprise

(c)

temperature during different expressions are given. On the right is a diagram which
allows us to distinguish between facial expressions by using vegetative criteria.
(After Ekman et al., 'Autonomic nervous system activity'.)

cent. It is capable of recognizing the structure of a face. If it is presented with a simplified face consisting of two eyes, eyebrows, a nose and a mouth, it turns its head. Its movements are proportional to how nearly the model resembles a real face. If the eyes are put in the place of the mouth, the baby's rotational head movements diminish. All movement stops when the characteristic traits are suppressed.[34]

The recognition of the mother's face is innate in the baby, but the mother also shows innate behaviour. It is no exaggeration to say that the mother and her child are genetically prepared to exchange smiles. According to Henry, the smile is the cement used by mother and child to concretize the social unit.[35] A whole repertoire of expressions programmed before birth light up the face of the baby, which must content itself with the mother's voice and caresses in response to its smiles, because its vision is so imperfect. A baby under a month old can discriminate between speech sounds. The development of language, with its universal phonemes and similar word organization from one culture to another, shows that the child is programmed to speak with innate nervous structures which determine the learning of syntax rules and allow it to use pronouns correctly even if the parents make mistakes.[36] Expectation of a response is also programmed, in the same way as the expression itself. Brazelton has shown that when this expectation is not satisfied by an unresponsive mother, the baby is troubled and rapidly ceases to smile.[37]

Body language is not limited to facial expressions. Eibl-Eibesfeldt has shown that many other gestures are innate and form the framework for interpersonal communication.[38] The baby, in its interaction with the mother, has a variety of cerebral processes capable of expressing the functions of affective and referential communication. Programmed emotions, like language and gestures, form the basis of what socio-linguists call intersubjectivity. Functionalist linguistic theories recognize that we cannot understand how language functions if we are incapable of seeing more than the objective realities denoted by words.[39] What good would passions be if we could not express them in words? 'I am because I am moved and because you know it', as Descartes would not have said . . .

Notes

1 W. James, *The Principles of Psychology*, New York, 1890.
2 J.P. Sartre, *Esquisse d'une théorie des émotions*, Paris, 1965.
3 J. Panksepp, 'Toward a general psychobiological theory of emotions', *Behav. Brain Sci.*, 5, 407–67, 1982.
4 G. Mandler, 'The search for emotion', in L. Levi (ed.), *Emotions: Their Parameters and Measurement*, New York, 1975.
5 E. Blass, 'Prenatal and post-natal determinants of suckling and sexual behaviours in rats', in *Ethologie 85 (Nineteenth International Ethological Conference)*, Toulouse, 1985.
6 Ibid.

7 Ibid.

8 It is possible to induce lactation in virgin rats by presenting them repeatedly with young needing to be fed. After a few days, the female rat, which has already adopted maternal behaviour, begins to lactate (C. Montagnese, U. 176, INSERM, unpublished results). The structural modifications in the female rat brain described by Théodosis can then be observed (D.T. Théodosis et al., 'Possible morphological bases for synchronization of neuronal firing in the rat supraoptic nucleus during lactation', *Neuroscience*, 6, 919–29, 1981).

9 R.S. Bridges, 'A quantitative analysis of the role of dosage sequences, and duration of estradiol and progesterone exposure in the regulation of maternal behavior in the rat', *Endocrinology*, 114, 930–40, 1984.

10 R.A. Hinde, *Biological Bases of Human Social Behavior*, New York, 1974.

11 M.H. Klauss et al., 'Maternal attachment: importance of the first post-partum days', *New Engl. J. Med.*, 286, 460–3, 1972.

12 P. De Chateau, 'Neonatal care routines: influences on maternal and infant behavior and on breast feeding', Thesis, UMEA University, Switzerland, 1976.

13 Klauss et al., 'Maternal attachment'.

14 J. Bowlby, *Attachment and Loss*, London, 1970.

15 H.F. Harlow and M.K. Harlow, 'The affectional systems', in A.M. Schrier, H.F. Harlow and F. Stollnitz (eds), *Behavior of Non-Human Primates: Modern Research Trends*, New York, 1965.

16 B.A. Hamburg, 'The biosocial bases of sex difference', in S.L. Washburn and E.R. McCown (eds), *Perspectives on Human Evolution: Biosocial Perspectives*, New York, 1978.

17 R.H. Rahe, 'Subject's recent life changes and their future illness reports', *Ann. Clin. Res.*, 4, 250–65, 1972.

18 M. Frankenhaeuser and B. Gardell, 'Underload and overload in working life: outline of a multidisciplinary approach', *J. Human Stress*, 2, 35–46, 1976.

19 H. Anisman, 'Time dependent variations in aversively motivated behaviors: non associative effects of cholinergic and catecholaminergic activity', *Psychol. Rev.*, 82, 359–85, 1975.

20 R.L. Conner et al., 'Stress, lighting and neuroendocrine function', *Nature, Lond.*, 234, 584–6, 1971.

21 J.P. Henry and P.M. Stephens, *Stress, Health and the Social Environment*, New York, 1977. This remarkable work is a veritable mine of information not only on the biology of stress but also on the sociobiology of illnesses.

22 E.T. Rolls, *The Brain and Reward*, Oxford, 1975.

23 B.J. Carroll, 'Limbic system – adrenal cortex regulation in depression and schizophrenia', *Psychosom. Med.*, 38, 106–21, 1976.

24 R.M. Sapolsky and B.S. MacEwen, 'Adrenal steroids and the hippocampus: involvement in stress and aging,' in R. Isaacson and K. Pribram (eds), *The Hippocampus*, New York, 1985.

25 R.C. Bolles and M.S. Fanselow, 'A perceptual–defensive–recuperative method of fear and pain', *Behav. Brain Sci.*, 3, 291–323, 1980.

26 M.S. Fanselow and R.C. Bolles, 'Naloxone and shock elicited freezing in the rat', *J. Comp. Physiol. Psychol.*, 93, 736–44, 1979.

27 J.P. Henry and J.P. Mechan, 'Psychosocial stimuli, physiological specificity and cardio-vascular disease', in H. Weiner, M.A. Hojer and A.J. Stunkard (eds), *Brain Behavior and Bodily Diseases*, New York, 1981.

28 S. Schachter, 'Cognition and peripheralist – centralist controversies in

motivation and emotion', in S. Gazzaniga and C. Blakemore (eds), *Handbook of Psychobiology*, New York, 1975.

29   C.R. Darwin, *The Expressions of the Emotions in Man and Animals*, London, 1872.

30   G.B. Duchenne de Boulogne, *Mécanisme de la physionomie humaine ou analyse électrophysiologique de l'expression des passions*, Baillière, Paris, 1876.

31   P. Ekman, 'Universals and cultural differences in facial expressions of emotion', in J.K. Cole (ed.), *Nebraska Symposium on Motivation*, Lincoln, NB, 1972.

32   P. Ekman et al., 'Autonomic nervous system activity distinguishes among emotions', *Science*, 221, 1208–10, 1983.

33   R.B. Zajone, 'Emotion and facial efference: a theory reclaimed', *Science*, 228, 15–20, 1985. Ekman's work and the revamping of Waynbaum's theory give a scientific basis to physiognomy as a science which tries to establish links between temperament, character or personality, and facial features. If facial expressions exert an influence on the organism it may be worth our while to put a good face on things to keep ourselves in good health!

34   D.G. Freedman, *Human Infancy: An Evolutionary Perspective*, New York, 1974.

35   Henry and Stephens, *Stress, Health and the Social Environment*.

36   H.F. Harlow et al., *Psychology*, San Francisco, CA, 1971.

37   T.B. Brazelton et al., 'Early mother infant reciprocity', in *Parent–Infant Interactions (Ciba Foundation Symposium No. 33)*, Amsterdam, 1975.

38   Eibl-Eibesfeldt, *The Ethology of Man*, New York, 1975.

39   C. Travarthen, 'The structure of motives for human communication in infancy: a ground-plan for human ethology', in *Ethologie 85 (Nineteenth International Ethological Conference)*, Toulouse, 1985.

Epilogue

This book ends with the enigmatic face of the cavalier Rampin (figure 62). On his face we can see what is called a primitive smile, the expression to be found on the statues of all early civilizations. It is as if this representation were inscribed in the genetic programme of the artist exactly like the smile on the face of the new-born baby. As a manifestation of the artist's central state, this face sculpted from stone illustrates the miraculous balance of a being at the heart of a world in the making.

FIGURE 62   Archaic smile. Greek sculpture of the sixth century BC: 'Rampin head'.
(Courtesy The Louvre.)

Appendix 1

The Main Hormones in Man (Excluding the Hypothalamic Neurohormones)

Glands	Hormones	Targets or functions
Adenohypophysis	Prolactin (PRL)*	Mammary glands
	Growth hormone	Growth, metabolism
	Corticotropic hormone* (ACTH)	Adrenal cortex
	Luteinizing hormone (LH)	Gonads (ovaries, testicles)
	Follicle-stimulating hormone (FSH)	Gonads (ovaries, testicles)
	Thyroid-stimulating hormone (TSH)	Thyroid
	β-endorphin*	
Neurohypophysis	Vasopressin*	Kidney and blood vessels
	Oxytocin*	Mammary glands, uterus
Thyroid	Thyroxine (T_3, T_4)	Development and metabolism
	Calcitonin	Kidney, skeleton
Parathyroid	Parathormone	Phosphorus and calcium metabolism
Adrenal cortex	Glucocorticoids	Sugar, protein and fat metabolism
	Mineralocorticoids	Water and salt balance in the organism
	Androgens	
Adrenal medulla	Adrenaline*	Heart
	Noradrenaline*	Blood vessels, glucose release

Glands	Hormones	Targets or functions
Ovaries Follicles	Oestrogens	Development and maintenance of sexual characteristics, reproduction, behaviour
Corpus luteum	Progesterone	Development and maintenance of sexual characteristics, reproduction, behaviour
Testicles	Testosterone	Development and maintenance of sexual characteristics, reproduction, behaviour

Pancreas;
  α cells
  β cells
  δ cells
	Glucagon
	Insulin*
	Somatostatin
		Glucose release
		Utilization of glucose

Stomach and intestine	Vasoactive intestinal peptide (VIP)* Cholecystokinin (CCK)* Gastrin Substance P* Neurotensin* Bombesin Secretin Motilin	
Various tissues	Angiotensin* Bradykinin CGRP* Peptide Y*	Blood vessels, adrenal cortex Blood vessels

The hormones marked with an asterisk are also present in the central nervous system.

Appendix 2

Main Hormonal Substances Deriving from the Modification of an Amino Acid Molecule

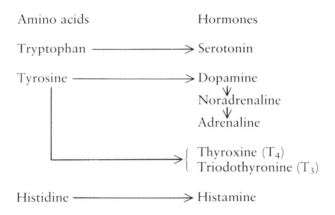

Appendix 3

Evolution of Biochemical Elements in Nervous and Endocrine Systems

Higher plants	Unicellular plants	Unicellular animals	Invertebrates				Vertebrates
Alfalfa	Mushrooms Yeast	Protozoa Amoebas	Sponges	Worms	Molluscs	Insects	
							Glands
			Neurons				
Hormonal peptides and messenger molecules							
Neurotransmitter molecules							

After D. Le Roith, J. Shiloach and J. Roth, *Peptides*, 3, 211, 1982.

1 Thyroliberin (THR)
Pyroglu – His – Pro NH$_2$

2 Luliberin (LH-RH)
Pyroglu – His – Try – Ser – Tyr – Gly – Leu – Arg – Pro – Gly NH$_2$

3 Somatostatin (SRIF)
H – Ala – Gly – Cys – Lys – Asn – Phe – Phe
                     | |
                    S   Trp
                    S   Lys
HO – Cys – Ser – Thr – Phe – Trh

4 Corticoliberin (CHR)
Forty-one amino acids

5 Somatoliberin (somatocrinin) or GH-RH

Appendix 4
Hypothalamo-hypophyseal Factors

Hypothalamic factors accepted from the biological point of view

1 Structurally identified hormones:
   TRH, LH-RH, SRIF, CRH, GH-RH.
2 Functionally recognized hormones which are not structurally identified:
   PIF, PRF.
3 Possible hormones which have not been demonstrated:
   MSH-IF, MSH-RF.
4 Hormones with no primary effect:
   substance P, neurotensin, angiotensin, endorphins and encephalins.
5 Classic neurotransmitters:
   dopamine, serotonin, GABA, noradrenaline etc.

Structurally identified hypothalamic hormones

The abbreviations His, Pro etc. indicate amino acids. Conventionally, F indicates a biologically accepted factor (IF, inhibiting factor; RF, release factor). H indicates a structurally identified factor (hormone). The letters T, LH, P, GH, MSH indicate respectively the thyroid, gonads, prolactin, growth hormone and melanocyte-stimulating hormone.

Appendix 5
Endomorphines

Endomorphines include the separate substances which have the analgesic properties of morphine, common structural characteristics and are manufactured by the organism in the central nervous system in particular (endogenous origin). They are grouped in three categories according to their precursor.

1 Derivatives of pro-opiomelanocortin: the cleavage of this large precursor produces β-endorphin, a peptide of thirty-one amino acids, in certain hypophyseal cells and in the hypothalamus.
2 Derivatives of proencephalin A: the best known are leu- and met-encephalin, peptides of five amino acids. These peptides are widely distributed in the brain and spinal cord where they are responsible for neurotransmission.
3 Derivatives of proencephalin B: above all dynorphin and β-neo-endorphin. They are present in many cerebral structures, and located in different neurons from those containing proencephalin A derivatives.

The various endomorphines are released by neurons which synthesize them and act on their targets, in the brain or on the periphery, through specific opiate receptors of which there seem to exist at least three types, K, μ and δ. Receptors are classified according to their preferential affinity for certain opioid molecules and naloxone, an antagonist to morphine, and according to the prevalence of certain pharmacological effects in experimental conditions.

Index